Words of Praise for
Catching God's Thoughts

Catching God's Thoughts is full of rich gems for those on the spiritual path. In a thought provoking manner, Allen David Young invites the reader to tap into his/her own intuitive faculties through an understanding and use of visioning and the I Ching. Different approaches to discerning divine guidance are presented in a reader-friendly manner that assists one in accessing the realm of divine thought.

Dr. Joan Steadman, Spiritual Leader—Oakland Center for Spiritual Living

Allen David Young is passionate about helping regular people realize their spiritual potential and he does so in *Catching God's Thoughts* by introducing them to a practical—and enjoyable—system of listening for guidance. He addresses the desire many have to combine intellect and intuition when seeking guidance, and also, he balances this affirmative spiritual process with a mindful consideration of the shadow part of life. This book stimulates creative thinking, and promotes deep inquiry into the nature of being.

Dr. Edward Viljoen, co-author of *Seeing Good at Work*, Spiritual Leader—Santa Rosa Center for Spiritual Living

I enjoyed reading the me o
archetypal and historical char ,
Moses, Abraham, et al. I find e
are instructional ways in whi r
meanings. People who are schooled and interested in the I Ching will find the diagrammatic element of associations with characters, elements and categories a good guide on ways to think.

Dr. Margaret Stortz, author of *Lights Along the Way*, Former President of United Churches of Religious Science

Dr. Young has written a delightfully useable book. He walks the user across the bridge between intuition and spirituality, linking the two shores with efficiency and grace. *Catching God's Thoughts* has proven to be an invaluable addition to my spiritual toolbox.

Dr. David Bruner, Spiritual Director—San Jose Center for Spiritual Living

I value this work. It is in the spirit of bettering the human condition. I found it worthy of critical reflection.

Rev. Archie Smith, Jr., M.S.W, Ph.D., author of *Navigating the Deep Rivers: Spirituality in African American Families,* Professor of Pastoral Counseling and Psychology—Pacific School of Religion

CATCHING GOD'S THOUGHTS

Visioning with Elements of the I Ching

Allen David Young, Ph. D.

January 2012

ISBN 978-0-7414-6852-9
ISBN 978-0-7414-9600-3

Printed in the United States of America

Published January 2012

INFINITY PUBLISHING
1094 New DeHaven Street, Suite 100
West Conshohocken, PA 19428-2713
Toll-free (877) BUY BOOK
Local Phone (610) 941-9999
Fax (610) 941-9959
Info@buybooksontheweb.com
www.buybooksontheweb.com

Contents

Acknowledgments

My one-year of study with the Berkeley Psychic Institute (BPI) created the opening for me to seek union with the Divine. Even though this program was about clairvoyant training it paved the way to my interest in dreams, exploring my deeper feelings about life, intuition, and the beginning of my serious interest in spiritual growth. As such, I want to acknowledge the founder of BPI and the person who taught me to do clairvoyant readings, the late Reverend Lewis Bostwick. Even though individuals come to their interest in spiritual growth in different ways the process begins with getting in touch with ones feelings.

After my departure from BPI, I enrolled at Pacific School of Religion and the Graduate Theological Union in Berkeley (GTU) a month later. I then started my formal study of religion by taking classes from various seminaries within the Union in the summer term. At the end of my first year I met Dr. Howard Thurman and took his weeklong intensive class titled, *Mysticism and Social Change.* To this day, he remains the most influential mystic that I have met and learned from in person. From him I discovered that nothing in life is more important than the search for God. I credit him with putting mysticism in my lap, raising profound questions, and giving profound insights about the mystic's experience of the meaning of God. I am forever grateful for the late Thurman's wisdom and presence in my life.

The seeds for this work were planted in the summer of 1978 when I studied with Howard Thurman. I credit him with introducing me to mysticism and giving me a context for thinking about its practical applications. He encouraged my interest in building bridges between spirituality and intuition. As I expressed my interest in mysticism but lacked of knowledge about the subject matter he provided comfort by explaining that when he began to study mysticism in the 1930 it was not yet a valid discipline. Since then a lot has happened to advance the subject and it is easier for newcomers to learn about direct communion with the Divine. Even though mainstream religious communities have little tolerance for mystics or occult practitioners, each group has historically gained valuable insights from the other.

I want to thank Strephon Kaplan Williams for leading the numerous dream groups I attended, for teaching me how to interpret dreams, and about the psychology of C. G. Jung in the intensive yearlong training with his Jungian-Senoi Institute in Berkeley.

I am very grateful for the many enlightened teachers who shared their wisdom with me over the past 30-years. Of the many teachers from the West I most thankful for the wisdom imparted by authors of the Bible, Howard Thurman, Ernest Holmes, Carl Gustav Jung, Joel Goldsmith, and Emanuel Swedenborg. My most profound teachers from the East include authors of the I Ching as a book of wisdom, Lao Tzu, Guatama Buddha, and Paramahansa Yogananda.

I want to acknowledge the Reverends Margaret Stortz, Victor Postalaki, and Elouise Oliver from the Oakland Center for Spiritual Living for their teachings in preparing me to become a Science of Mind Practitioner. I am also grateful for the numerous Holmes Institute teachers who led the way in my journey through the three-year master's degree program in consciousness studies:

Reverends: Deborah Johnson, Michael Bernard Beckwith, Joan Steadman, Mary Murray Shelton, and Edward Viljoen. In addition, I give great thanks to Amit Goswami, Stephan Hoeller, Robert Frager, and Alan Wallace for their specialized knowledge in helping to raise my consciousness in the areas of Science and Spirituality, Gnosticism, Spiritual Psychology, and Buddhism.

I want to thank the two thousand plus clients and students who allowed me to express my soul's potential through my nation wide vision centered counseling practice, intuition training workshops, and dream groups over the years. Finally, I want to acknowledge the members of Illuminata Center for Spiritual Living and senior minister Carolyn Jolly Douglas who have loved and supported me in sharing my consciousness with them over the past five years.

Introduction

In the pages that follow this book makes apparent how you can listen to God directly for enlightenment and guidance when you don't know what to do, and for assurance that what you are about to do will work out well. The process of training yourself to hear, feel, see, and intuit God's ideas for your life or for any endeavor you seek to understand, called visioning, is a growing spiritual practice now used by people ready to take the next step beyond visualization as presented in the popular book *The Secret* by Rhonda Byrne, et al. [1]. Visioning has emerged naturally because a growing number of people have an interest in spiritual insights and solutions for their lives, and the world in general. I have expanded visioning in a way that helps intuition and the intellect work together to answer questions with greater reliability than visioning alone. In addition to using examples from the lives of real people and situations, the intuitive methods in this book become known through applications to the universal social problems of underemployment, illegal immigration, and fighting terrorism. When viewed from spiritual perspectives, the use of intuition greatly enhances how to get, comprehend, and discern God's ideas.

Throughout the spiritual history of humanity visioning and some form of divination like the I Ching have been used to answer the questions raised by individuals at all levels of awareness. In this book rational intuition is the result of combining "the Change"—a simplified new version of the I Ching—with the visioning process to give you a reliable way to capture divine ideas and understand their meaning. Each approach has its advantage and one approach may be better suited for your purpose than the other. The intuitive discernment of answers that only rely on visions takes longer to understand because you need several visions to sort out recurring themes and reach acceptable conclusions. Getting answers to questions that rely on the Change alone are easy to discern but have few vision insights.

Visioning and the Change start with the premise that you're open-minded about what you want, where to go, or what to do, and as such you seek to catch divine ideas for inspiration and answers. Visioning is a form of inner observing that takes place when the conscious mind is quiet. A vision is a "dream" you have while semiconscious, or awake, and focused on listening to the divine. It is a form of thinking without words. Visioning and the Change are methods for listening to the ever-present divine broadcast. As long as you have the desire to receive and follow God's ideas, you have the right attitude for each method. The answer to the question of how often and how long to do visioning varies from person to person. A good rule of thumb is to do it as often as you can if you need guidance and answers to questions.

My journey is a microcosm of the journey made by humanity in its history to become civilized. It follows the creation of the Bible by its first authors who listened to the unconscious through visions and dreams, and then graduated over time to understanding this wisdom. My journey, and the journey of humanity, has parallels to the historical developments of the Bible and the I Ching or Book of Changes in Chinese. Just as biblical authors worked with visioning long before creating the Bible, early creators of the I Ching used it as an oracle to listen to the unconscious long before any religion was established to teach us about God. Over three thousand years of seasoned wisdom came about as many authors applied themselves to explaining the oracle and creating its spiritual and philosophical backbone. The development of the Book of Changes first as a book of divination used mainly by pagans, and then as a book of wisdom, gave birth to Taoism and Confucianism which in turn supported the growth of Buddhism.

The Change and I Ching are close relatives but they are significantly different. The Change simplifies the basic structure of the I Ching, eliminates moving lines and reinterprets the ancient Chinese philosophical descriptions of the trigrams and hexagram signs in light of the teachings of Jesus and Jungian psychology. The Change offers an intellectual understanding of visioning, and along with visioning provides a rational understanding of intuitive insights and the experience of oneness.

For those unfamiliar with the I Ching, the Change offers an excellent way to get divine insights quickly. Although I present examples in chapters four, six, and ten let me mention it here. Consulting the Change only requires you to flip or toss one coin six times and record whether each random landing is Heads (representing a Yang line _______) or Tails (representing a Yin line ___ ___). You will get one of 64 patterns or hexagram symbols to answer your question. If, for example, you get three Heads followed by three Tails you would look up the hexagram number for this pattern in the table titled "Matrix of Trigrams and Hexagram Numbers" at the end of chapter ten. The page just before the table explains how to use it. In this case, the first three lines represent Heaven, the upper three lines represent Earth, and the six lines together represent Hexagram 11 titled *Prospering*.

Intuitive knowledge is immediate, direct, and not an interference from logic. As you speed up the rate of catching and understanding God's ideas, you'll speed up the rate of manifesting God's thoughts. Manifestation is all about transforming ideas into forms on one hand, and releasing forms to receive new ideas on the other hand. It is not limited to the activity of holding an idea in mind until put into physical, emotional, mental or spiritual form. Manifestation goes beyond the activity of parachuting down from the heavens, intending to land on the spot marked X, or traveling into outer space to planet Y.

Central to the visioning process as made popular by Michael Bernard Beckwith, founder of Agape International Spiritual Center, is asking the right questions. Beckwith uses four basic questions for the visioning process, and encourages people to adapt the process for their environment and purposes: "What is God's idea of itself as my life? What must I become to manifest this vision? What must I release to become this vision? What gifts and talents do I now possess that can be used to serve this vision?"

In his CD titled *The Life Visioning Process, Session One,* Beckwith describes the spiritual journey as consisting of four stages of consciousness and spiritual growth—Victim, Manifester, Channel, and Being [2]. People in the Victim stage tend to believe that circumstances such as uncontrolled emotions and other people control of their lives, and things are done to them and imposed upon them by others people. They ask questions such as why did God let this happen? What did I do wrong? Why me, or why do bad things happen to me? People in this stage have no spiritual practice or they are spiritual beginners whose practice has not yet taken them beyond this stage of consciousness. In general, people in the Victim stage have low self-esteem, great difficulty with personal relationships, unfulfilling jobs, material insecurities, and poor psychological health.

People in the Manifester stage learn to gain control over their emotions, take dominion over their lives, and recognize that they are no longer victims of circumstances or outside influences. Learning to master this stage is the central message of *The Secret* by Byrne, et al. [3]. Even though uncontrolled events happen to people in this stage, they understand that outside events have no power over their lives. People at this stage have higher self-esteem and confidence than those at the Victim stage, and their consciousness has shifted from being at the effect of conditions to being the cause of conditions. They ask questions such as how does this or that belief limit my growth. Why am I not accepting success in this or that area of my life, and what can I do to change? Are my thoughts about myself negative or positive? Typical spiritual practices for people at this stage include affirmative prayer, visualization and spiritual education. People in this stage often focus on attracting stuff and having things such as greater material comfort, better relationships, better health, etc.

While this book is not for spiritual beginners in the Victim stage, it is well suited for people in the Manifester, Channel and Being stages. This book offers many examples of Manifester stage questions and answers, but most illustrations highlight the Channel and Being stages. People in these two stages ask questions such as, what is God's plan for my life or my project. What must I release to manifest God's ideas? What must I become to help God express itself as me? In his little book titled *Mysticism and the Experience of Love,* Howard Thurman makes the point that the mystical experience of letting go is a limited form of life denial, and that in the most profound sense it becomes life affirming [4].

Although Beckwith presents the Channel and Being stages as distinct levels of consciousness, they are essentially the same or third stage of consciousness. They differ mainly by the degree to which people make use of spiritual practices such as sacred study, rational intuition, visioning, and other methods for catching divine ideas. Being stage people see themselves as one with God at all times, and as such gain access to God's ideas daily, whereas those in the Channel stage don't acknowledge the Divine connection as often. No one stays in any one stage all the time. For instance, people in the Being stage may find themselves in the Manifester and even Victim Stage in some areas of their live. People who live mainly in the Victim stage may find themselves inspired by a vision or new knowledge that temporarily moves them into the Manifester or Channel stage.

Downward manifestation begins with the illusion of separateness and temporary amnesia about our connection with the Divine. It is a form of visualization in the sense that the descent of spirit into matter is no longer a potential, but a known. Visualization is about personal development, individual recognition, and discovering one's uniqueness.

People in the Manifester stage of consciousness pursue this course to create self-recognition, loving relationships, emotional security and material possessions. The main benefit of downward manifestation is also its main cost, namely that of getting the things you want. The saying, "be careful what you pray for as you might get it," means that getting what you want also brings the responsibility of accepting what you get. For example, when I joined the Navy I got what I wanted. I got to travel, make and save money, and a host of good veteran benefits. But I didn't think my job would require me to assemble mines and torpedoes, follow orders I didn't agree with or that I'd never like being on ships. The Manifester benefit is that of using the power of the universe to get what you want rather than support what the universe wants. In sustained downward manifestation efforts, the will of God takes a back seat to your will.

Upward manifestation begins with some form of visioning and involves movement toward unity. Whether you seek to acquire the riches and blessings of the Kingdom of Heaven or to acquire material blessing visioning brings priceless results. Once downward manifestation is complete, the journey toward upward manifestation or evolution begins. It is not called evolution because life evolves from matter, but because its potential already exists in matter and this potential is being uncovered. It is a journey toward self-discovery, self-actualization, and transcendence. People in the Channel and Being stages learn to let go of their attachments to the material, emotional, relational and self important aspects of life that hold them back from the goal of self-realization. The main difficulty of this journey is also its main gift—that of replacing personal desires expressed as "my will be done" with "thy will be done." The fear is that to do God's will you have to give up the things you want. While this fear is valid, many things are false about it. The following story of two waves illustrates the consciousness of upward manifestation. As the first wave approached the shoreline, it began to cry. The second wave asks, "Why are you crying?" The first wave replies, "I'm crying because I'm going to die when I reach the shoreline." The second wave then says, "Oh, I known your problem. You think of your self as a wave instead of the ocean." To catch and understand God's view you need to release or transcend your idea and get behind God's view as if it were yours.

The intuitive methods of visioning and the Change used in this book give voice to the deeper mind. Each approach has its advantage and one approach may be better suited for your purpose than the other. For instance, without the assistance of another perspective visioning gives rise to multiple interpretations and fits the saying 'a picture is worth a thousand words.' The intuitive discernment of answers that only rely on visions takes longer to understand because you need many visions to sort out recurring themes and reach acceptable conclusions. Getting answers to questions that rely on the Change alone are easy to discern but limit the deeper minds vocabulary for expressing its message.

After the introduction the first chapter titled, "Seeking God," is a summation of my initial awakening and spiritual journey, how it progressed, and where I'm coming from with this book. This journey describes the main events surrounding my psychic development studies, my life altering lucid dream, and my quantum leap from the rational world of business to intuitive spirituality.

Chapter two, titled "Accept the Mystery," deals with learning to accept and reconcile the reality of the shadow. This chapter coaches you about the nature of God so that it comes not as a force that says no but as an expected companion to your life. It explains how to live your life with meaning based on the accepting all of your parts through visioning and the Change. Strange though it may seem "Accept the Mystery" tells us that there are no absolutes in seeking self-discovery, and that the most productive area for growth is through the experience of letting go. The message here is that when you accept that God has better ideas than you do, many things are replaced by something far better than you could have imagined.

Chapters three and four, titled "Catch the Vision" and "Manifest the Vision," describe the use of visioning for getting spiritual insights and solutions. The third chapter, "Catch the Vision," points out the origin visions, introduces the visioning process, and explains the nature of visioning process questions. "Catch the Vision" discusses the role of visions and dreams in humanity and in relation to God. It lays out the difference between visioning and visualization, and how the two can work together to produce the best results. In keeping with the central theme of this book, this chapter makes the case that visualization is the assertive path to getting what you want from the Universe while visioning is the receptive path of helping the Universe to express itself.

The fourth chapter, titled "Manifest the Vision," begins by defining the eight stages of the visioning process and the relationship between these stages and meditation and concentration. It points out how visioning differs from ordinary intuitive insights. "Manifest the Vision" presents examples of the visioning process and ways that people use the process for their lives, projects, and setting mission goals for organizations. In addition to discussing how to make spiritual discernment decisions and interpret visions, this chapter offers advice on how to set up visioning groups.

The fifth chapter, titled "The Change and Visioning," begins with a short history of the I Ching or Book of Changes in Chinese as an oracle and its development and use as a Book of Wisdom. It explains why I created the Change to replace the traditional form and content of the I Ching. Visioning and the Change are both concerned with manifesting unity more than with manifesting personal material success, especially if that success is likely to cause difficulties to others or adversely affect our character or peace of mind. The Change offers an intellectual understanding of visioning, and along with visioning provides a rational understanding of intuitive insights and the experience of oneness. The Change not only simplifies the I Ching's use and form but also reinterprets its message based on biblical and psychological wisdom. The chapter ends by explaining the difference between information conveyed by visions and hexagrams, and hexagram answers.

The sixth chapter, titled "Elements of the Change," expands the traditional eight-trigram signs based on adding the life stories of the eight biblical patriarchs from Abraham to Jesus, and C.G. Jung's eight psychological types to make the ancient Chinese interpretations more relevant to Western minds. The trigrams offer at least one of eight universal perspectives for every question and hexagram. Because two trigrams make a hexagram, you can understand hexagrams through the trigram pair that produces it. Finally, "Elements of the Change" shows how hexagrams and vision come together to deepen your understanding of God's ideas.

Chapter seven, titled "Vision Centered Counseling and Healing," presents real-life examples of spiritual solutions to issues faced by a sampling of my counseling clients. These illustrations apply visioning and the Change to ordinary folks. After assisting clients in asking their questions, they are answered directly by the Divine in its ancient universal language of symbols (including Change hexagrams), and then interpreted for their situation. I hope that these real-life cases show how you can receive God's ideas and get spiritual solutions for your personal questions and projects.

Chapter eight, titled "Well-known Personalities," shows the Divine's ideas about the personalities, personal assets, and lifetime goals: President Barack Obama, Warren Buffett, and President George "W" Bush. The message is that when you know something about the person you are trying to understand the visioning process comes to life to deepen your knowledge. After giving mini biographical sketches, I discuss the Divine insights based on information from visioning with the Change to answer questions about their aura and personality, personal assets, and life goals. The process of getting answers to questions in the chapter can be adapted to understanding yourself and others.

Chapter nine, titled "Spiritual Solutions for Social Problems," applies visioning with the Change to three universal social problems and shows the Divine view on how society can tackle and resolve these problems: Underemployment, Illegal immigration, and Fighting Terrorism. The questions and answers to these universal problems begin with a summary of how society experts understand the problems. The intuitive insights to answer these questions present the Divine view. They are examples of how you can use the methods to receive information from the deeper mind to understand these social problems and adapt the process to answering your questions about other social issues.

The tenth and final chapter, titled "Consulting the Change," presents three ways to get hexagram answers to your questions. While the method you use will depend upon your questions and the information wanted there is no need to make anything happen as the answer you seek is already in the mind of God. My new interpretations of all 64 hexagrams appear in the pages following this chapter. As already mentioned I have expanded the original Chinese meanings to include the teachings of Jesus, Old Testament stories, and insights from C.G. Jung's psychological types. These new interpretations have greater relevance for Western minds today than the ancient hexagram interpretations.

The binary opposites from ancient Chinese and Western cosmologies such as light and dark, heaven and earth, yang and yin, etc. form the basis of I Ching and the Bible, and define us in the most basic ways. Since God needs humanity to shed its light and express its nature, humanity must reinterpret God's nature and message in new ways in order to receive new revelations. The more you listen to the Divine, the more it reveals new insights. As long as you think about the Divine in new ways, it reveals new ideas.

While this book combines visioning and the Change for hearing God's ideas the results from these methods are still subject to interpretation. If for example, ten people get together for visioning you will see ten different visioning styles. If ten interpreters of visions interpret what they received, you will get ten different explanations. Like the I Ching, the Change is useful with or without the addition of visions. The meaning assigned to your vision or insight from the Change is what you say it is, and this meaning may change over time. Your understanding of God's nature will always have an impact on interpretations of intuitive insights. Insights that come through your awareness of sacred teachings will usually have deeper spiritual meaning than those that comes through secular teachings.

People who use intuitive methods for enlightenment should take a moment to center and contemplate the Light Within. Doing so is like requesting permission to ask your question, giving thanks in advance, and becoming aligned with God's will. As you focus your attention on receiving and discerning visions or hexagram signs, you can use visualization and your will to manifest this intuitive insight.

Properly used, visioning and the Change will help you align your will with the Divine will. This does not mean giving up your ideas and desires at all. It simply means accepting that God has a better way of getting the things you want than you do. Because God is the source of all goodness and always does the right thing, manifesting goodness in your life will always come about when you consistently know and embrace God's ideas. Although it appears to be a paradox God is the source of all problems, known and unknown, and God is the best solution to all problems.

In general, you should be skeptical of the things you desire. Before pursuing big things, you should ask yourself (God within) if it's appropriate or beneficial to you. Before spending a lot of energy being attached to the things you want it's better to spend a little time asking the Divine for its opinion. Is it a good idea or desire to have what I want in the way I want it? If the answer is yes, you can bring it into manifestation with a high probability of goodness and success. If the answer is no, you can still push for manifestation even though success may be doubtful.

1

Seeking God

We must not allow any consideration whatever,
any institution, or organization, or any book,
or any man or woman, to come between us
and our direct seeking for God.
—Emmet Fox

This book offers spiritual seekers a reliable yet simplified way to listen to God or the self within for enlightenment and guidance. The time-honored methods presented here are designed to provide you with direct access to specific guidance when you don't know what to do and for assurance that what you are about to do will work out well. *Catching God's Thoughts: Visioning with Elements of the I Ching* helps every seeker discover and express the will of the Divine resident within them. When you follow the Divine, you live up to your greatest potential and nurture all life. You are enlightened by not only intuitive insights but also what you learn about the nature of Ultimate Reality and how you apply these ideas when interacting with yourself, others, and the environment. The fabric of this book is made of wisdom from the East and West that has been around for thousands of years, but reshaped by my spiritual journey.

To make sense out of this book let me outline the steps leading up to my awakening, the awakening itself, and what followed. The stage was set for me to begin my spiritual journey the moment I let the prospect of running for the Oakland City Council in February 1975 go to my head. With no forethought, l let other people talk me into the race. Within days, I had a campaign manager, volunteer workers to help me run for city council, and a dozen friends lined up to make donations and give fund raising parties. In spite of contributions and fund raising, I still bank rolled about half of the needed costs and ended the campaign in debt. In the blink of an eye my quiet academic life as a 29-year old professor and business school dean at California State University, Hayward became very public. When my Dr. Allen and campaign slogan "Intelligent Change" went up on billboards across the city, the whole nature of the campaign changed and it seemed as if the entire city of Oakland knew who I was. Even though I was barely into the political arena, a number of people were looking to me as Oakland's first black mayor. In no time I was giving political speeches, attending fund raising parties, and granting countless media interviews. I quickly learned how big the city was and how difficult it was to collect votes from its four hundred thousand citizens. Each section of the city had different interests and it took skill to say the right things to the various groups. Instant popularity came with the territory of being a political candidate. I enjoyed the recognition of feeling important, and only realized after election that I was not prepared for all that attention. It was as if I suddenly inherited being the leader and center of a new political movement.

Within six months, this political experience turned my life inside out for the better. A major blow to my ego came from losing the election. This led me to get help in understanding why I got involved in first place and what I should do with my life. I wanted help to learn about myself, and the choices I made. I was embarrassed that I jumped into such a big event without thinking much about it. As a little time passed, I saw this chapter in my life as an awakening and gift from the dark side. It was the first of many transformational steps from the unconscious to the conscious realm. I was relieved that I wasn't elected and completely turned off by the process. The fact that I got 45 percent of the vote made the effort worthwhile to my ego and supporters, but the debts I accumulated demanded payment. I had no plan for the steps I took toward financial recovery and self-discovery. The steps I took showed up as I opened my self to what seemed to be the right direction. Shortly after the campaign, I had to deal with dissolving my marriage, leaving my associate dean of the business school position, and taking a second job at the Federal Reserve Bank to earn enough money to pay off my debts.

These back-to-back losses' set the stage for my awakening and were enough to shove me in the new direction of self-discovery. The more I learned about my self, the less interest I had in business as usual. My initial help came from learning to do psychic readings. After a year, I set aside this work to study religion and psychology at the GTU in Berkeley. I thought about using this study as a stepping-stone to ministry but changed my mind after being in the program for just over one year. At the same time, I took the one-year intensive program to work with dreams and Jungian Psychology at the Jungian-Senoi Institute in Berkeley.

Soon after getting my first psychic reading from an instructor at the Berkeley Psychic Institute (BPI), I signed up for its yearlong program in clairvoyant training. I did so because I was impressed with the reading on the status of my life, personality, interests and abilities. If I could read people the way he read me, I thought, I would avoid bad decisions, make good decisions and change my life. After this experience, I was fired up and eager to learn. At the time, I did not intend to become a psychic. I simply thought that training my intuition and doing readings would help me do a better job at understanding people and situations. For a short while, I even thought I would use my acquired skill to select good romantic partners. This actually worked in the short-run, but was no substitute for day-to-day interactions and experience. I soon found that readings were only an aid to point you in the right direction and should not be confused with knowledge. As I got into my psychic work, I developed an interest in dreams and re-discovered my interest in religion. As my interest in religion grew my psychic studies took a backseat, and the differences between them increased. Because understanding religion and dreams were far beyond my psychic studies, and I knew they were important, I needed to go elsewhere to find how these subjects could get me closer to God. Further along in my spiritual journey I learned that clairvoyance and visioning have much in common, but that visioning is always focused on catching and expressing God's will whereas clairvoyance is not.

Of the many elements that put me on the spiritual path, the most important element was my sincere request to God for union with God. If I knew better, I would have done so earlier, but now I knew it was time to unite my life with God. Thanks to a little black pocket book titled *The Impersonal Life,* by Joseph S. Benner the first state of my request was answered [1]. As I finished this book, I reaffirmed my request to unite with God with understanding and conviction, and then had the following lucid dream before I fell asleep on June 26, 1977.

> *A large white light entered my bedroom as I stood on a platform above my bed. The white light became Jesus. I saw an umbilical cord flow down from my navel as an observer to the navel of my physical body. The chord became a silver color and grew in thickness. I felt a strengthening in my attachment to this chord. I then saw all of my possessions before me: My home, property, job, my nearly completed clairvoyant training program at the Berkeley Psychic Institute (BPI), three girl friends and my academic degrees. As I stood next to Jesus and looked down at myself lying in bed Jesus said, "Now that you see yourself and the choices you have made are you ready to follow me, your true guide within?" I quickly answered, "Yes." He then asked, "Are you*

ready to give up all you possessions." I hesitated a moment and again said, "Yes." He then said, "Cut the silver chord and follow me?" In silence and fear I said, "No" to my self. I picked up the belief from BPI that one only detaches from the silver cord at death, and I did not want to die. Jesus just waited behind me. It was a momentary stand off. I then thought to myself, "I may never get another chance like this again." I then created a razor blade and cut the cord.

This lucid dream altered my life completely and revealed to me that I was now on a spiritual path to God. This dream responded to what I was seeking, revealed my status in life, and gave me the choice to accept or not accept what I was seeking. Since that moment of awakening, I have not been the same. It was as if God literally became another being in my inner space and took up half of my psyche. To say that I was in awe of what just happened is an understatement. This dream put me into another reality unlike any I had known before. Later that evening I had a short second dream that gave me absolute confidence that what I just experienced was real and that my journey had begun:

A woman dressed in white led me to a special series of rooms in a large hotel. She asked me to take a shower, leave my old friends behind, and prepare my self for living in my new home with God.

To this day, I am grateful for these two life-altering dreams, and thank God for allowing me to share its life since that moment. Within days, I ended my training program at BPI and let go of my three girl friends. My interest in learning to do clairvoyant readings quickly became secondary to my interest in religious education and finding God. I chose to drop out of the psychic course immediately, even though I had completed 95 percent of the requirements and planned to graduate. With a feeling of guilt about my three girl friends and realizing that I had a sex addiction illness, I sat in a chair and made a spoken promise to God the following morning that I would become celibate until I healed my addiction and habit of needing multiple intimate relationships. At the same time I set my sights on attending the GTU and started my class work toward the end of the summer.

After being a student at the GTU for an entire year, I met Howard Thurman in his class on *Mysticism and Social Change.* I had heard a great deal about him before this class and he lived up to his reputation as one of the nation's greatest mystics. This one-week intensive course shifted the focus of my awareness from the subject of organized religion to mysticism. The course affirmed my growing interest toward direct communion with the Divine through dream interpretation work and Jungian Psychology. When I told Dr. Thurman about my plans to leave the GTU and work with dreams he showed great interest. He said he didn't know what God had in store for me and he hoped he'd be around for another ten years to see. Unfortunately he made is transition the next year. When I asked about his view of my hero C.G. Jung, he said that he didn't see him as a mystic but thought highly of his work with dreams and depth psychology as a path to God. He added that I was headed toward serious self-discovery and on to God's scent. The thing that I remember most about him, that I had not experienced before I met him nor since, was the awareness of a loving presence that is part of this world, and yet bigger than this world. In my brief dealings with him I felt that I was in the presence of a saint.

In my year of work with the Jungian-Senoi Institute I practiced and learned to interpret dreams for myself and others. Even though I have interpreted thousands of dreams and led many dream groups, I remain in awe of dreams and find there is still much to learn from them.

I felt the connection between what I learned at BPI and the GTU but it came with conflict because I couldn't articulate what it was. The psychic training at BPI approached the human soul by learning to read its emotional and energy body, but nothing about mysticism. The program at the GTU approached the human soul by presenting psychological and theological knowledge about God and gave me my first exposure to the I Ching through Father Robert Ochs, a priest teaching at the Jesuit Seminary, and to mysticism through Howard Thurman. My third year of independent study with Strephon Kaplan Williams' Jungian-Senoi taught me about dream interpretation and provided me with Jung's depth psychology view of the human soul. By honoring the religious and occult approaches, Jung's depth psychology perspective helped me put together what I got from BPI and the GTU. Based mainly on the training here I started my intuitive counseling and training business, the Aquarian Institute, which continues to this day. Like most people who teach and counsel others, I have done so because this is what I love and need to learn. While I have taught courses to many students over the years in intuition training, dream interpretation, meditation, psychological astrology, tarot, and the Change—my new version of the I Ching—most of my service consists of vision centered counseling by phone with clients throughout the country. Over the years, I have given over 25,000 intuitive consultations to over 2,000 clients.

Since 1989, I grew with my counseling practice and integrated the Science of Mind philosophy into my intuitive experiences. As I continue my sacred education and spiritual practices, my service to humanity continues to shift in a way that incorporates what I am becoming. I continue to learn as a student and teacher of the broadly defined Science of Mind philosophy. When it comes to bridging the various disciplines or taking sides with one over the other, I recall an answer to a question put to the Dali Lama by one of my teachers of Buddhism, Alan Wallace. When asked, "Why don't you recruit non-Buddhist to Buddhism in your travels across the country?" His response was that since Buddhism had much to offer all people and all religions right where they are there's no need for any one to change religions. He added that Buddhist ideas are universal and can be beneficial to all religions.

I aligned myself with the First Church of Religious Science in Oakland, a trans-denominational spiritual philosophy, now called the Oakland Center for Spiritual Living in 1989. Over my fifteen years of being a member, until 2004, I learned about the teachings of its founder Ernest Holmes and author *The Science of Mind* [2]. In my early association to this Christian philosophy with a mystical spin, I became a licensed Science of Mind Practitioner, graduate of the Holmes Institute's Master of Consciousness Studies program, and Science of Mind minister. My training and practice as a practitioner deserves mention because it is the foundation of my experience with visualization, the visioning process, and the basic ideas on these subjects in this book. Even though my approach to God started with learning effective ways to listen to God through other intuitive methods, I have integrated these methods into the visioning process.

When you don't study the true nature of the Divine, the concept of God is dimmed. All the troubles of the world, especially spiritual troubles such as impatience, hopelessness, and despair, have root in the failure to see the nature of God clearly. My journey has brought me in touch with some of the many approaches to knowing God and the names we call the Creator of the Universe. In mysticism, religion, and spirituality the names God, Godhead, The Divine, Spirit, Soul, Love, Absolute or Ultimate Reality, Lord, Christ, Allah, Brahman, Jehovah, Yahweh, Tao, and King of Kings are among the most popular. People who identify with religion will be comfortable with using many of these names in referring to the Creator. People who shy away from religion but accept the role psychology has played in understanding the human soul are often at peace with name for the Creator such as The Self, The Transcendent, The Unconscious, The Eternal, The Deeper Mind and the Psyche. Individuals who don't accept religion or psychology as their primary link to the human soul or Creator—namely those in the fields of classical philosophy, the occult, the new science and pantheism—will use different terms for the Creator. These names include The Universe, Being or Supreme Being, Higher Power, The Source, The One, The Creator, Life, Truth, Existence, Energy, Deity, The Way, Principle, Mind and First Cause.

All of these names are imperfect and misleading as we cannot define Ultimate Reality. All Divine names provide points of light for which the soul yearns when it says "God," yet every definition of God leads to heresy because the intellect cannot fully comprehend the mystery of God. Despite these limitations, the use of different names will continue and serve the benefit of expanding our concepts of God beyond limited forms and childish habits. In his book, *The Creative Encounter* Howard Thurman says, "It is my belief that in the Presence of God there is neither male nor female, white nor black, Gentile not Jew, Protestant nor Catholic, Hindu, Buddhist, nor Moslem, but a human spirit stripped to the literal substance of itself before God."

Accepting God

Strange though it may seem, one of the most productive avenues for growth is through the experience of letting go. Letting go is like dying and you can practice death every day. How do you do that? Death is nothing more than withdrawing our consciousness from things. If you practice doing this a little every day, you can receive more consciousness. You can practice through meditation, visioning, or the Change as a start. In each case you start with the premise that God knows more than you do and if your mind is quiet and open insights will come to offer you a better way. Every time you sleep at night you experience a little death as well. Every morning you awaken with a dream that offers wisdom to enlighten you about life. You can accept it and in doing so you experience another death. Anytime you say, "thy will be done" you're opening yourself to a small death. The more you practice letting go, the easier is becomes. You can also think of letting go as the three "G's;" namely, giving back, getting off it, and getting lost. Giving back means to be of service and to tithe or give to your spiritual source. Getting off it refers to letting go of your position and letting God enlighten you on what position to have. This may take a little time but with patience and sincerity, God will get you to new places. Getting lost refers to walking away without engaging the adversary. If this is not possible, you may need to incorporate the previous method of getting off it.

When you practice seeking God's ideas on an ongoing basis, you continuously reinforce a new way of being. This constant seeking and letting go of your desire to do things your way is the key to the door of fulfillment. You must learn to draw on the Divine to define yourself based on the feedback you receive from it rather than trying to fit yourself into ill-fitting stereotyped roles. The world is in desperate need of people whose level of growth and faith in Spirit is sufficient to enable them to learn to live with and serve others cooperatively and lovingly. Humanity will advance only through commitment and involvement of individuals in their own and others spiritual growth and development as human beings. This means the development of loving and caring relationships in which participants are as committed to the spiritual growth and happiness of others as to their own. To gain everything from Spirit you must give up everything. What you must give up is all that is not truly you. It also means giving up accepting someone or something because of external judgments or ego judgments, rather than God's perspective. By understanding and becoming what Spirit wants you will become your true self; a self who is at peace and who is able to truly love and serve.

Ultimately you must learn to give up your need for approval from love ones and others, and look to the deeper self for evaluations of success and failure. When you truly understand that material things, relationships, and your desires are not the source of your fulfillment, and may be taken at any time without notice then you must live each day knowing that God is the source and substance of your life. If you make it a habit of listening to God and have patience, hope, and faith, you'll receive an ever-increasing consciousness to give you strength and guidance. The act of letting go and letting God is like sitting before a curtain that covers the thing you seek until the curtain opens. Whether God gives you a vision to open the curtain or you get an insight from some other source on what you need to become, you must be willing to release your way of thinking. Although there's always a bigger truth beyond the closed curtain we are often unwilling to let go of the ego's perspective and let God have its way. We are often unwilling to turn to the other person and say, "you could be right." As Wayne Dyer described in his public TV presentation titled *The Power of Intention*, "the ego is that part of your personality that edges God out."

The following story will help to illustrate the subtle and not so subtle misunderstanding and often resistance people have to change. A modern day wealthy man had a counseling session with a spiritual counselor and asked what he should do to received God's riches and blessings? The question is similar to the one the rich man in the New Testament asked Jesus what he needed to do to enter the kingdom of God. Jesus told the rich man he needed to do two things: First, to follow the commandments, which was no problem as the man had done so since his childhood; and second, to give his wealth to the poor, take up the cross and follow him. The man was sad and walked away because he had many possessions. His disciples were astonished at what he said and asked, "Who then can be saved?" Jesus answered by saying, "With men it is impossible, but not with God: for with God all things are possible." This New Testament story is just as true to day than it was two thousand years ago.

Regarding our story, the spiritual counselor told the modern day rich man there is good news and bad news. The good news is that this is the twenty first century so you can keep your stuff. It does no good to give up your stuff and become a poor man. As the rich man smiled the counselor added, the bad news is that you must give up the way you think. When the wealthy man asked how he was suppose to do that the counselor tells him that God can make use of your wealth, talents, and life to serve others in ways far better than you could ever do, and in the process give you riches and blessings beyond what you can imagine. He adds that this won't happen until you learn to truly get out of the way and follow what God gives you to do. For this to happen, you must learn to live in close contact with your intuitive and spiritual nature and do some letting go in order to make room for the new things that come up for you to do. In other words, you must think in terms of a cooperative relationship with spirit where you seek to become the riches and blessing God has for you on the one hand, and seek to contribute and help others become what they need to become on the other hand. It is not enough to think purely in terms is what is in it for you, but in full participation with Spirit becoming part of your life in a new way.

The need to release and let go will always be with us. The highest spiritual values of life can originate from the thoughts and study of transformation. The most persistent questions that humanity explores through its myths and religions are those pertaining to the growth that comes from transforming or changing old habits, rebirth and death. You may be able to delay the change that comes from letting go but you cannot escape it. Even the people who put a high value on being in control of the things in their lives must accept that they are subject to the forces of change as well. Just about everybody has some answer to the question, why is it so hard to give up control or let go? All would agree that it is difficult to release the thoughts and things we want because loss is scary. In spite of the fact that it's going to happen from time to time anyway doesn't mean we're willing to accept doing so. It is hard to change what you don't acknowledge and it always will be so even when you have learned to accept transformation as an integral part of life because a big part of change means loss of the familiar. But if you can learn to accept God's view of your life so that it comes not as a force that says no but as an expected companion to your life, then you can also learn to live your live with meaning and full appreciation of the limits of your view of life.

Affirmative Prayer of Acceptance

Take a moment to relax and put your attention on these thoughts: There's only one life, one absolute reality, one mind, and one universe that's everywhere present. The center present in all life is present within you and within all life where ever it exists. Everything and every no thing lives, moves, and has its being in the infinite whole that is everywhere. There's not one spot where the whole is not. There are no seams in the whole, only the illusion of parts, fragments and separateness.

The more you dwell upon the oneness of all life and unity of the whole the more you will see that you are the place where all life comes together. The more you seek the Light Within the brighter it becomes. The more you desire to know and experience its presence the more it reveals itself to you. The center of the universe is right where you are. You share the center and circumference of the entire universe.

When your mind is quiet and at peace, you can hear, sense, see and feel the message of the universe. While in the silence, you can tune in the intelligence of the universe and understand its thoughts. The divine broadcast is always present and announces again and again that all life is connected to the same source, all life lives in the one, and all life has access to the one. As you continue to dwell on the idea that you are one with the infinite, it reveals its truth to you.

I now accept that I can receive the divine broadcast and know the thoughts of my soul. I recognize that what I seek will come into my consciousness and manifest in my life. Knowing that I have access to all that I am willing to receive I release the stuff that stands in the way.

In that quite place of mind repeat these words, "I give thanks for all that I have and seek to receive. And so it is."

2

Accept the Mystery

We are so overwhelmed by the personal but vast impact of the particularity of living objects that we are scarcely aware of a much more profound fact in our midst and that is that life itself is alive.
—Howard Thurman

This chapter is about a subject that we all know something about. All of us have unwanted, dark and shadow emotions and we experience them with regularity. So let's talk about the nature of these feared and upside down emotions. What are they? Why do you have them? How can you benefit from accepting their existence? The prophet Isaiah refers to the presence of these emotions at the beginning of creation when he says, *"I form the light, and create darkness: I make peace and create evil: I the Lord do all these things"* [1]. Here, God tells us that he made the right side up and up side down, the light and the dark, the highs and the lows, and all other things.

Every tree is rooted in the cold dark earth. The tree may be beautiful, bear sweet fruit, and grow the most breath taking flowers, but its rooted in an unattractive substance. The spirit is radiant and we heap our praises upon it, but it too is rooted in frail bodies that are subject to pain, grow weak, and often have bad habits and negative emotions. The sun rises out of the darkness and everything beautiful in life comes out of something ugly by comparison. The more you look at the under side the more your definition and perspective of beauty changes. Just as fear is the underside of courage, the Devil is the base side or God turned upside down. Fear and the shadow can be your friends when viewed in the right way.

People have become one sided. We say that good is inside and bad is outside. However, if God is everything how is this even possible? Whenever you're having a bad experience you should think of it as an opportunity for something good. Everything that's up in life was down at some point. You can only talk about up in terms of down and good in terms of evil. One supports the other. In the beginning, God brought the world into existence through binary pairs. The problem with humanity has come to be its identification with one side of the pair at the exclusion of the other. Religion in general and as a whole thinks in terms of absolutes. Religion is often about absolute laws—a right way to do things and a wrong way, a good way and a bad way. The Old Testament contains many stories of punishment as the result of violating the law. In the New Testament Jesus modifies the laws to integrate the opposites. He came to fulfill the law by liberating humanity from one-sided thinking.

In true self-discovery, as in following God's will, there are no absolutes. Everything depends upon the consciousness that you bring to the table. Conventional religion is based on either/or thinking. Either you're for me or against me, either yes or no. However, Spirit says, *"why not both as both exist."* Visioning and other intuitive methods for listening to the divine bring to light a paradox about consciousness. What we know now was previously unknown and a mystery to us. As we come to known the unknown the paradox is this: consciousness or the known excludes the unconscious and the known excludes the unknown. For instance, the more education you get the more you realize that there is much more that you don't know.

This seems to explain why people tend to be more humble with greater knowledge. Consciousness causes us to define reality in terms of right and wrong. The unconscious is the true home of upside down emotions. It's not good or bad, it just is. The unconscious is both either/or, yes and no. It's only defined when we define it, and only becomes something only when we say it's something.

The persona is that part of the total personality that you identify with, the part that you like. It is your mask and the most conscious part of who you are. However, behind every conscious part there's an unconscious part called the shadow. No matter what you like about your personality, there's always an opposing part that you don't like. Whenever you see a friend, there's an aspect of that friend that's an enemy. You can only be conscious of a certain amount of reality and the rest remains unconscious to you. The unconscious is where your troubles lie until and unless you can make friends with it and embrace it in some way. But most of us don't want to face the unconscious because it's mysterious, unknown, and scary. Even though we want to sweep it under the rug or lock it in a closet it's a necessary part of life. The idea of sin and making mistakes are part of the unconscious, and a necessary part of growing up.

Many Meanings

Unlike the Old Testament teachings from Moses that place emphasis on the persona and demands obedience to the law, the teaching of Jesus integrate persona and shadow and in the process stress obedience and disobedience. This may sound shocking but it's true. Sometimes you have to do things the wrong way first before you learn the right way. In most cases, you can only learn about good by having knowledge of evil. Among the best examples of integrating the dark, upside down emotions in the New Testament are those found in the parables. Jesus used this clever way of explaining things in about fifty percent of his teaching. Parables are like dreams in that they have a cartoon like presentation with direct and indirect meanings to make you think about the message. When asked by his disciples why he spoke in parables he explained that black and white explanations limit thinking about other meanings. Like dreams, the parable causes people to think in expanded ways. With dream interpretations, for instance, there are often several layers of interpretation. The saying, ‘a picture is worth a thousand words’ makes this point.

The parable of the Prodigal Son illustrates this idea. As the story goes, a certain man had two sons [2]. The younger son asks his father for his inheritance so he could enjoy his life now. His father agreed and gave him his portion. The younger son left his father’s household and lived a riotous life in a foreign country. After a while, there was a famine in the land and he quickly became broke. He did what we could to earn a living and found employment as a pig feeder. When he came to his senses, he decided to return home, apologized for his mistake, and asked his father if he could work as his servant. Upon hearing this, his father was happy to see him and gave a big banquet to welcome this son back into the household. His older brother was angry about how well his younger brother was treated, and complained to his father. His father tried to calm things down by explaining that he had enjoyed the household alone, that his inheritance was still forthcoming, and that his love for him had not waned. He added that he was happy to have the younger son come home and the family restored.

Most people hear this story and conclude that the son who stayed home was good and the one who left was bad. However, there’s more to the parable when you ask additional questions. Why did the young son leave the home in the first place? Was it simply because he was young and restless? Is it possible that he had a bad relationship with his father and didn’t feel welcomed in the household? Maybe his father showed favoritism toward the older son and ignored him. Maybe the young son felt he could do better on his own. His father could have said no and simply refused to give him the inheritance. Just because the son asked, didn’t mean the father had to agree. That his father said yes was not the son's fault. When the young son lost all his money you might conclude that he was careless, but there was a famine in the land and it is likely that everyone had losses. For example, many homes and retirement accounts lost their value, and investments were down in the 2007-2009 worldwide recession. Even if the young son was not foolish with his money, the famine may have caused his funds to disappear quickly. We can ask questions about the son's relationship with his father. What is it? Maybe he had a bad relationship with his son and this was the price for sonship. Perhaps his father didn't appreciate the younger son. Perhaps he wanted to get rid of him at the time. Maybe he felt threatened by the younger son's presence. The older son was upset because he never left his father's household. He complained about the banquet that his father was giving to celebrate his younger brother's homecoming. He felt that he never did the bad things his younger brother did, yet his father gave him no banquet. What was the older son's problem?

Integrating Shadow and Persona

The shadow for people with negative habits and emotional addictions contains spiritual truth and self-knowledge. Until people learn about, make peace with, and express this side of their nature the shadow will remain as the feared and unwanted side of their personality. While the shadow is often a threat, it is easy to see that in this case it can be a boon to you if you can relate to it in the proper way. The shadow for spiritual people who are free of emotional addictions and many of the ills that afflict those who are not aware of their oneness with God and the power within them is the ruthless tendency to see people victimized by negative habits as dummies. Comprehensive spiritual education teaches you about spiritual laws, being one with God, and that at the highest level you can know God's thoughts and become God. Most spiritual people conform more or less to these truths, and even deny being a victim and negative thinking. Spiritual teachings go further and urge us to be happy, loving and wise, etc. In attempting to conform to some ideals, many spiritual people reject that they can be unhappy, victimized, and unconscious.

There are differences in the ways people change and release bad habits just as there are differences in the ways people receive guidance from the Divine and introduce new behaviors. The differences depend on differences between consciousness of spirit and unconsciousness and between disciplined and undisciplined living. Choosing to seek and follow Spirit is the path of the deathless; choosing to follow the ego is the path to death. When the light of true knowledge and the deeper mind dispels the darkness of ignorance, peace ensues. When you accept that God has better ideas than you do your thoughts and things have less importance, and something far more glorious than you could have imagined replaces them. People freed from the fetters of following their emotions and all their attendant anxieties, who seek Spirit's guidance as a companion to fulfillment, are on the path to mastering the art of letting go. Only when you fully and willingly choose to follow God's will you have the courage to become what you are destined to be.

The following story of a neighbor is an example of integrating the shadow and persona. Mike prides himself as being a religious man and spends long hours with his church every Sunday. One evening I went out to catch a late movie and saw Mike standing in the street in front of his house pacing back and forth. When I asked him what was going on he pointed to a car blocking his driveway in such a way that he couldn't get his truck out. He said he was waiting for the Tow Company and police to come and take the car away. He explained that the visiting owner told him she would move the car nearly an hour ago. Just before I left to catch my movie, I said it's good you called the Tow Company and that ought to teach the woman a lesson. The next morning I asked Mike how things worked out. He explained that the Tow Company and police arrived about half-hour after I left.

Instead of having them tow her car, he asked if they would go to her house with him to give her one last chance to move her car. They agreed and the woman quickly came out and moved her car. At that point, the tow truck and police left the scene. To his amazement, the woman partially parked her car in his driveway again. I said wow, what did you do about that? Well I'm such a nice guy that I just let the car stay their all night. I chuckled and thought to myself, was Mike expressing his persona or shadow? Is it possible to be the "good guy" and express the shadow as well? I believe the answer is yes, but it depends on the person and their feelings about what is going on. In this case, Mike was the nice guy whose shadow was not accepting the actions of the woman who disrespected his property. Had he followed through with having the car towed he would still have been the polite fellow he wants to be and not the uptight and polite shadow-suppressing fellow he ended up being.

People contain within themselves the full range of potential human behavior and personality traits, but exclude some potentials for the sake of developing a specific conscious personality. Take the Great Commandment, for instance [3]. It would not be necessary to have a commandment saying, *"love God with all your heart, mind, strength, and soul; and love your neighbor as your self,"* unless it was likely that you might not do these things. If you follow the Great Commandment, those unloving and hateful psychological tendencies excluded by the Great Commandment are included in the shadow personality. The necessity of integrating the shadow and the dark, unwanted aspects of personality and life as a whole is explained by Lao Tzu in his simple observation, *"a good person is a bad person's teacher and a bad person is a good person's charge"* [4]. You can also see the transformational value in seeking God's help to integrate upside down emotions in the original title of Terry Cole-Whittaker's book *Every Saint Has a Past, Every Sinner a Future* which was later changed to *Dare To Be Great.*

The bible presents Jesus as a man without sin, as the flawless example of a person who made no mistakes. He set a high standard for us to follow and his example allows humanity to elevate its consciousness. Yet even Jesus had a shadow. He expressed his shadow in such a way that it serves as a lesson to us. In the following two stories, he shows us how to call an evil, evil by expressing his shadow in a healthy way. The first story is the one where he encounters the Money Changers in the temple. He enters the temple near the end of his ministry, sees many people selling and buying and he overthrew the tables of the moneychangers and the seats of those that sold doves. As he does so he says, *"It is written, my house shall be called of all nations the house of prayer, but you have made it a den of thieves."* [5]. He was angry and had a temper tantrum. Instead of stuffing his feelings and keeping his lips sealed, he expressed his upset. Had he not done so his shadow may have grown and become less manageable. Like a pressure cooker with a tight lid, he may have exploded in a larger way that caused physical harm to others. By expressing your capacity for anger in a controlled manner and integrating it into your conscious personality like Jesus, it will help you become a stronger more resolute person.

When the Pharisees confronted Jesus, they asked him why he worked on the Sabbath by picking corn and later by healing a man with a withered hand. Even though they were angry at his actions, he did so anyway and responded to their question by asking, *"Is it lawful on the Sabbath day to do good or evil? To save life, or destroy it?"* [6]. In going against the established law he was expressing the unwanted shadow. Had he not introduced a larger way of thinking about the law, its shadow would have become more dangerous because the conscious personality would continue to lose touch with it. His mission to teach about love by going beyond the rigid black and white thinking of the law is essentially an expression of the shadow. Jesus whole purpose to fulfill the law by teaching love gives us an excellent example of the difficulty and benefits of integrating shadow and persona.

Releasing Negativity

Being around negative and unhappy people rubs off on you like catching a cold. In addition, to make matters worse, people remember negative thoughts, like insults and criticisms, more than positive thoughts like compliments and encouragement. The following example will illustrate this point. I once attended a Buddhist talk in San Francisco. One of the participants asked the speaker how he should deal with his lingering upset at the person who cut in front of him to steal a parking space as he arrived for the talk. He ended up needing to park an extra block away. The speaker thanked him for making it to the talk then asked, "How far did you come to attend the lecture and how many other drivers did you have to deal with?" The man replied, "Hundreds if you count the people I had to look out for and that looked out me on the freeway and bridge from the East Bay and through town." The teacher then asked, "Did anything go wrong with all those people?" The man replied, "Well no, everyone did the right thing." The teacher then asked, "Why do you focus on that one negative encounter instead of the hundreds where things went right?" The room went silent, for a moment, as the man never answered the teacher's question.

Most people have this kind of negative bias. Although one insult can overpower a hundred compliments, you can do many things to get beyond negative thinking and this kind of limited focus. It's not easy or natural, but you can replace pessimism with optimism, negative behavior with positive behavior and false belief with true belief. To do so, calls for learning from good teachers and practice. To do so, demands a significant degree of self-regulation or learning new ways of thinking and acting. Visioning and the Change are powerful tools that can be used for answering questions like, "What is God's idea about the thing I can do to love and care for others?" "What is God's vision for the kind of service I can provide to others with enthusiasm and passion?" "What must I learn and become to be happy?" Just thinking about past moments of feeling deeply loved and cared for by another, or times when you loved and cared for another or felt enthusiastic about where you were doing will move you toward happiness, ease, liberation and even healing. In his book titled *Excuses Begone*!, Dr. Wayne Dyer tells us that we can practice not believing everything we think by asking, "Is it true?" "Can I prove its true?" and "How would my life look if it's not true and I had other options?" [7].

Negative thinking refers to ego-centered thoughts or decisions that shrink and by nature limit who you are. Because beliefs are the framework for the thoughts you think, the only thing worse than thinking negative thoughts is having negative or false beliefs. For better or worse, people are bound to keep thinking about the things they believe. Even though it's a bad idea to believe most of the things we think, we do it anyway. People believe its okay, for instance, to dwell on being a victim, to complain, to criticize, to resent or regret past actions, to make excuses, to blame others, etc. After all you have a right to do so. But you also have a right to dwell on other things and to change. It's not difficult to understand why Buddha says that all suffering comes from believing your thoughts.

Researchers on the subject tell us that about 95 percent of our daily thoughts are the same thoughts we had yesterday, the day before, and the day before that, etc. We are habitual thinkers and as already mentioned we tend to believe what we think without question. The following story illustrates how most people think. A woman drove into her driveway late at night and it was dark outside. She opens her car door and steps on something squishy. Without hesitation, she fearfully assumes it's a snake and slams the car door shut. She's so afraid that she sleeps in her car over night. At daybreak, she backs up the car a bit, rolls down the window and sees that she stepped on a water hose. She is relieved that it was not a snake but it never occurred to her to hold off her original judgment and see if it was true. Like many people, her habitual thoughts led to negative thinking and habitual stress.

The way to happiness is a subject at the heart of every religious tradition and every discipline that studies the human soul. Because true happiness comes from within, visioning and related methods for catching God's ideas can lead the way. When you look outside of yourself suffering sets in and you can never find the fulfillment you seek. Unlike the outer categories of happiness such as "material happiness," "false happiness," and "unhappiness," spiritual happiness is permanent and attainable by anyone willing to release the things that rob them of happiness. The main thieves are negative thinking, blaming other people and circumstances for our problems and bad habits. Happiness is an inside job and when you look for it outside you will not find genuine happiness. When you look for ways to make more money and acquire things thinking that this will give you the happiness you want you get a temporary happiness high that may last for a while but can't be sustained by these outside sources. Instead of changing the way we think about things, most people look outside for possessions such as a car or house or relationship feeling that this will make them happy, and it does for a while.

Questionable Answers

A common occurrence is that some answers are unexpected, resisted, and outright rejected. When this happens, it raises the question, "Is there another answer to my question?" While there is always more than one answer to any given question and more than one way to look at anything, this does not imply a different answer to the question. Rather, it may be a variation of the answer. Even though the text of each hexagram differs, the bottom line meanings may not be that different. When people ask different experts the same question the answers they give will likely be more similar than different, but rarely the same answer.

The answer to some questions may be puzzling because they don't fit with the possibilities you expect. Some answers are mysterious because there is no answer. For instance, when you ask seek answers to visioning questions and receive nothing at all or draw a blank or see only dark space or perhaps get a dizzy sensation, the answer is unknown. While this can be puzzling, you should remember that everything means something and nothing means something as well. It may mean that you are not ready to receive the answer to your question or that the answer is simply unknowable to you at the time of your request. As already discussed regarding either/or questions, asking a question in no way guarantees an answer in the way that you want it.

When you ask a question at a given point in time and space it comes with the consciousness of that moment, and you can never duplicate that consciousness. That is, because the universe is always changing and evolving just as we are changing and evolving as part of the universe; the present can never be identical to the past. In pointing out that the original situation cannot be duplicated, C.G. Jung says, "One ought not go to cadavers to study life" [8].

When the answer to your question is truly unclear the question may be asked a second time. If you don't understand the vision you get you can set it aside and ask the for another vision. Only after accepting or considering the first answer is right, even though it is initially unwanted or not understood, should you seek another answer for clarity. In most cases, it is better to have patience, reflect on the answer given, and perhaps re-phrase and re-ask the original question. You might ask yourself, "Is this the best way to ask the question?" or "How does this answer make sense?"

In cases where the second answer to the same question is completely different from the first, I view the second answer as the more correct answer. Although you cannot forget the first answer, you should accept that the second answer contains the most up-to-date information. If you repeatedly ask the same or nearly the same question the answer you get will change. For example, if the Change gives several warnings to avoid a certain course and you continue to ask the question about pursuing that course, a subsequent answer may suggest that you ignore the warning or that it's now a good idea to move in the direction that was previously denied. It's as if the universe is saying, "I tried to tell you but since you refused to listen its time to do it your way so you can finally learn what I've been trying to tell you."

3

Catch the Vision

In the widest sense every thing is a symbol of that which constitutes its inner being.
—Thomas Troward

In this book, visions and intuitive insights are regarded as revelations from God. From the Divine perspective, people with spiritual experience will have a better understanding of what the Divine has to say. The Bible regards visions, dreams, angels, and intuition to catch God's ideas in much the same way, and as a whole, they tell the story of how God makes its way from the invisible realm into the visible realm. Through visions and the like, the biblical story was told through prophets and wise individuals who caught them and passed them on through oral and written traditions. It is fair to say that without visions and other intuitive encounters we would have no Bible, no Judaism, no Christianity, no Islam, and no spiritual traditions. Only after their personal intuitive experiences with the Divine did people of the bible, and the priests who wrote it, think long and serious about God. They gave meaning to their experiences and called these collected interpretations the Bible.

The Garden of Eden allegory gives us an example of how humankind moved from unity and vision to separation and no vision. In this story, the tree of life stands for unity and the tree of knowledge of good and evil represents separation. The more you cherish the tree of knowledge the more you move toward separation and the more you embrace the tree of life the more you move toward unity. In psychological terms, the daily choices you make between ego and self are much like choosing between the tree of knowledge and the tree of life. Manifestations of unity show up as aligning yourself with the will of God and releasing the need to be in control and get what you want. Separation comes about when you ignore the Self or God's will. The Garden of Eden and tree of life represent spiritual ideas, intuitive thinking, and vision. Being out of the Eden and the tree of knowledge of good and evil represent material desires, sensual feelings, and living without vision [1]. Since the beginning humanity has been in constant back and forth movement between separation and unity, self and ego, vision and visualization.

Getting things from the Universe through the power of desire is an act of separation from the whole. When you support the will of the Divine by seeking its vision you are giving support to the whole and moving toward unity. Just as the visualization of desires is the opposite of letting visions show the way, separation is the opposite of unity. In visioning, you are catching God's ideas and letting go of whatever attachments are necessary to embody these ideas. Whereas visualization is the process of clarifying or manifesting what already exists in potential for an individual, visioning is the process of clarifying what the whole reveals. When visioning becomes your spiritual practice, manifesting the things you desire takes a back seat to manifesting the Divine.

In the beginning, the unknown Universe wanted to see and know itself. In order to do so it had to separate part of its unknown self from its state of wholeness. The unknown part became things and the things in time needed to recognize the wholeness to complete the cycle of seeing and knowing. For individual things to return to the whole of the unknown they must release their desire for form. When your desire to see and know the Divine exceeds your desire for things, you have taken the first step toward reunion. As you support God in manifesting its will, you become one with God and in turn manifest your highest fulfillment. Your highest fulfillment, identity, the Source, and God in are fact one in the same.

The Creation of Visioning

Most people find the world of dreams and daydreams acceptable because everyone has them, but tend to look down upon visions, and divination. Although we all live with the world of inner activity at all times, most people ignore its presence. That some ways of getting messages from within are acceptable while not others are is largely a matter of how the person receiving them understands them, and how they come to those who receive them. Many people who experience dreams and visions don't communicate their content or even try for fear of being ostracized. While visioning and dreams are among the most direct methods of understanding the inner life most people are not interested in visioning and even fewer have an interest in dreaming. Of the many thoughts and feelings people have about the subject they rarely include the prospect of spiritual growth or understanding the joy in reunion with the Divine.

Dreaming is a necessary part of living and when properly understood can help you to release the grip that your personality and ego has on your life. Dreaming like visioning is a cure for pessimistic or negative thinking. Most people choose not to remember dreams because the language is confusing and they don't tell you want you want to hear. While it is not required that you remember your dreams you must dream. On average, people spend about one and a half hours in Rapid Eye Movement (REM) sleep. Dreaming occurs in the REM portion of sleep while the eyes are in constant movement as in waking life. If prevented from going into REM sleep, you will soon begin to hallucinate, develop neuroses, and lose your sanity. Simply put, dreams awaken you to life, maintain your sanity, and are God's way of asking you to re-examine the way you think about things and to keep your life in order for daily living.

For people who are spiritually inclined, dreams, like visions, give true freedom of choice and unlimited opportunities to manifest divinity. At a minimum dreams tell us about our shadow and what is happening in daily life that we are unconscious about. When you work with a dream the first question you should ask is, how could it be related to my life or the questions I am asking about my life? This requires you to step back and answer questions such as, what is going on, what am I doing or what am I planning to do? For those seeking reunion with the divine, dreams like visions offer spiritual solutions to every problem, and allow you to experience and serve God. Ordinary dreams tell you about aspects of your personality, life activities and choices, and what you don't know. When your attitude is one of unity and you pay attention, your dreams become the voice of God. *The Talmud* says, "The dream not interpreted is like a letter from God not read." The spiritual practice of catching divine ideas through visions or dreams gives form to divinity and attracts whatever is needed to expand that form.

The hidden world of dreams and visions which resides in the unconscious is a much larger realm than can be imagined, one that has a complete life of its own running parallel to the ordinary life we live day to day. Dreams are the secret source of thoughts. Unlike visions which are largely given through daydream states, dreams which come when you sleep influence you in ways that are all the more powerful because of being uncensored, more hidden, unexpected and thought provoking than visions. C.G. Jung's model of the Psyche tells us how the conscious and unconscious parts of our personality and life relate to one another. His study of the soul helps you to understand how your persona (the roles you play and your identity) on the one hand, your shadow (undesirable roles and traits which oppose the persona) on the other hand, and ego (your choice maker or personal will), relate to the Self (Almighty God within you). When viewed as an iceberg, the smaller portion above the water or conscious realm contains the persona and ego while the much larger unconscious realm, below the water, contains the shadow and the Self. Most people know far more about their persona or mask, while the shadow is unwanted, feared and suppressed, and they are unconscious for the most part, regarding what it has to say about their deepest secrets and intentions.

When your spiritual practice makes use of visioning and intuitive tools like the Change, you'll move toward a life of unity with the Self where no one aspect of personality (ego, persona or shadow) is allowed to dominate in expression at the expense of other aspects. Those who seek to catch and express wisdom from the Self, or God's ideas, will face many opportunities to manifest the divine and transform their state of being from lesser to greater joy, health and fulfillment.

Because every aspect of your identity lives within the whole of the Psyche, you can choose to receive and express any part of the whole at any time. The degree to which you receive the whole depends upon the degree to which your ego makes the choice to do so. The more your desires are in charge the more your choices will be defined by limited awareness, and the more you release control to serve divinity the more your choices are defined by the whole.

Visioning and Visualization

Many people see visioning and visualization as similar but they are as different as letting go and getting things, listening and speaking. Visualization refers to wordless thoughts directed toward a desired goal, whereas visioning is receptive and open-ended. Visualization takes the assertive path of getting what you want from the Universe; visioning takes the receptive path of helping the Universe express itself. Visioning starts with the premise that you're open-minded about what you want, where to go, or what to do, and as such you seek to catch divine ideas for inspiration and answers.

With visualization, you are using the laws of the Universe to manifest your needs and wants. You can command what you want into existence by holding a thought or picture of what you want in mind, remaining focused on it, and taking appropriate actions as needed to assist in its manifestation. Albeit simplified, the visualization process works like Aladdin's' magic lantern. You rub the magic lantern to get the genies attention. When the genie pops out and says, "Your wish is my command." You say what you want and the genie grants your wish. In visualization, you can understand the genie as the blind king and all-powerful Self who awaits instructions from the ego. In visioning, the aim is being, not doing. Instead of using the power for good in the Universe to get what you want, you ask the power to use you. You acknowledge there is a power for good in the universe, but instead of using it, you choose to support it. The law of attraction governs both Visioning and visualization. Visioning attracts God's ideas to the receptive mind. When the things you visualize accord with the nature and will of God you will attract them.

As her reminder, and no doubt to remind others, my mother use to wear a button that said, "Pray until Something Happens." This was her way of visualizing. While this is still a good reminder, talking to God through prayer also calls for listening to God for the answer, which may not be the answer you want. Another method of visualization known as outlining takes place by keeping a clear picture of the things you want. You can do this by putting up a picture of the car, house, or environment you want to have as a constant visual reminder in places such as your kitchen or above our desk or in your bedroom. Whether its money, better health or loving relationships, what ever you keep your focus upon comes into existence in a way that fits with your identity, situation, and what you allow yourself to have. Where your attention goes, energy flows and manifestation follows. If you are not clear about what you want, your manifestation will not make sense to you. For example, a man who used affirmations and prayer to attract more love into his life than he had ever experienced got his answer in a few months. While he was expecting a love relationship, he received invitations to parties, compliments on his good looks, and a feeling that people wanted to be his friend. After getting many invitations to participate in relating he felt overwhelmed by his sudden popularity and asked God to back off.

After reviewing hundreds of scientific experiments on prayer in his book *Healing Words,* Larry Dossey, MD concludes that prayer, a form of affirmation and visualization, works one-hundred percent of the time in a statistically significant way [2]. Yet we know that most prayers like most visualization efforts don't give us the exact results we seek. These facts don't diminish the need for visualization, praying or simply asking for one very good reason. The likelihood of getting what you want is always greater if you ask for it. Although the odds of winning a lottery are a million times less than the odds of prayer being answered, you can't win if you don't play.

Throughout the Old and New Testaments we hear that people don't have what they need or want because they have not asked for them. When you do ask, you won't get what you want as much as what you are because your identity defines what you can attract. You cannot manifest things that are unlike your true inner nature even though you may want to do so. Getting what you want through visualization is not unlike piecing together a complex jigsaw puzzle. With a sustained focus, the pieces will come together and the picture will manifest. Even though visualization puts your attention on the goal, it takes visioning to shine light on the unknown. Discovering your path in life and your identity is an on-going work that calls for visioning or some kind of direct intuitive contact with the architect of identity, God itself. Those who have yet to discover their true identity should know that God knows what it is, and if they catch God's ideas about the plans they have before acting on them they can discern whether this plan or that plan is consistent with their true nature.

Visioning is an effective tool for helping you see what changes need making, what you need to release, and how you can go about doing so. It is the interface between mind and matter, thoughts and things, and between you and God. It can help you understand the problems, questions or needs indicated by your circumstances, and develop healthy ways to meet those needs. Prayer can be of great assistance to both visualization and visioning efforts. Dossey summarized numerous research studies that concluded that directed and non-directed prayer methods are both effective and practically identical to visualization and visioning [3].

The directed approach is like visualization in that it tends to use many words to focus on what you want to manifest. For example, If you want to have money, it may be necessary to know how much money to ask for. Do you ask for a small, reasonable, outrageous amount? Do you ask for the money to come to you in expected or unexpected ways? Do you need it, sooner, later, etc.?

The non-directed approach, like visioning, is one of listening for answers to open ended questions such as, "What is God's idea about itself expressing through me as money?" Visioning uses few words and essentially asks, "May the best thing happen regarding my interests" or "Thy will be done" or "let it be." The studies reviewed by Dossey conclude that non-direct prayer is quantitatively more effective and gives results twice as great when compared to the direct approach [4]. His research findings suggest that open-ended visioning methods are about twice as effective as visualization methods.

Visioning is the process of listening to the ever-present divine broadcast. As long as you have the desire to receive and follow God's ideas, you have the right attitude for visioning. The answer to the question of how often and how long to do visioning varies from person to person. A good rule of thumb is to do it as often as you can if you need answers to difficult or moderate questions, and while dealing with daily routines such as deciding how to accomplish various tasks, spend your day, or set priorities. You can do this because the universe contains infinite wisdom and energy that can't be depleted. When you integrate visioning and visualization, the results are stunning. When you catch God's thoughts about your ideas, you can know in advance how your visualization efforts will materialize and make appropriate adjustment based on this added insight. Those who learn to balance visioning and visualization will do so more often, more enthusiastically, and more carefully. In addition, they will get the best results.

Unity and Separation

Because of conflicts between ego and self or your plans and God's plans, there's always a need for resolution and self-improvement. In the language of ego and self, the ego exists in a box that represents our individual comfort zone and habits. Thinking of the Self as the world and the ego as a country offers an analogy for understanding unity and separation. The ego contains beliefs, ways of thinking, and personal traits that define our ways of being in the world. When you need help from beyond your ego but remain unaware of what is available it's like being thirsty for a drink while swimming in a lake. The help is there but not recognized. When the ego desires things and makes choices with little awareness of how they may affect others, and the world in general it remains separated from the Self. For instance, when any country engages in destructive behavior the effect is global, and if any country discovers a medical breakthrough the whole world benefits. When the ego chooses to act in ways that serve the Self the result is good for all.

The parable of the talents serves as an example of unity and separation. As the parable goes, a nobleman left three of his servants in charge of one, two and five talents respectively while he went away for a long trip. The talents represent Divine potentials. Upon his return, he asked each servant for an accounting of what he did with the talent(s) left in their care. The servant given five talents expanded them to ten, the servant given two talents increased them to four, but the servant given one talent did nothing. That servant was afraid of losing his only talent so he buried it and returned it in tact to the nobleman. The nobleman had good things to say to the servants who multiplied their talents and, as a reward, made them ruler of many things. However, he scolded the servant who did nothing with his one talent and took it away. He explained that those that have will attract more, and they will have abundance, but those that have not even that shall be taken away. Simply put, this story is about faith in spiritual ideas and illustrates the age-old saying, 'use it or lose it.' The choice always becomes one of inviting the vision and growth with self-awareness or sticking with your limited ego-awareness. When we use our gifts to serve Spirit we participate in manifesting unity. When you're afraid to let go of your plans and trust God you manifest the losses associated with separation.

Just as too much separation creates problems of isolation, too much unity can deny individuality. The Buddhist teaching that all suffering is the result of believing your thoughts and wanting things serves as another example of the relation between unity and separation. The teaching implies that when you give up thoughts about doing things your way the circumstances of your life changes from contraction to expansion, from suffering to joy, and from doing to being. Through visioning, you can learn what needs to be released and kept in order to assist the Divine in manifesting its kingdom. Growth replaces whatever you release, and what ever is manifested in the name of the Divine meets your needs as well as those of the Divine. When you are unwilling to let go and let God's will have its way you suffer, but when you are willing to let go suffering falls by the wayside. I say "willing" because some of the things you have and want can be of great value in co-creating with God.

The nature of separation and unity can be understood by simply seeing unity as the whole and separation as part of the whole. If you start with an understanding of the whole, knowing the part and its relationship to the whole is straightforward. Understanding the whole allows you to answer questions about the meaning of the whole and its parts. If you begin with an understanding of the part, you can speculate about the whole. The more parts or samples you examine from the whole the more you'll know about the whole. In the world of separation, people think by collecting information samples from the particular whole they want to understand and then make educated guesses or predictions about that whole. For example, you can make good predictions about an entire group by defining the whole you want to know and then taking a sample from that whole. In the world of unity, understanding subjects and questions calls for taking samples as well. However, here the samples are in the form of intuitive insights such as visions, hexagrams or dreams. While we don't get objective data from the inner world we can still make good predictions about it. A small sampling of divine insights on most subjects will give good ideas about what the Divine thinks about that subject.

Allowing the Vision

Albert Einstein constantly performed what he called "thought experiments," using visual images. "Imagination is more important than knowledge," he once said, acknowledging that he arrived at his most creative insights not through reason but through imagination. One of my favorite TV ads, created by Citicorp that says, "Every night you go to sleep but your dreams are wide awake, visions never sleep, opportunities never sleep, goals never sleep, hopes never sleep." The ad tells us that visions are always available to us.

It is common to hear people say, "I don't have dreams." Even though night dreams and daydreaming take place daily most people don't remember them and few understand what they mean when remembered. A similar situation applies to the realm of visions. Whenever you focus on remembering and understanding night dreams, you will learn to do so. The same applies to visioning, but the process is easier. Visioning becomes stronger with focus and experience, and over a few weeks or months of working with them you will get better. Visioning is just like anything else that is new to you, like learning to paint or play a musical instrument. At first it feels unfamiliar and strange, but the more you do it, the more comfortable it becomes, until you can do it automatically without effort. The key is to relax, allow your mind to daydream and accept what comes up. The idea is to "fake it until you make it." If you get something, it means something, if you get nothing it means something. If you get nothing you might ask, "What would I get if I could get something?"

The visioning process as made popular by Michael Bernard Beckwith, founder of Agape International Spiritual Center, is an eight-step process. As outlined in his CD titled *The Life Visioning Process, Session 2* the process begins with being centered, and spending some time in the silence to establish the awareness of God's presence and your oneness with the source of life [5]. This may take a few moments or up to perhaps ten minutes or so. Once you establish this connection there are four standard questions to be asked in a state of inner listening, observing and openness to God's ideas for your life. To honor what is received the visioned insights should be written down. Everyone is different. Some insights take the form of images, feeling tones, words phrases, perhaps whole scenes, and so forth. There is no one format and you don't need to be clairvoyant to do visioning. Beckwith offers the following four questions for the visioning process, and encourages people to adapt the process for their environment and purposes.

1. What is God's idea of itself as my life?
2. What must I become to manifest this vision?
3. What must I release to become this vision?

4. What gifts and talents do I now possess that can be used to serve this vision?

After getting insights for these questions, it's important to remain in the silence and give thanks for what has been received. You are giving thanks not for the future, but for what is already happening in the Mind of God.

Visioning begins with the four questions just given, but the process of hearing God's ideas applies to other questions. For instance, the first question can be "What is God's idea about this subject, person, relationship, project, etc.?" Visioning questions that begin with, "What is God's idea about…?" might conclude with "How is this or that to be accomplished?" or "What is hindering the progress of this or that project?" "If this or that action is taken, what will be the result?" "What can be done to resolve this or that situation?" Unlike either/or questions that may be addressed by the Change, visioning is better suited for open-ended questions. Spiritual discernment questions, a form of visioning which is better suited to the Change addressed in the Chapters four and five, may be asked in an either/or or decision-making format. In visioning, you are always opening to a Divine idea of what you are or subject you are visioning about. You always start from the premise that God has a better idea than you do, and that you are volunteering yourself to manifest its ideas and let go of your personal ideas of how things should be.

Learning to vision will help you become more aware of the background behind your questions, your perspectives, potential choices, and even how you feel. Visioning will help you clear your mind and open up to new ideas, possibilities, and new ways of solving problems. Compared to intuition and visions received in the form of hexagrams from the Change, the formless nature of visions allows you to draw more deeply upon your creativity. Although the meaning of individual visions are not easy to discern with confidence, the process of collecting several visions moves you in the direction God is already going. Through visioning you can learn to relax and release the need to control any situation whether you have a preference or not for the outcome. Releasing the ego honors the soul and elevating the ego dishonors the soul. You can use vision to help you determine how your activities in life or habitual ways of doing things contribute to your circumstances or problems.

Vision, divination, intuition insights and the like point you in the right direction and give you the right opinion. While they show you how to get beyond the ignorance of not knowing what's going on or where to go, they won't give a detailed roadmap. Roadmaps can only come from a teachers, learning, or guides that have made the journey. Visioning is a big step, but only the first step toward finding what you seek. If for instance I am lost in the woods and don't have a clue of how to get out visioning, like a compass, will point me in the right direction. In *The Creative Encounter* Thurman says, "In the living of my life I establish more and more levels of understanding of the Creator as I achieve in fact what I seen in vision." [6]

Even though a compass is not good enough to get you where you need to go, there is no limit to how much it can be used and in time the compass alone may get you to your destination. If it takes a thousand steps to get out of the woods from where you stand, visioning can lead the way with small steps and in time with a quantum leap. With faith, persistence, and patience the light of visions reveal what you need along the way. Visioning can be applied to any person, thing, or situation that can be seen, touched, smelled, heard, tasted or experienced in any way. Vision binds us together and keeps us moving in the right direction. At a minimum, it puts you in the ballpark and points the way as in north, south, east or west, but it's up to you to take the steps. What would happen if there is no vision or no one to point us in the right direction? In Proverbs 29:18 King Solomon answers this question by saying, "Where there is no vision the people perish." Solomon's answer is good advice and may be understood as a universal law.

4

Manifest the Vision

Everything in the unconscious
seeks outward manifestation.
—C.G. Jung

As mentioned in the previous chapter there is no one way to do visioning or get visions, but eight stages can be identified. To better understand the mechanics of catching and manifesting visions let's talk about the stages common to all forms of the visioning, concentration, meditation and inner observation in general. Taken apart and examined we can describe them in the following way.

Stage 1: The process begins with the belief that you can receive information from the Source of all knowledge. According to Ernest Holmes in *Creative Mind and Success*, if the process of sitting in the silence to get centered and receive guidance from Spirit is trusted, everything that follows will usually fall into place even if it is unexpected [1].

Stage 2: Place your attention on the question, person, place, object or situation, etc. you have in mind and keep your focus on it long enough to complete the next two stages.

Stage 3: Increase your focus on the details about that object or subject. This implies noticing more and more details about it such as what is revealed, how it feel, its color, its look or sense, and so on.

Stage 4: Unify or become one with the question, object or situation in mind. In short, put yourself in the picture. You may temporarily lose or forget yourself because you are tuning out the world around you. What sets visioning apart from other methods of gaining access to riches of the inner world is that it always seek to commune with God. When the uses of mental imagery, intuition, and even clairvoyance and lucid dreaming are applied to catching God's ideas they can be understood as visioning. When centered in the divine, and focused on catching God's ideas you are engaged in a form of visioning.

Stage 5: This intermediate stage requires you to catch the vision and describe your insight to another person, write it down, sketch it out, or a least commit it to memory. At this intermediate stage, there may be no need to take the vision any further. You have reached the starting point of new meaning, direction and purpose. You may choose to let go of previous ideas or ways of doing things in light of the information revealed.

The last three steps deal with manifestation. Because clarification and manifestation mean the same thing, to clarify is to manifest. In stressing the need for empirical verification of our intuitive experiences, Howard Thurman guards against the danger of subjective private meaning. In *The Creative Encounter* he asks, "How may a person know he is not being deceived? Is there any way by which he may know beyond doubt, and, therefore, with verification, that what he experiences is authentic and genuine?"

Stage 6: Analyze and interpret the vision insight you got in the previous stage by answering the question, "What does it mean or could it mean to me?" Depending on the nature of the vision, answering this question may be difficult and one filled with uncertainty. The saying, 'a picture is a thousand words' applies in this situation. For people who make time there are numerous ways to go about getting the meaning such as being open to what comes to you, sharing the vision with another, looking into books on symbol interpretation, using other intuitive information, or asking for additional visions to clarify those which are less understood. It may take several sessions to collect additional visions but additional insights often provide clarity about what is revealed.

Stage 7: Verify your insights by getting validation from an independent source. If you have enough information, check out the reality of the insight with the person, subject, or situation, etc. that you focused on, and find out if it makes sense. At this point, the use of logic and feelings can be a great help in understanding what it means.

Stage 8: Take action to manifest the vision. Give it a voice, a body, a place in the world by becoming the vision. In this way, you support the Divine and its desire to manifest heaven on earth.

In David Spangler's excellent little book titled *The Laws of Manifestation* he describes the spiritual process of downward and upward manifestation [2]. Upward manifestation involves movement toward unity or wholeness. It is a journey toward self-discovery, self-actualization, and transcendence. Those who take this journey are trying to let go of their attachments to the material, emotional, relational and self-important aspects of life that hold them back from the goal of self-realization. Their aim is to release their desire for ordinary human needs—basic and tangible physical possessions, financial security and safety, loving relationships and friendships, and to be respected and looked up to by others. The main shortcoming of this journey is also its main gift, namely that of replacing personal desires often expressed as "my will be done" with "thy will be done." The fear is that in order to do God's will you will have to take a back seat and give up the things you want. While this fear may be present, you should eliminate what is false about it.

The journey toward individuality is one of separation from the Divine and downward manifestation. It is taking the road to personal development, individual recognition, and discovering one's uniqueness. Those who take this path are trying to create self-recognition, loving relationships, emotional security and material possessions. Their aim is the polar opposite and reverse order of upward manifestation in that they are attempting to attract things to themselves—self-esteem and recognition, relationships, financial security and safety, and tangible possessions.

Becoming the Vision

Divine ideas, like other ideas, cannot be manifested without help from others. Manifesting or becoming an idea is a cooperative process because you need the agreement and participation of others to clarify the idea and make it of interest to them. For example, I may need your assistance to catch God's idea, interpret my dream, or consult the Book of Changes. If you have an idea for the invention of a new product such as a car powered by your thoughts, other people must accept your invention before it can be manifested. In this case, you will need to meet with people interested in your idea, give demonstrations, get patents, get investors, designers, engineers, people to produce and market the idea, customers willing to buy what you have put together, etc. Those with faith in the Divine will be more inclined to act upon and even share their ideas without complete understanding because they know that additional information will show up when needed. Those with limited faith will likely hold back until they can completely grasp the bigger picture. Just because something makes sense to me does not mean it will make sense to you. Whether it makes sense will depend on you and me being on the same page and speaking the same language. If you have an idea and want to share it with me or others you should think about it first and then present it in a way that makes sense to both of us.

The advantage that God has in presenting images, dreams, and intuitive impressions in a variety of forms is that God's language is universal. For example, regardless of culture the images of summer and winter, young and old, or climbing and falling have universal meaning. Once the person who receives it understands an idea, additional steps must be taken to express it in a form that others recognize. The form will depend on the idea itself and can be expressed in a variety of ways, e.g. a change in direction, a change in behavior, a decision to express oneself in writing or speaking or through an act of kindness or resistance.

Catching God's ideas through intuition and visioning is analogous to fishing in that there are many ways to fish, several places to go fishing, and countless fish to catch. Fishing from the waters edge is symbolic of intuition that is close to the conscious mind such as visioning, while fishing from boats refers to a deeper level of intuition such as that seen in dreaming. Fishing with a pole is symbolic of individual or single question visioning whereas fishing with nets represents group or multiple question visioning. People who fish for entertainment resemble those who approach visioning with small needs to embody what spirit has to offer, whereas those who fish for a living have big needs to embody what spirit is giving. Like God's ideas, the fish already exist but we don't see them or know what we'll catch until we open ourselves to the process. People who cherish catching divine ideas, like the seasoned fisherman, have great faith in the unseen, ask the right questions, and know from experience that they will get what they seek. Whether you use a fishing pole or net you must still depend upon the source to provide that which you seek. When you approach the divine with an open mind to its ideas, you will attract what you need to assist you in becoming the manifestation. When you approach the Divine with your own ideas, and ask for its thoughts about them, whatever you need will be attracted to assist you in manifesting what you seek.

In the face of strong desires the ego overpowers the soul (God's will) unless steps are taken or have been taken to put the soul in a stronger position. For example, many years ago I met an attractive woman at a nightclub and we spent an hour or so dancing and having great conversation. We exchanged telephone numbers and after leaving the club, I was excited as I imagined what would follow in the coming days. I looked forward to calling and confirming that I'd be at the office party she was having with her new law practice partners a few days later.

I was reluctant to consider God's opinion because I didn't want cold water thrown on my new passion. However, based on experience I knew that ignorance is not bliss. If I did not at least listen to the Divine I would be choosing my desires and lose the possibility of following God's wisdom from the outset. I knew that my emotions would cloud and perhaps overpower the visioning in this situation so I opted to use the I Ching to catch God's wisdom as a more objective alternative. Since I had not developed any deep roots, it was not too difficult to consult the I Ching the next morning. When I did so, I was shocked when I received the hexagram *Adversity (47)* with no moving lines. This insight applied to both the present and the future.

For those unfamiliar with the I Ching and want to use it sooner rather than later, let me take a moment to explain how you can consult it, as I did. I consulted the Change by flipping a penny six times, and recorded whether the penny landed Heads or Tails each time. The pattern I got was Tail, Head, Tail, Head, Head, and Tail. Since Heads represents a yang or straight line, and Tails represents yin or a broken line, I recorded this pattern as follows.

Tail ___ ___
Head _______
Head _______
Tail ___ ___
Head _______
Tail ___ ___

This pattern is one of the 64 possible patterns or hexagrams that you can get from flipping one coin six times. Although it's not necessary to consult the Change a second time, in most cases, I wanted to see if the future would be different in this case so I consulted. I was so eager to get a complete picture that I repeated the process of flipping the coin six times and again received Hexagram 47. I was amazed at this direct response. With this second result, I knew there were no changing lines, no difference between the present and future, and nothing to do but let go. As you will note in the last section of Chapter 10 titled "Finding Your Hexagram Number" this sequence or pattern of the six lines is Hexagram 47 titled *Adversity* and the meaning of this hexagram follows the tenth chapter. .

My confidence in the Change helped me to deal with this dilemma. Do I follow my attraction or let go based on the Divine insight I received? I asked. For a brief while I did both. I allowed myself to feel the desire and without letting it grow unchecked, I caught God's idea. However, based on this insight and after reviewing the evening and my situation I decided not to call or follow thorough. The self-inflicted blow to my ego was worth it as the insight helped me to look at why things would have likely gone downhill had I followed my desire. As it turned out, I was looking for this woman to pull me out of the depression I had fallen into because of separating from with my wife about a month earlier.

I was lonely and blinded by the beautiful form before me. Even though there was no turning back to the marriage, our relationship was not really over and going forward would have created a big mess for all concerned parties and me. With the passing of a little more time, it was clear that Spirit helped me make the right decision. Had I gone forward and experienced the "Adversity" I could still turn to Spirit later for guidance on what to do, but the problem would have been much bigger. Spirit didn't tell me not go forward with my desire, only what I would likely experience if I chose to do so.

In most cases, the use of visioning before visualizing is the best thing you can do to be in alignment with the universe and gain its full support in your endeavors. It is active listening to the Divine through visioning related methods and not desire driven visualization that is the ruling faculty of humanity. The central tenet of this book is that when you listen to the inner voice and follow its guidance before taking on significant ventures, significant mistakes will be avoided.

In his book *Up from Eden,* Philosopher Ken Wilber has emphasized that descent, or moving from unity to separation, of consciousness must take place before ascent, or moving from separation to unity, can take place [3]. Even though it is tempting to create solely through visualization and many people are attracted to doing so, it is a serious mistake to ignore visioning. The use of will power is a necessary power to exercise throughout life and we need it to manifest ideas, a form of downward manifestation and to release our attachment to things, a form of upward manifestation.

Ways to do Visioning

As already mentioned there are many ways to do visioning and with each way you get a different view of the Divine message. When you truly seek to catch God's ideas through automatic writing, for instance, you are using a form of visioning. Here you pick up your pen and write without thinking or censoring the dialogue; your hand becomes the mouthpiece for communicating the vision. Much has been said about this form of catching Divine ideas and there are many books and courses on the subjects of inner wisdom dialoguing, journaling and automatic writing.

Art Therapy uses a method called blindfold drawing to gain access to the riches of the Self. I used the method to gain insights on my purpose in life by selecting multicolored crayons while blindfolded and then drawing while still blindfolded. After completing the drawing, I took off the blindfold to see in the colors selected, how I used them, how the picture looked, and the meaning it conveyed. Even though I had a sense of what I was drawing, I had no idea of what colors I was using and how the various pieces fit together. As long as we have a tool or way to allow visions to break through to the conscious mind from the unconscious, it's a process like visioning.

In my counseling practice, I often use the I Ching and tarot cards to expand upon the content of the visions received. For those who want to live in harmony with the Universe but find it difficult to discern from direct observation and experience the value of visioning is invaluable. The magic is not only in the tool or method but in the spiritual consciousness of users. The purpose of using them is to see and evaluate things from more than one perspective. In addition, the result, I believe, is a higher level of precision than any single approach or perspective offers. The systems of 78 tarot cards and 64 hexagrams from the Book of Changes represent universal conditions in the cosmos that are divined or selected at random they and serve as excellent aids for those who use them as tools for catching divine ideas. While the combination of insights they offer are finite in number, compared to the potentially infinite combination of images and intuitive based visions, their finiteness often gives interpretations that are more straightforward. The lack of form and structure in the ordinary visioning process may tempt the ego into playing with less than a full deck, where as the limited number or tarot cards and hexagrams represent playing with a "full deck."

The visioning process assumes that God is always right and knows more than you know even though you may not like the visioned insight. The process always begins with a question like, "What is God's idea for this person, project, organization, etc.?" By catching God's thoughts and thinking like God, you realize God's power. Visioning may be adapted to clarify problems and how solve them, get insights into open-ended questions, relationships, into life situations, and so forth. Visioning may be for personal reasons or in groups of two or more to create shared visions.

Typical visioning questions give insights into ones place regarding the vision, and guidance to assist in manifesting the vision. After recording your visions, you can go back and begin to interpret them as much as you want or simply let them be, and give thanks to the source from which they came.

There are two basic ways to do visioning. You can begin by asking several questions and then answer them with one vision. You can also ask and answer questions one at a time. In the first case, the answer or insight for the first, second, third, forth, and subsequent questions would be identical. I prefer the slower one visioning for one question approach, but I have found that it works remarkably well to catch one vision as the answer to several questions. This approach is sometimes necessary when we need the insight and simply don't have time for the step by step approach.

Visioning Examples

Visioning works best when the process is accepted. But, how do you honor the process in a community that does not understand it and may resist its use? How do you keep a consciousness of unity while living in a world of separation? As a practical manner, the solution to these dilemmas is learning to wear two hats. One hat in the spiritual world and the other in the material world, one by the ego and the other by the self, one for unity and one for separation. You must learn to put on the separation hat when dealing with matters of separation and return to the unity hat in matters of unity. Some examples are in order.

The creation of the Agape International Spiritual Center—This application of visioning that brought the process into the light of day for numerous spiritual centers and the people associated with them. As mentioned in *The Life Visioning Process, Session One* the Agape story started with a few people in Michael Bernard Beckwith's living room in July 1986 and grew to ten thousand people locally and over twenty thousand internationally [4]. What the visioning team had in common was a willingness to listen to the Divine broadcast. For about a year, before offering any public service, the group participated in the visioning process to catch the vision of their transformational spiritual community. They realized that they couldn't have anything they were unwilling to become. What came up was that the nature of their spiritual center was to reveal a new evolution in human consciousness. As Beckwith put it, "We had no resources, no building, and no land." What manifested from their years of visioning was a description of Agape, what they had to become, and then their first service in November 1986 with only seventeen dollars in the bank.

The Agape visioning sessions sought answers to many of the same questions until clear ideas emerged. The process took time because many divine ideas can't be understood in one session and the visions need to be discerned and clarified before planning can take shape. It is not unusual for some ideas to be reinterpreted as new visions, insights, and questions emerge. Even though it is tempting to rush out and act on new insights, it takes patience to ensure that the Divine is understood. As with most visioning it takes time for the ego to adjust to what the soul wants to bring forth and to release its opinions in favor of manifesting the visions. Since many ego-generated ideas will not be affirmed by the soul it is important to remain open and detached. In many cases ego-generated ideas are based on appearances and often overlook the wisdom of high impact vision-generated ideas that are often simple, unexciting and right before you.

The creation of a Mind-Body Healing Center—A number of its members asked the leader of a spiritual community if they could set up a Mind-Body Healing Center. He asked volunteers to make plans on what to do and forty people showed up at the first meeting. He asked that participants conduct visioning sessions once a week for the next two months week to get a consensus vision of God's ideas for the Body-Mind Center. Although most people participated in the process at the first meeting, only ten returned to continue the visioning process. The ten dwindled to a group of five who met regularly to carry out the visioning process and concluded that the participants who dropped out were doers willing to carry out plans but had no interest in visioning. After another three months of visioning working plans began to emerge on the center's purpose, services and how it was to be created.

Even though the visioning core continued to do visioning the non-visioning participants were invited back to assist in the manifestation process. Two distinct groups emerged: One focused mainly on visioning and the other on carrying out the vision. The group that didn't feel comfortable with the visioning process was less focused on how to serve and sporadic in their participation. It's as if they went along for the ride. Those who did the visioning ended up doing most of the work because they owned the visions and knew they were central to Mind-Body Healing Center. The visioning core talked about visioning, the meaning of their visions, and ways to present their vision centered plans to the non-visioning participants. The combined group focused mainly on strategy and carrying out the details of manifesting the center.

Visioning versus psychic readings—One example of an obstacle to visioning comes from the way I use to present my title as a counselor to others. Before going to ministry school, I publicly presented myself as a psychic reader and healer, and gave my name as Allen David Young, MBA, PhD. After earning the title of minister when I graduated from the Holmes Institute of Consciousness Studies I started using the title of Rev. before my name. I earned the title and wanted potential clients to recognize that my services offered a greater emphasis on spiritual consciousness. From a marketing perspective, this was a big mistake. Since most people that use psychic reading services do so for non-religious purposes my use of the reverend title placed a wall between us. It was as if the market I had successfully reached out to for years was now responding by saying, "I'm looking for a psychic reading not religious counseling."

After a year or so of using the Reverend title to the largely secular audience and losing a lot new business, the market place dictated that I stop using that title. I found that the people who saw me as Reverend Allen often projected their concepts of what a minister should be on to me. Some thought I should be more generous with my time, offer free prayer and readings on demand, and even walk on water so-to-speak. As long as I accepted the projections everything was fine, but when I didn't we had to deal with our shadows and everyone was disappointed. Their shadow was that I charged too much for my services, that I wasn't the nice guy minister type they expected, and that I was selling religion. My shadow was that they didn't want to pay what I determined my services were worth and wanted me to play the traditional role of minister as they saw it. Some thought ill about the relationship between psychic readings and religion. I concluded that I needed to wear my minister hat in spiritual communities and my business hat in my public psychic counseling practice. The reality of unity, oneness and vision is not one that works in an environment of people who don't understand the nature of visioning.

Integrating two communities—I participated in a spiritual integration community conference aimed at reuniting two spiritual communities, United Centers for Spiritual Living and International Centers for Spiritual Living. The two groups had been one spiritual organization, but they separated some forty years ago over internal differences. Throughout the meeting, various participants asked those in charge a variety of questions about how the integration process would take place, what the new organization would become, how the educational requirements would be integrated, etc. The leaders responded repeatedly that this would depend upon visioning input from the participants. Toward the end of the conference, about four-hundred representatives made up of ministers, practitioners and laity who attended the conference participated in a community visioning exercise. The leader of the large group visioning session paraphrased the individual questions and gave community participants about thirty minutes or so to draw or write out their vision answers with crayons, and then share them within small groups of ten.

Participants then posted their visions on the auditorium walls for all to see.

As I looked around the room, I marveled at the massive display of artistry, colors and creativity. While each presentation was different in often striking ways it was evident, as I walked around the large room, the degree of continuity among visions. Additional, but smaller integration meetings and visioning sessions took place to bring the two organizations together. What I took away from this experience is that after the question is asked, the deeper mind reveals its ideas in such a manner that every individual catches God's ideas in their own way and communicates what they got with amazing similarities. Once the vision is released it's available to everyone, individual or community. It's there for every one to see or hear if they have the eyes and ears for doing so.

Being susceptible to scams—One of my clients came to me to deal with one of the painful problems that most people face at lease once. After going through another financial scam, she wanted my assistance in understanding why she was so susceptible to scams and what could be done to guard against them in the future. She had faith in my intuitive ability and wanted a reading on how to think about and correct her situation. To begin the reading I got three vision insights to address her first question as follows:

-a deer standing in a wooded area
-sheep walking through a business district
-someone living an isolated life high in the hills beyond city life below

After discussing the first two images, we agreed on their meaning. In a straightforward way they suggested that being scammed was the result of presenting a sheepish attitude to others and being open to victimization because of inadequate self knowledge. Sheep are known for their vulnerability and being easily led. The sheep in the business district represent her tendency to trust others to be responsible with her money and simply not thinking about the possibility that many people look out for themselves. I mentioned that some people by nature are predators and others prey. I added that all of life depends on predators devouring prey, and that life must consume life to live. I nodded my head in agreement when she remarked that being a prey or predator has some advantages, just as leaders and followers, strong and weak each have advantages. While this was not a pleasant description, she felt it gave her an enlightened way to think about why she is scammed.

The scene of living an isolated life in the hills is similar to the first two images but adds a different perspective. It implies that hillside living was related to her spiritual interests and tendency to see life through rose colored glasses, and that these interests ought to be integrated with living in the city below. It's as if her isolated life of innocence on the hillside gave her no experience with the realities below.

The visioned solution to the swindle dilemma showed up as the following mental pictures:

-Someone following others from a distance
-A large grandfather clock
-A flagpole between two people

The first image suggests that by allowing others to take the lead she could get a better sense of where they are going and whether their leadership would serve her. If she took the lead she may get her way in the short run, but find it difficult to know their intentions. She agreed that it is educational to observe people who lead.

The grandfather clock in the second vision suggests giving things time to unfold. Along with the first image it implies that the solution to her problem calls for a trust, but verify approach. She agreed by saying, "My problem has to do with taking people at their word."

The flagpole is symbolic of independence. In general, this image hints at putting her interests and life first and keeping her independence. As a whole, these resolution visions suggest that she needs to reconsider her tendency to trust without verification.

Discerning the Vision

As already discussed, visioning is an intuitive process in which you open yourself to catch God's idea in the form of visions. You come into the process after spending some time in the silence, centering yourself in spirit, and then putting your attention on the questions that you want God to answer. You are not telling God what you want, rather you are open to receiving the highest spiritual vision or idea which may come in the form of hearing a message, seeing images, or having a feeling. Visioning questions are open-ended and in general include, but are not limited to, these four: "What is God's idea for my life or this situation?" "What must I become, know or embody to live the vision?" "What must I release to embody the vision?" "What gifts, talents, and capacities do I have to service the vision?" For beginners and some people who do visioning there is no need to make sense of the vision. However, it's important to share, write down or record every vision in some way to honor the gift. Next to discussing your visions with a like-minded person, one of the biggest aids to discerning visions is getting other intuitive perspectives from tools like the Change or Tarot, or collecting enough visions to discover emerging patterns.

The content of the collective mind is represented in consciousness in the form of pronounced preferences and definite ways of looking at things. The vision and its discernment make up a large portion of our total relationship with the Divine and determine most of our spiritual awareness and behavior in life. Perceiving visions determines what people get or receive from the Self and discerning their meaning determines what they decide to do about it. Those who prefer discerning or judging more than perception will likely experience difficulty in perceiving, and those who prefer perception more than judging will likely have trouble in discerning. When visions are seen but not understood they remain in the unconscious and may be overlooked. When day or night vision or dreams remain uninterpreted, they repeat themselves until they are understood. The complete process of visioning calls for suspending the ego to catch the vision and then bringing back the ego to assist in discerning the vision. When visioning stops at catching the vision or you jump to conclusions by prematurely discerning the vision you lose contact with its full content and may not see it as intended but rather in terms of your own self-imposed biases.

Discerning the meaning of visions takes much longer than the process of catching visions. Just as it may take only a few seconds or minutes to have a dream, interpreting its meaning always takes longer.

Being extroverted or introverted can play a role in how we go about discerning visions. For extroverts, what a person is within him or her self is normally less decisive than objective and external factors. People with introverted attitudes are inclined toward inborn psychic and subjective factors. Although introverted consciousness is aware of external conditions, it selects subjective elements as the decisive ones. Because people have the ability to express both attitudes when they choose or need to do so, the problems associated with each attitude can be resolved. However, those who are unwilling to release their attachment to extroverted or introverted preferences diminish their ability to catch the vision and discern its meaning. The extrovert whose natural energy flows outward toward people and things, may have the problem of keeping still and focused on the inner silence long enough to catch the vision or discerning visions in literal terms. The introvert whose natural energy flows inward toward privacy and being alone, may have the problem of validating the meaning of visions based on objective standards.

Visioning is available to all people. Visioning is always for transformation and eliminating which comes about as you shift your perception of reality. Through it, you move from the past to the now, from a smaller place to a bigger place, and release something every day. Unlike the pursuit of learning, spiritual discernment and growth leads to unlearning, eliminating rather than attaining. Because you are already one with God, you don't need to make things happen. All you need to do is trust that which already exists in the universe. As Joseph Campbell says, "We must be willing to give up the life we have planned in order to receive the life that is waiting for us."

Visioning in Groups or Alone

The best way to understand the universal language of symbols and images is to work with them. Anyone can learn to speak that language and gain access to the power and riches of the universe within. Not only do visions tell you who you are and where you're going, they can help you learn what you need to change in order to grow spiritually. They offer you an opportunity to understand your negative as well as positive character traits. To work with visions you must know how to read and interpret them in order to discern this wisdom. If a person has no desire to change or experience spiritual growth and transformation, then the messages of the soul are harder to detect. Training your intuitive and vision skills is one of the best things you can do to foster your personal and spiritual development.

Although most visioning takes place alone, most people learn the process in a group settings. There are three types of visioning groups and each requires at least two people who trust in the process and are willing to practice. The smallest group would be the one-on-one counseling setting where one person facilitates or takes the lead by offering vision-based insights to address the other person's questions. In this intimate group, each person depends upon the other and each commits themselves to their role in the relationship. Larger visioning groups take the form of support groups in which participants are committed to the growth and well-being of others, or visioning teams who come together to co-create or share the same vision.

Most visioning groups take place in homes or office settings if led by a facilitator, but telephone conference calls and on line works as well. Individuals seeking assessments and spiritual solutions to their problems alone or in counseling settings, and in visioning support groups can address just about any topics. If group meetings are limited to two hours, the size of the group should not be more than six people for starters. If everyone wants to have the group do visioning and give answers to their questions the meeting time may get out of hand. When the entire group agrees to do visioning on a few questions you can spend more time answering the same questions. However, when individual members have questions they want answered the number of questions per individual need to be limited. For large groups it will be necessary to limit the questions or divide the group into smaller sections. Participants should agree in advance on the frequency of meeting and length of time for each group. I have been in groups that meet once a week, once every two weeks, and even once a month for more and less than one hour.

While it is not necessary to begin visioning groups or individual sessions with a centering meditation and prayer, doing so honors the source and helps you step into the consciousness of oneness. This process may vary from two or three minutes to fifteen minutes. As you sit in the silence, you should do so with the knowledge that Spirit knows every thing you need to know and do. You should give thanks for the company of those in the group and for the visions, intuitions, insights and even dreams which have and will come to awaken you to life. After the centering meditation and prayer, the group begins with each participant giving a check in to let others know what is going on in their life and what they are working on.

In the case of visioning support groups, requests for help can come from each member. If individual members wish to have group members share their visions and insights the group must first agree to do so. When participants seeking feedback come to the group with a dream instead of questions, he or she can tell the dream if the group consents, and then ask for help in the form of visions and rational observations which help to understand its meaning. When you listen to another's vision or dream it is important to listen in silence with your whole self until the speaker has finished sharing. Then restate what the speaker has said and wait for confirmation before speaking. Actively listening does not come naturally unless you practice it. Listening is a learned skill. The tendency to interrupt, criticize or use humor should be avoided.

Depending on the size of the group and how well the participants feel about the work and one another it may be necessary to use a timekeeper so that every member has a chance to speak and make his or her contribution. It's usually helpful to keep track of the time and curb side conversations, interruptions, and preoccupations with subjects outside the group. If someone is preoccupied in a way that takes them away from the group, or if they have another agenda, it should be brought to the attention of the group. The timekeeper or facilitator should also respect time, group guidelines, and start and end the group meeting on time.

After each vision is shared with the group, those who have something to offer should practice asking for permission to speak and use statements like "if this were my vision." Since the visioner has the final word about what the vision means there is no value in rudeness. It is often helpful to ask the clarifying questions about the vision such as, "What does this scene or person in the vision mean to you? How do you feel about this or that aspect of the vision? I have found it helps to use dream symbol dictionaries to interpret symbols I don't understand. Because the interpretation of a vision is more important than the vision itself, it's best to work with people who care about your growth. If you don't understand the messages being conveyed there is no need to rush an interpretation as additional visioning often adds perspective and meaning.

5

The Change and Visioning

In view of the I Ching's extreme age and
its Chinese origin, I cannot consider its archaic,
symbolic, and flowery language abnormal.
—C.G. Jung

At the outset, the Book of Changes or I Ching in Chinese was a non-religious tool for catching the wisdom of the unknown. It took final shape before distinctions between one religion and another had arisen, namely before Taoism, Confucianism, and Buddhism. The separate meanings of "I" and "Ching" give us another insight into the meaning of the Book of Changes. While the words "I" and "Ching" have several meanings, among the central meanings are *individual appropriateness* (for I) and *oneness with the center* (for Ching). These two words tell us that the I Ching deals with dispensing guidance on the individual's relationship to the center or whole. Supported by the highest spiritual values, the I Ching allows any reasonably open-minded person who is serious about seeking God, and willing to follow a few simple requirements, to understand God's ideas.

Beyond making use of the I Ching's matrix of 64 hexagram signs for understanding the universal parts of the Tao my simplified new version of the I Ching called "the

Change" is related but significantly different. The Change is an offspring of the traditional I Ching but uses completely new interpretations for the trigrams and hexagram signs, and eliminates the 384 moving lines.

From the outset, the idea behind the Book of Changes was a collection of yang and yin signs used as an oracle that confined itself to yes and no answers. Like the binary opposites present in the beginning of Genesis and repeated throughout the Old Testament in the form of light and dark, heaven and earth, good and evil, etc., the yang and yin signs were divided further to expand the initial yes and no answers for greater clarity. The simple collection of yang and yin signs evolved into two types of yes's and two types of no's or four signs. The most obvious meaning of this division is a strong or weak version of yes or no. As the need for clarity continued, the yang and yin signs were divided again so that the four signs became eight. This third division of the binary opposites, yang and yin, gave rise to the eight trigrams we have today. Over time, they came to represent images of all that happens in heaven and earth. The 64 hexagrams of the I Ching came into existence by simply combining the eight trigrams in eight ways. By doing so, they determine 64 different, yet typical life situations. Through correctly discerning and following insights given by the I Ching, you can align yourself with God's ideas and choose to follow where God is already going.

The trigrams and hexagrams represent universal archetypes or stages of consciousness. In this book, the eight trigrams, the eight patriarchs in the bible including Jesus, and the eight psychological types from Jungian psychology characterize these stages of consciousness in similar ways. Each patriarch has many similarities to the original ideas given for the eight trigrams but offers the Western mind a way to understand the trigrams. The roles played by patriarchs personify the trigrams and can be read against the background of the history of the Near East from the early part of the second millennium until the time of Jesus as written in the Bible and documented from Biblical sources.

To offer the benefits of the I Ching as an extended way of visioning I have revised the Chinese style, language and meanings of the eight trigrams and sixty-four trigram pairs or hexagrams. These modifications give rise to what I have called the Change, which amounts to reinterpreting the traditional eight trigrams symbols in ways that are more accessible to the Western mind, and tell us that the spirit is not bound to one place or the I Ching to any one form. They include the central teachings of Jesus, contributions of the Biblical patriarchs, and associations with the Jungian personality types. In his effort to present the I Ching to those who are Biblically oriented, *Secrets of the I Ching* by Dr. Joseph Murphy reinterprets the hexagrams based upon applicable Bible passages [1]. My hope in adding applicable Bible passages to expand upon the meaning of hexagrams is to promote greater ease in using the Book of Changes for those who are spiritually oriented and open to catching God's ideas. Isabel Briggs Myers with Peter B. Myers [2] presents the original meanings of the types described in detail by Jung in a more down to earth fashion in *Gifts Differing.*

Before the I Ching became a book of wisdom, it was a book of oracles used by pagans, sorcerers, and psychics. For people with limited to advanced spiritual education, the I Ching remains as a method of developing intuition. It does so by focusing on archetypal images and describing the seeds of transformation that exist in the current state. Over time, the I Ching became both a book of divination and a book of wisdom. This second level of development came about through the seasoned wisdom of thousands of years applied to explaining the oracle.

As a book of wisdom, the I Ching is largely the result of commentaries written by China's most distinguished philosophers, including Lao Tzu, the Taoist and Confucius known as the Ten Wings or expositions. These commentaries contain the substance of the oldest literature relating to the Book of Changes and serves to give it its spiritual and philosophical backbone. According to the Ten Wings, "the

Changes is a Book from which one may not hold aloof." Its authors tell us that whoever has realized what the Changes have to offer, be he a philosopher, a psychologists, a member of the clergy, a social reformer, a pragmatic statesmen, other professional or nonprofessional, or even an empire builder, will not be able to live without the Changes again.

In addition to its uses as a divination tool the Book of Changes is of far greater significance as a Book of Wisdom and serves to further our intuitive understanding of conditions in the world and to penetrate the depth and nature of Spirit. Fritjof Capra, author of *The Tao of Physics* claims, "Only the Vedas and the Bible can compare to the I Ching in aura of respect and as a revered scripture." The I Ching provides the philosophical background for the Change and offers an intellectual understanding of oneness.

The development and use of the I Ching as a Book of Wisdom was greatly influenced Lao Tzu and Confucius. In his book titled *I Ching: The Book of Change,* John Blofeld discusses the I Ching's background and the difference between the Taoist and Confucian strands of the I Ching [3]. Their contributions are summarized here.

Taoist Influence	**Confucian Influence**
Lao Tzu (540-460 B.C)	Confucius (551-479 B.C.)
Father of Taoism	Father of Confucianism
Taoist Religion (450 B.C. to present)	Confucianism (450 B.C. to present)
Chinese Buddhism (400 B.C. to present)	The Ten Wings (221 B.C. to 1700 A.D.)
Various Schools (300 B.C. to 200 A.D.)	1st & 2nd Wings, Judgment
	3rd & 4th Wings, The Image
Government Applications	5th & 6th Wings, Great Treatise
Military Applications	7th Wing, Words of the Text
Legal Applications	8th Wing, Trigram Discussion
	9th Wing, Hexagram Sequence
Zen School of Buddhism (200 B.C. to present)	10th Wing, Miscellaneous Notes on the Hexagrams

Although Buddhism is popular in China its teachings are not present in the Book of Changes because it did not reach China until long after the I Ching took final form and many insights from Taoism and Confucianism were already added to the I Ching.

The most scholarly book on the subject is the unrivaled translation by the Christian missionary Richard Wilhelm and Cary F. Baynes and one worth exploring [4]. It has consistently been in print since its first English publication in 1950 and is under constant scrutiny by scholars for things that might need revision. In his excellent forward to the book, the great psychiatrist C.G. Jung presents four interesting perspectives [5]. First, he personifies the Book by asking for its assessment about its present situation and his intention to present it to the Western mind. The I Ching answers his question as follows:

> *It tells me of its religious significance, of the fact that at present it is unknown and misjudged, of its hope of being restored to a place of honor—this last obviously with a sidelong glance at my as yet unwritten forward, and above all at the English translation.*

Second, Jung points out that most methods of divination with the I Ching aim at self-knowledge but like many divination methods which rely on intuition, such as tarot, the interpretation of dreams, and clairvoyance it has also been put to superstitious use and is open to every kind of misuse by the frivolous–minded and immature. Third, in using the phrase "exploring the unconscious" he suggests that the function of the I Ching is to draw from the unconscious whatever is necessary for correct understanding of the problem posed and its solution. Fourth, in pointing out that there are multiple answers to his question or any question Jung also asserts that not all answers and by implication, not all interpretations are equally significant. Since the original situation of the questioner cannot be reproduced in time or awareness there is only a first and single answer. In other words, it is impossible to replicate the conditions that were present after consulting the I Ching.

Yang, Yin and Change

The Taoist symbol of a circle showing white on one side containing a small black spot within it, and black on the other side with a small white spot within it, illustrates the interaction between yang and yin. This symbol of the Universe says that half the universe is made of light or yang energy and half is made of dark or yin energy. The small black and white spots tell us that we never have an entire yang or yin situation. When divided into three parts the Taoist symbol suggests that we get solid expressions of yang and yin throughout the universe about one third of the time, and a close to equal mixture of the two about one third of the time. The union of yang and yin represents wholeness and separation, and has much in common with making distinctions between yang and yin. Movement toward the energy of light or matter has much in common with the movement toward yang or yin. The English translations of yang and yin as young and old respectively tells us that half the universe is made of young energy and half of old energy. Examples and qualities of yang and yin follow.

Yang	**Yin**
Wave	Particle
Intuition	Sensing
Masculine	Feminine
Mind	Matter
Sunny	Shady
Animus	Anima
Expanding	Contracting
Upward	Downward
North	South
East	West
Thinking	Feeling

This list is of course only partial and does not tell us the degree of yang or yin. The yang components of an object is everything perceived by the senses, and the yin components is everything hidden from the senses. Just as thinking contains more yang than yin and feeling contains more yin than yang, it is possible to be in a place of partial unity moving toward separation or partial separation moving toward unity. When making the journey from a place of unity toward separation or downward manifestation we are coming from oneness and choosing to separate yang and yin, or either/or consciousness. When changing from separation back to unity or upward manifestation we are moving toward oneness and choosing to unite yang and yin.

The journey from unity to separation and vice versa has been taking place since the beginning of creation. The journey from spirit into matter is nothing short of the creative process. The creative process begins in a place of unity or pure spirit and proceeds in stages of changes with no discernable appearance. All things depend upon and emanate from this initial place of unity. In this beginning or first stage there are only possibilities which have yet to be recognized by consciousness.

The second stage to emerge is that of intuitive insight and vision which comes about by catching God's ideas. We can understand this stage as the first step toward separation and manifestation. It is the tiny spark, the initial impulse to speak before speaking.

The third stage gives us an expanded perspective of the tiny point of insight revealed in stage two. This stage is the beginning of understanding. Here you choose to become what Spirit needs to manifest through you. This is the place where new thoughts, beliefs and concepts take shape, and where intuitive insights and visions become clarified.

At the fourth stage, your understanding gains the added power of a focused will. This concentration of will, purpose, and the cooperation needed with other people produces the energy for manifestation to occur.

The fifth stage, called manifestation, comes about through participation and co-creation with Spirit and through cooperative relationships with other people. This stage completes the journey of transformation from the unity of spirit into its separate aspects as matter. It is the journey taken by no-things to things, from image to form, and from vision to manifestation.

Now that spirit has become itself in form the, journey from separation back to unity begins. This journey represents the true meaning of yoga: "reunion" with the Self that's been separated from the ego. The return trip to spirit has five stages that deal with retracing the steps we took in the journey from union. Because the starting point in this journey is separation and the world of matter, it always starts with the releasing of conscious attachments.

The first stage in this change is getting the right opinion. Without this basic understanding of where you need to go, nothing happens and you will remain in a state of separation and ignorance until you learn something different. To begin we must learn about the human soul and know that we are related to and a part of something much bigger and wiser than we are.

The second stage of listening to and controlling your emotions begins when you meet the requirements of the first stage. An example of emotional control would be making the choice to understand my upset with someone or something as coming from me rather than an external situation. This stage is difficult because we are addicted to our emotions and controlled by the thoughts that produce them. In order to continue the journey of unification with Spirit you must renounce your servitude to physicality and emotions.

The third stage begins when you learn to control your emotions. This means understanding the correct ways to relate to others and yourself. Until you are able to control your emotions, it is difficult to have good personal relationships, correctly participate, or accurately observe others.

In the fourth stage we learn to set goals, pursue our visions and dreams, and embrace our purpose in life. This stage marks the high point of creative self-expression, helping others and playing our part on the world stage.

The fifth stage of self-realization and transcendence completes to journey of reunification. At this stage, you must learn to let go of your attachments to the previous four stages and to material things in general. Mastery of this stage goes by many names such as the attainment of Christ, Krishna or Buddha Consciousness; individuation; wholeness; bliss; etc. It is the journey yin makes back to yang, matter back to mind and forms back to spirit.

Attaining Unity

As in visioning, the Change goes beyond cyclic or natural development laws and the law of karma or cause and effect. Because insights from intuition and visioning give us direct knowing and lead to real understanding, they transcend the past, fate or the alignment of stars. Even though divination results from the Change often point to change governed by karma and cyclic development, their intuitive nature transcends them and allows for quantum leaps in growth and awareness. The Chinese philosophers who describe the I Ching imply that performing many duties to serve God is identical serving the collective. In the end, those who seek and accept divine guidance through the Change will allow all 64 hexagrams or aspects of the universe and their personality to express themselves. In doing this, they gain an awareness of the previously suppressed side of their nature. These people will achieve a high level of self-knowledge; they will come to know themselves at both conscious and unconscious levels. They learn to understand the dark or shadow side of their nature and bring it into consciousness.

According to Stephan Hoeller's work with the Gnostic Gospels titled *Jung and the Lost Gospels,* the purpose of attaining unity is to re-establish the connection that existed in human beings before the separation of the sexes, as symbolized by the dividing of Adam and Eve in the story of Genesis.

> *At the time when Eve was in Adam then there was no death: but when she was separated from him death came to exist. If completion shall occur again, and the earlier identity is attained, then death will be no more. [Saying 71]*

In the beginning when Eve was in Adam, there was no separation. Christ came so that he might take away the separation which was there from the beginning and thus again reunite the two [6]. In practical terms the Change helps those who consistently rely on its wisdom unite the opposites of masculine and feminine, yang and yin, light and dark, etc. Those who attain unity will take up residence in the Kingdom of Heaven forever and make the transition from serving Jesus Christ as master to become his twin brother or twin sister. If you rely upon the Change for guidance to advise you on how to attain improper goals, its responses will lead you away rather than toward unity and you may end up joining the company of those who regard the I Ching as meaningless superstition.

The Change has much in common with C. G. Jung's beautiful model of psychological types and his theory of unity called "individuation." In Jung's book titled *Psychological Types*, we see a pattern of relationship that is identical to the pattern found among the trigrams and trigram combinations (hexagrams). The eight primary trigrams and sixty-four hexagrams represent the equivalent psychological types or preferences found in the Change and universe of human consciousness [7]. In many of our basic orientations toward the world, only one or two of the eight trigram types or attitudes assumes dominance and comes to rule behavior and consciousness. The tendency for individuals to specialize in expressing only part of the whole comes about because of the binary opposites, i.e., light and dark, heaven and earth, etc., set in motion at the very beginning of creation. The other non-dominate types become part of the unconscious where they are still capable of influencing behavior.

Just as most people prefer one polarity to the other and one or two trigrams to the others, they prefer a few hexagrams attitudes to the others. This comes about because a person cannot consistently react to the world using both polarities at the same time. However, there are many cases where incompatible attitudes have a way of sharing the limelight. Its not that we can't help ourselves or change, it's just that we were created with this tendency. Whether a particular hexagram will strike us as desirable or undesirable will depend upon whether the hexagram is carrying out what we have in mind. In the end, no polarity or hexagram is undesirable since all parts of the universe are indispensable. Increase without decrease, creation without destruction, or advancing without retreating would lead to such an accumulation that life would become impossible.

Moving toward unity is central to the Change in that all trigram combinations express themselves without regard to your historical preferences. In asking for divine guidance through the Change, in the end there is no dominance of any preferred attitudes. In every case of asking for help and following the guidance received, the range of all component parts or patterns in the universe come into harmonious balance in time. Because you end up making a conscious choice to adopt all trigram combinations, individual differences disappear and you no longer fit any one category. As a process, reunion integrates both conscious and unconscious attitudes toward the universe. Everything is coming into existence, developing, decaying, or going out of existence.

In Using the Change to reveal the future you are asking the Universe to calculate the general trend and give you the best way to become one with that trend. This trend represents what the Universe is already doing. This comes about by relating whatever situation you have in mind to the predictable cycle of events to which it belongs. It is not getting out of life what you want, but the acceptance of ultimate reality. Those who purse this path to reunion will face many doubts but the result is wholeness.

Hexagram or Vision

Visioning can be used to expand the meaning of hexagrams from the Change and hexagrams can be used to expand the meanings from visioning. You can deepen your insights by the structured approach of using visioning after consulting the Change or the unstructured approach of consulting the Change after visioning.

The structured approach calls for consulting the Change first to catch God's ideas about the question, and then using visioning to expand your understanding of the hexagrams' answer to your question. You do this by holding an image of the hexagram in the mind's eye and allowing additional impressions of its meaning to come forward. These additional images or impressions will usually add greater understanding of both the hexagram and the vision. Even though the resulting vision will add more insight to the original question, the hexagrams have already shaped the answer. If for example you hear or come to know things about a certain subject before you begin to do visioning, you can't help but include that subject.

The unstructured approach calls for catching God's ideas through visioning first, and then using the Change to expand upon this insight. This is the same as getting a second reading from another person on the same question. Here the visioning process is incomplete until you answer the same question with the Change. Visioning that takes place before creating hexagrams tends to be open-ended and broadly defined. Visioning after creating hexagrams tends to be limited and narrowly defined. When the vision and hexagram seem unrelated, and you just don't get the connection, the question arises as to which one we give more attention. In most of these cases, I pay more attention to the visions when a single hexagram is involved and less to the visions when there are two hexagrams.

When you are aware of what both perspectives have to offer, your perception of the subject matter is greater than either the hexagram or vision by itself. Instead of simply reading the text of the sixty-four hexagrams, those who use visioning as well will get better results. Even though many people will not see mental images or pictures while visioning it is completely acceptable to receive feelings, words, phrases, intuitive hunches, nothing at all, or other spontaneous forms of input. Everything you get means something, including nothing, which usually means the answer is uncertain.

Intuition is the process of exploring the unknown and sensing possibilities that might not be readily apparent. Even though we are conscious of only a small portion of what is, this changes when we let go of the conscious mind by opening the door to intuition. The process of visioning, inner observation and getting insights from the Mind of God, takes place when the conscious mind is still and focused upon receiving answers to question such as "What is God's idea about the subject of this question?" "What must I become?" What must I release?" and "What other information do I need in this moment?" To get a sense of what is going on you must go to the deeper mind and set up communication with it through your intuition. You should write out any insights you get to honor the Source and give thanks for the insight received. As you open the door to your intuition, you gain access to the secret world within which has a complete life of its own. This life runs parallel to the ordinary life you live from day to day and is the source of infinite wisdom.

People who shy away from the use of visioning in favor of written hexagram text may face difficulties in relating the answers given to the questions they ask. Those who stick with the literal words of hexagram texts will perceive things differently than those who read between the lines to broader meaning. It is not that one way is wrong and another right but that different people see the world through the lens of their own internal make up and beliefs. For instance, Chinese culture tends to rely on intuitive thought processes from an inner-directed perspective; and Western culture tends rely on the outer directed perspective of logic.

Reading the Hexagram Answer

With the proper perception and judgment, you can activate the divine power within to overcome every obstacle in your experience. In this book, perceiving the divine comes by way of collecting vision and hexagram insights. While the perception of visions often includes what you see mentally, it also consists of what you hear in your inner ear, sensations, emotions you feel, and even what you smell and taste in your imagination. It doesn't matter how you vision, just that you learn to recognize and work with your own visioning. Judging refers to the process of forming an opinion by discerning the things you perceive and deciding what action to take. Perceiving and judging are necessary for understanding, and presented here in the spirit of honoring that individuals differ in their approach to arriving at meaning.

People who consider first whether the vision or hexagram answer to their question is consistent and logical are using a thinking approach to spiritual discernment. Those who consider first whether insights are pleasing or displeasing, helpful or harmful are using a feeling approach. The feeling approach is constantly seeking an image or divine idea that may have no clear existence in reality. It strives after inner intensity and looks beyond appearances that do not fit with its aim. Everything about thinking is equally true for feeling except one is intellectual and the other emotional. The process of discerning the meaning of God's ideas through visioning and hexagrams is one of necessity for drawing conclusions and deciding what to do about the insights we receive. When we lack complete knowledge, judgments are necessary to give us the right direction and opinion until we know more.

People who tend to confine their attention to what is literal in the hexagram or vision are using a sensing approach to perceiving. Sensing perceives the black and white meaning suggested by the idea, rather than its appearance as a symbol. People who prefer a more intuitive approach will likely read between and beyond the lines of the insights received to possibilities that come to mind. With intuition, one's attention is on a vision whose reality is not physical but psychic. The focus is on perceiving visions and images, and there is little or no immediate concern with external possibilities. Intuition and sensation have little inclination to make a moral problem of perception—that is up to judging.

Visioning based on hexagrams alone can be of great value for many decision oriented questions and most either/or type questions. For other questions, spiritual discernment based on literal hexagram interpretations alone is not easy and the chances of misunderstanding may be too great. In general, attempts to catch God's ideas through the thinking approach that seems for many people the only possible approach to knowledge are sure to miss the mark. I have encouraged those who want to broaden their understanding of divine insights to use the Change with visioning. Training of your intuition for inspiration and spiritual guidance will be helpful in expanding your perspective. Whether you access the universe within through visioning, deep meditations, directing your imagination in waking life, consulting the Change, or other methods, you are using your intuition. All of these intuitive sources come through mindfulness—the act of stopping, listening, looking within, and accepting divine insights.

People who find it difficult to use the visioning process and their intuition can still get a great deal of insight if they meditate and study to expand their understanding. This approach may take more time but if a number of texts are available for review and moving lines are included, insights will emerge. With the right attitude toward the divine, people who use a mainly rational approach will likely get useful results whereas those who use visioning but have the wrong attitude will get poor results.

The meanings of the 64 hexagrams and moving lines tend to be consistent among the numerous renditions of books in print on the subject. Reading another view will give you a more complete picture of what the hexagram means. Many websites offer explanations and interpretations of various hexagrams as well. Even if an insight doesn't make sense right away it should be recorded anyway and reviewed later. If your interpretation does not answer the question you are asking, it's not because the Change gave you the wrong answer rather it's because you don't yet understand the answer. Since the Divine is never wrong the problem is not with the insight given, but your lack of understanding.

Although the full I Ching as a divination tool or book of wisdom is beyond the scope of this book, it can be of great value for those who invest the time in learning to access its wisdom. At those occasional times when I want to consult the I Ching for this perspective, I rely on the Wilhelm/Baynes translation titled *The I Ching of Book of Changes.* These occasions come up when I need to take a break from visioning, or want an unclouded view, or simply want to mix things up a bit. To deepen my understanding of the changing lines, when needed, I use the translation by John Blofeld titled *I Ching: The Book of Change*. Although the Blofeld book is weak on hexagram meanings, it does a superb job in translating the original Chinese interpretations of the 384 moving lines.

6

Elements of the Change

In China, as in Japan, Korea and Vietnam which have a predominantly Chinese-style civilization, the Book of Change has been in constant use from remote antiquity until the present.
—John Blofeld

The conscious use of the Change assures mastery over the lesser conditions of karma because it makes use of higher laws and greater powers. This comes about because the divine transcends the time-space limits of karma and brings forth its judgments and wisdom for its purposes. While using the Change alone cannot accurately answer all questions without intuition, it demands less from intuition than visioning. Only when you are detached from the outcome by temporarily withdrawing from your hopes, fears and expectations about answers will you have true intuition.

Each of the 64 hexagrams consists of six lines and two trigram archetypes. All trigrams consist of three yang and yin lines. The possible combinations of these three lines represent the eight trigrams. At the most basic level, you can understand the meaning of each hexagram through the meaning of its trigrams and their position. Both trigrams and hexagrams represent collectively inherited unconscious ideas, patterns of thought, and images that are universally present in individual psyches. Just as each trigram contains the other seven, in that movement is possible from any one to the other by changing any line from yang to yin or vice versa, all hexagrams contain the other 63. This is possible because the combination of eight lower and eight upper trigrams or eight times eight is 64.

The lower trigram is made of the first three hexagram lines and by itself represents the inner world, thoughts, feelings and points of view. It points to what you are seeking and striving to get. This trigram shows the nature of your position, motives, desires and the pattern of choices you are making in the situation regarding the hexagram as a whole. The upper trigram is made of the last three hexagram lines and by itself represents the outer world of forms, things, effects and the manifest universe. It represents collective agreements, the established order, the environment of your position and your understanding of its intentions. The form of the upper trigram and hexagram as a whole is the out picturing of the desires set in motion in the lower trigram.

Getting hexagrams from the Change is a valid and needed alternative to visioning. Interpreting information from visioning is a sizeable challenge for many, while interpreting information from the Change tends to be easy. This comes about because visioning offers an unlimited variety of perspectives, but the Change limits you to 64 grand symbols or hexagrams. To answer questions based on the Change you need to flip or toss a single coin (typically a penny) six times and record whether the random landing is Heads or Tails each time. The pattern of Heads (represented by a straight yang line) or Tails (represented by a broken yin line) will identify one of the 64 hexagrams. You will see how to find your hexagram number in the last two pages of Chapter 10 titled "Finding your Hexagram Number." The meanings of all 64 hexagrams follow this section. The two examples that follow should be helpful in understanding how you get hexagrams and how they are made of two trigrams.

Tail ___ ___
Tail ___ ___
Tail ___ ___
Tail ___ ___
Head _______
Tail ___ ___

The first illustration of the trigram approach comes from *Teamwork (7).* All hexagram interpretations follow Chapter 10. In Hexagram 7, we seek to understand symbol Earth above Water. The presence of Water below earth brings to mind images of an underground stream, wells and tree root systems delivering water to sustain life. In Jungian psychology terms, the existence of Water below Earth can be seen in situations where one's personal attitude of introverted feeling, with its attributes of mystery and personal desires, must support the established order as a team member. In this hexagram Water below Earth is a sign that established group objectives represented by Earth above should have a higher priority than the individual goals implied by Water below. Your position in the lower trigram is like the team member who needs to work with and serve a team or collective organization linked by inherited circumstances or choice. This trigram combination suggests the need for your contribution and cooperation in order for the established group to achieve its mission. If your goals are aligned with the team, you will share its success even though you have limited opportunity for self-expression.

The second illustration of the trigram approach to understanding hexagrams comes from *Building the New (50)* Hexagram 50 came about from the following pattern.

Head _______
Tail ___ ___
Head _______
Head _______
Head _______
Tail ___ ___

The combination of Wind below Fire hints at warm atmospheres in nature or in human interactions, and the potential for clarity as signified by the mid-day Sun. In Jung's terminology, the presence of Wind below Fire is represented by situations where your attitude is one of introverted thinking. This attitude has the tendency to ask questions and create prospects that lead to new perspectives, and must find a way to express itself in an environment whose attitude of extroverted thinking demands you to focus on the details of concrete facts and practical solutions to problems. In this hexagram, Wind in the lower trigram and Fire above may be understood as a message that the objective facts outside have a higher value than your inner thoughts represented by Wind below. Your role in the lower Wind trigram is that of the person who extends the hand of fellowship to greet authority figures and leaders represented by Fire above. This trigram paring suggests that your position is also like the friendly leader who welcomes and is acquainted with people in positions of power and authority.

Rating your Hexagram

The purpose of assigning judgments to I Ching hexagrams was to put its original images into words in an effort to help those who use it make decisions on when to desist from a harmful course of action or pursue a helpful course. For similar reason, I have assigned judgments to the 64 Change hexagrams that follow in this book. In this book, the judgments have a more simplified, straightforward, and limited use than we see in the traditional I Ching. The five basic judgments indicate whether a given action will bring positive or negative results and make it possible for users to discern in advance the most beneficial course of action that may not be obvious. The judgments, patterned after academic achievement grades (A, A-, B, C+, C-, D, and F) are *excellent, better than average, average, below average, and failure.* Some of the judgments are refined by plus or minus signs. For example the *average* judgment may be graded *average* + or *average* – to indicate slightly above or below *average.* While most of the *excellent* judgments are simply *excellent,* Hexagram 27, Nourishment and Hexagram 48, The Well are given the *excellent–* judgment to indicate slightly less than excellent.

While limited in scope, the easiest way to interpret the hexagrams relies on judgment categories. The use of graded judgments makes the most sense when you ask well-defined fork in the road decision-making questions and what if type questions. This kind of spiritual discernment calls for making use of the five graded judgment categories. Graded judgments for each hexagram are included in the summary meanings at the beginning of the hexagram.

When people ask questions such as "What will I experience if I take this or that action?" or "How will I experience the approaching situation or person?" the judgment grade has significant value. When people ask guidance type questions such as "What am I to do?" or "What is the nature of this situation or person?" judgments grades are less relevant. The judgments are only summary pointers to close-ended questions that can be answered with either/or responses. For the person who reads and discerns the meaning of the hexagram, and those who already understand its meaning, the judgments are implied. People who seek wisdom to open-ended questions that ask for guidance will find little or no value in the judgments.

The Eight Trigram Answers

The eight trigrams represent collectively inherited unconscious ideas, patterns of thought, and images that are universally present in individual psyches. As already mentioned the trigrams are personified mainly through the teachings of Jesus and also the lives of the historical patriarchs Abraham, Isaac, Jacob, Joseph, Aaron, Moses, and David to expand upon the nature based images and meanings found in the original Book of Changes. In addition, the psychological types developed by C.G. Jung are helpful in explaining some of the trigrams.

The main difference between the trigrams and biblical patriarchs is rooted in the difference between Chinese cosmology and the Bible. The Chinese assign no human, moral, or historical qualities to the trigrams. In the beginning of Genesis light is good, implying that darkness is bad, but the Chinese creation of yang and yin principles making no claim to morality. This distinction continues as the authors of Genesis describe God himself as a human like storyteller who used the lives of the people submissive to him to describe his divine plot.

In the view of Lao Tzu and Confucius, the eight trigrams are images more than objects representing states of change in the unseen world. The trigram meanings that follow are nearly identical to the text for Hexagrams 1, 2, 29, 30, 51, 52, 57 and 58. In these eight hexagrams, the upper and lower trigrams are identical. These meanings are less evident in the remaining hexagrams for two reasons. First, in this book the meanings of the remaining fifty-six hexagrams revolve around the teachings and stories attributed to Jesus, and second, the upper and lower trigrams are different in these hexagrams.

— —
——— *Lake*
——— Introverted Intuition, Abraham

Summary: Joyous; Knowledge; Wisdom; Gnosis; Values teaching and understanding of life; Subjective understanding of external situations; Faith; Devotion; Compassion; Insight. See *The Joyous (58).*

In the Bible, Abraham is the first patriarch and first individual in biblical history to both have an awareness and personal relationship with God. He was the first person to establish monotheism by recognizing that there's only one supreme God. The personification of Abraham as the LAKE trigram teaches that faith in the Inner Light and its guidance becomes part of consciousness when we are devoted to it. LAKE tells us that we can know human nature and God's thoughts by knowing the self within.

From the Jungian perspective, the greatest value of introverted intuition lies in the interpretation of life and the promotion of understanding. Intuition tends to regard immediate situations as prisons from which escape must be made, and it attempts to do so by making major changes based on its intuitive understanding of objective situations

The Israelite people know Abraham as "Father Abraham" because their bible and religion, along with Christianity and Islam descend from him [1]. God spoke to Abraham and chose him to be the patriarch of a new level in human consciousness and father of his people. This trigram represents the power of mind to make unlimited expressions of substance out of ideas received in faith. Abraham personifies the LAKE trigram. He represents faithful submission to the urge of Spirit until we develop communication with the mind of God and then receive assurances that Spirit guides us. LAKE represents intuition that is in direct contact with the Universal Mind and is thus our mental tool to comprehend Spirit and its ideas for each individual.

— —
— — *Thunder*
—— Extroverted Feeling, Isaac

Summary: Arousing movement; Unexpected and sudden awakenings; Judgments that discipline humanity; Related to existing traditions and collective ideals; Desire to create emotional harmony. See *Shocking (51).*

Isaac, son of Abraham became the second patriarch, and like all of the patriarchs that follow does so in a counterintuitive manner. When personified as Isaac, this trigram is symbolic of the conditions that represent sudden events that awaken us to new life experiences. As seen in the role played by Isaac it represents the unpredicted breakthrough of God's life from the unconscious into the conscious realm.

From the Jungian perspective the motivation of extroverted feeling does not live in the individual but outside in the collective ideals of the community. THUNDER represents the creative impetus of the individual, environment, or nation for whom it represents. On the psychological level, this trigram operates like the shadow and refers to the dark, feared, unwanted side of our personality. In general, its purpose is to destroy old patterns so that unexpressed aspects of our identity can bring about fulfillment.

The birth of Isaac changed the course of history. The whole meaning of his life is bound up with his father and his son Jacob in that his importance consists less of his actions than in the unexpected ways others act upon him. His role gives us an expanded view of the meaning of this trigram and its connection to the Lake and Fire trigrams. According to biblical history, Isaac was born when Sarah was ninety years old and Abraham was one-hundred, clearly past the age of bearing children, and Sarah was barren. Because there was no possibility of his conception under the natural course of things, Isaac's conception and birth was the result of a divine seed, not from flesh but from the will of God [2]. This came about because Abraham's first son Ishmael, conceived by his wife's servant for Abraham, was not to be the chosen seed and heir as previously thought While in his old age Isaac's second son Jacob, with the help of his mother, tricks him into giving up birthrights that were to go to his older brother.

———
— —   *Fire*
———   Extroverted Thinking, Jacob

Summary: Clinging; Attachment; Jacob's role; Extroverted Thinking; Leader; Person in Charge; Relies on tangible forms, reason, facts and accepted ideas; Making plans and solving problems. See *Attachments (30).*

The grandson of Abraham, Jacob is the third patriarch of the Israelite people and father of the twelve sons that form the tribes of Israel. When personified by Jacob, the FIRE trigram stands as a symbol of the soul's path from the lower nature of earth to the higher nature of heaven, and the study of religion. In Jungian terminology, the FIRE trigram refers to extroverted thinking and can be seen as the executive, planner, and practical problem solver. Its activities are dependent upon intellectual conclusions and objective data in the form of facts and accepted ideas. Historically, FIRE like the physical Sun is representative of leadership, the God-Principle, and has been the central deity of all peoples. The name Attachments for Hexagram 30 represents the ego, personal desires and will power. This trigram points to the beginning of gatherings in which leaders turn to the light to perceive others in the right way and thus govern the world. It implies receiving admiration from others as well as giving recognition to others based on mutual respect.

Jacob's rise to power was unethical but allowed Spirit to continue its dominion over the senses. His mother Rebecca helped Jacob get the birthright from his father Isaac because she sees that Jacob is quiet and has an interest in developing his spiritual and intellectual nature [3]. The events and circumstances throughout Jacob'*s* life are an enigma in that his memory and offspring continue to be looked down on and adored, accepted and rejected. The name Jacob represents learning to take the human journey or "Jacob's Ladder" back and forth between separation and unity.

— —
_____ *Water*
— — Introverted Feeling, Joseph

Summary: Abysmal; Mysterious; Intense emotions; Inner-directed; Misunderstood; An interest in the subjective elements of life; Values religion, loyalty, love, and deep relationships. See *The Abyss (29).*

The fourth patriarch Joseph personifies the WATER trigram. The WATER trigram, and the name Abysmal for Hexagram 29, represent inner world activities, emotions, and the unconscious. This Jungian type is often completely misunderstood and may appear cool and aloof. Subjective factors influence introverted feeling but this type adapts to objective situations by ignoring unacceptable elements in the environment. The story of Joseph serves an example of the turmoil and struggle associated with the Water trigram. His existence personifies how the understanding of dreams makes the link or bridge between Spirit and matter. While the role of dreams appears throughout the Bible, their importance takes root and bigger meanings in the patriarch Joseph.

Joseph's ten older brothers are jealous because he is Jacob's favorite son. They misunderstand his spiritual gifts, belittled and persecute him, tell his father that he is dead, and sell him into slavery to a high-ranking Egyptian official. Joseph is wrongly accused of trying to sleep with the Egyptian official's wife, and is thrown in prison for years. The Pharaoh of Egypt, bothered by two troublesome dreams, hears of Joseph's ability to understand dreams and summons him to interpret the dreams. Joseph successfully interprets the dreams, warning the Pharaoh that a great famine will strike Egypt in seven years [4]. Impressed, the Pharaoh appoints Joseph to be his highest official and Joseph leads a campaign throughout Egypt to set aside food in preparation for the famine. When Joseph's brothers go to Egypt to purchase food during the famine he eventually reveals his identity and persuades them to move to Egypt along with Jacob and the family of seventy. While in Egypt Jacob's descendants, (the Israelite people) grew rapidly over the next three hundred and fifty years to two million.

———
— — *Mountain*
— — Extroverted Sensation, Moses

Summary: Keeping Still; Extroverted Sensing; Values tangible things; Established orders, laws, traditions; Objective favored over the subjective; Authority figures; Sensible; Step-by-Step Approach. See *Keeping Still (52).*

Moses is the fifth patriarch and the first true hero we encounter in the Bible—a new type of hero, the religious priest. Moses personifies the MOUNTAIN trigram. He represents the tester whose purpose is to teach that in order to function both as an individual human and spiritual being we must abide by certain earthly and heavenly laws to govern our behavior.

From the Jungian perspective, extroverted sensation values actual objects rather than the subjective impressions of the objects. For this type, life is mainly under the influence of accidental outer events. It is through the principles of the MOUNTAIN trigram or Keeping Still as titled for Hexagram 52 that we learn to attain completion and perfection in the material world. Here growth takes place mainly through movements within the limits of our position and the execution of our earthly responsibilities

Moses' entry into history comes about 400 years after Joseph. Moses is raised as an Egyptian prince by the Pharaohs daughter but is aware of his Hebrew roots [5]. After killing an Egyptian who is beating an Israelite worker Moses flees Egypt for forty years. God speaks to Moses, informing him of his plan for Moses to return to Egypt and lead the Israelites out to the land promised to Abraham. Even though Moses is timid and resists he reluctantly returns to Egypt with Aaron as his eloquent spokesperson to organize the Israelites and asks the Pharaoh to let the Israelites go. After several tests and demonstrations of God power through Moses, the Pharaoh finally relents and releases the Israelites. It is widely accepted that Moses was the author of the Torah: the law of the Jewish people and the notion of law as a way of life.

———— *Wind*
———— Introverted Thinking, Aaron
— —

Summary: Gentle expansion and penetration through asking questions; Intelligent; Dissolving the rigid; Depends upon analysis, abstract ideas, theories, and archetypes; Looks for similarities. See *The Gentle (57).*

Moses' older brother Aaron becomes the sixth patriarch because he is the communicator of God's words and helps to establish common bonds between Moses and his people. Aaron personifies the WIND trigram. He represents the dissemination of commands and connections needed to establish common bonds between people. WIND or The Gentle as titled for Hexagram 57 represents talents that deal with various aspects of speaking, learning, commerce and writing.

Among the eight Jungian types, introverted thinking depends upon theories and ideas to make its decisions. This type uses its thinking to analyze the world, not to run it. Like Aaron, WIND is symbolic of communications, mediation, meetings between people and social contacts.

Aaron is only the spokesperson for his brother Moses, but able to express his thoughts in fitting language even before the highest, and carry out what his great brother Moses had planned. He appears only in a subordinate position but faithfully assists his brother in leading the Israelites out of their bondage in Egypt [6]. Aaron became the first priest and communicator of the Divine broadcast to the Israelites in that he spoke for God after getting God's messages through his servant Moses. The priest and many religious leaders have demonstrated forms of religious thoughts in traditional Judaism, Christianity, and Islam that follow the set of rules and the letter of the law with little or no thought of its practical uses, or its inner spiritual import. While the role of priest, rabbi, minister, etc., may not require direct communication with God it does call for the kind of

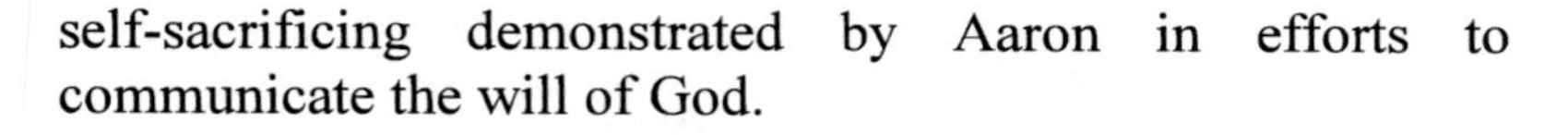

self-sacrificing demonstrated by Aaron in efforts to communicate the will of God.

— —
— — *Earth*
— — Introverted Sensing, David

Summary: Receptiveness; Subjective, ego-centered views of physical reality; Individualistic, inner-directed approach to life; Selective; Irrational attention on the manifest universe; Yielding, supportive and simple. See The *Receptive (2).*

David is the seventh and last of the Old Testament patriarchs. As personified by the patriarch David, this trigram represents divine love manifested in human consciousness. David personifies the EARTH trigram or the Receptive as titled in Hexagram 2. King David's life is one of modesty, obedience, simplicity, and mastery over obstacles.

This Jungian type is guided by its inner interest, tends to be irrational, and often sees things that others don't see. The EARTH trigram is symbolic of devotion, receptiveness, and supporting others. While Water relates to emotional security and the feeling of belonging, EARTH relates to practical, physical security, to actually possessing what one needs to survive in comfort.

God favors David because David, like Moses and Abraham, reinforces God's ongoing preference for the unseen over the seen, the lesser over the greater, inner faith over external circumstances, and David places a higher value on religious devotion than the physical world [7]. When David was in his youth and purity, he communed daily with God and closely reflected divine love. He had his faults, but historical records depict David as the most honorable of all the ancient kings of Israel. In addition to being King, he was an acclaimed warrior, founder of Jerusalem, famous singer, harp player and poet credited with the authorship of half of the Psalms. David could have become king much sooner but was unwilling to take the throne from the current ruler by physical force. Although Israel started out as a nation of loosely affiliated tribes led by priests and religious heroes, it became a nation-state lead by a centralized King.

———
——— *Heaven*
— — Extroverted Intuition, Jesus

Summary: Creativeness; Spirit manifesting in form; Practical intuition; Potential; Natural self-expression; Promotion of new ideas; Innovation; Outer-directed creativity; Aliveness; Enthusiasm. See *The Creative (1).*

Jesus is the eighth and last of the Biblical patriarchs. He represents the spiritual ideal of Christ Consciousness and God's plan for reuniting its human and divine nature. Jesus personifies the HEAVEN trigram. He represents conscious alignment with the Divine or Self. As seen in Jung's understanding of introverted intuition, extroverted intuition tends to regard immediate situations as prisons from which escape must be made. HEAVEN or The Creative as titled in Hexagram 1 represents creative potential, new beginnings and life itself.

The entire New Testament is devoted to the teachings, life and works of Jesus, and the mystery of his person. He offered spiritual solutions to every problem by getting his hands dirty. To the established religious authorities, nothing in Jesus' ministry fit the mold: associating with sinners, the sick, and the poor. Jesus is the new Adam and his mission was and is to show humanity the way to the time when Eve was in Adam, the time when death did not exist [8]. Simply put, his message is to unite through consciousness or the conscious mind to the unconscious mind. God, Allah, Brahma, and their personification as Jesus, Mohamed, Krishna and Buddha, are all agents of creation and apart from them both physical and spiritual life would recede into nothingness. His purpose was to fulfill the laws of Moses by replacing them with the laws of love and reunite humanity with God so they are made one.

Combining Hexagrams and Visions

In most cases, the hexagram and vision insights will compliment each other as answers to the same question. When contradictions show up between them that make no sense you can consult the Change for another hexagram or catch another vision to help clarify the difference. In the event that this becomes necessary it may be easier to consult the Change again and replace the first hexagram answer with the second hexagram answer. If the replacement hexagram or vision is misunderstood, it is best to stop trying to get an answer for now. You can contemplate the contradiction to see why it may make sense in a way that you were not thinking, reframe the question and ask it in another way or try getting an answer after some time has passed.

There is always a reason for contradictions between hexagram and vision insights when they exist. Contradictions are a natural part of life whose presence and mystery make us pause, take a deep breath, and get our bearings. Sometimes we get to know the basis for the opposition but most of the time it's not that important. After all, we're looking for an answer to our question more than an answer to why the hexagram and vision contradict one another or why one or the other doesn't make sense. The problem of contradictions between the hexagram and vision is like making a spelling error. Although we focus on the misspelled word, the problem is often the result of the sentence or context in which the word is used. It's as if the Universe is trying to tell us to step back and look at a bigger picture or context through the misspelled word or contradiction.

7

Vision Centered Counseling and Healing

Problems do not go away. They must be
worked through or else they remain, forever
a barrier to growth and development of the spirit.
—M. Scott Peck

Throughout this book visioning and the Change are tools for listening to God. As tools for spiritual guidance, they help us gain insights into the inner nature or soul's perspective on the questions we seek to answer. The examples in this chapter come from a sampling of my clients. The examples presented in this chapter will help you find answers to personal questions such as what is the status of my life, project or problem. Since the Universe responds to us on a question and answer basis, the consciousness of people who seek answers to their questions will play the biggest role. You can ask questions that have little transformation value as well as those that bring about opportunities for spiritual growth.

I started my intuitive work as a psychic counselor and integrated vision centered counseling as I grew in spiritual consciousness. My spiritual history is a mirror image of humanities spiritual history in that it progressed from ignorance about my relationship to the Divine, to pagan centered psychic development, to dogmatic religious understanding, and from those to the true spiritual liberation of mysticism and gnosis. Vision centered counseling has similarities to psychic counseling but differs in that visioning asks different questions, requires greater spiritual awareness, and comes from a place of serving the Divine rather than getting things from the Divine. Psychic counseling like vision centered counseling depends on intuition but requires less awareness of the spiritual world and often asks questions based on urges, emotions and physical desires. I find that the biggest challenge to vision centered counseling is that many clients that seek help are more interested in getting answers to ego centered rather than Spirit centered questions. I have found that compassion and patience to assist people at every level of consciousness is the best way to meet this challenge.

Anyone who lives in close contact with the indwelling Spirit can learn to catch and reveal God's thoughts. In his book *With Head and Heart* Thurman says, "All persons are mystics who can be broken through at any time by an encounter with the Divine" [1]. You can ask questions and listening to what it has to say. The most important consideration in choosing to work directly with the Soul and seeking help from it is the faith and belief you have in the process. Since much of what we get in life relates to what we believe, those with the greatest faith will get the greatest help.

Just as meditation, the Change, and visioning are ways of listening to God and receiving its ideas, prayer, affirmations and visualizations deal with talking to God and asking for its help. In a variation of the Lord's Prayer Jesus says, "Ask and it shall be given; seek and you shall find; knock and it shall be open to you" [2]. The key themes ask, seek and knock can be easily remembered as they spell out the word "ASK." In the totality of this teaching, he announces that God only gives good things to those who sincerely ask. The teaching implies that you can ask for anything so long as it is not against anyone. As you awaken to the spiritual truth that you are one in nature with God, this teaching becomes more obvious. Beyond using the power for good that is God, you can follow and support what God is already doing. You can use the power for good through prayer, affirmations and visualizations. You can support the power for good through meditation, the Change, visioning and other spiritual practices that make use of your intuition.

God's language is ancient and universal. Regardless of culture, wordless images and symbols represent the Divine as archetypes with universal meaning. Once the person who receives and understands the vision or hexagram from the Change, there is still a need to take additional steps to understand and express them in a form that others recognize.

The visioning insights given for the examples in this chapter and in the eighth and ninth chapters appear in the form of images, symbols, feelings, and hexagrams. They are the mother tongue in the mind of God speaking to answer the questions people raise. They function to influence the mind/body realities of my counseling clients and help us to understand divine ideas about many social and collective questions.

Rather than being irrelevant to behavior, information from the unconscious or deeper mind is the wellspring of behavior that is uniquely human. This information determines to a great measure the nature of who we are, what we're doing, and what we will become. The methods of visioning and the Change are tools to get information out of the deeper mind and set the direction for the whole person or body that we want to understand.

The deeper mind only speaks the universal language of imagery and symbols through tools such as visioning and hexagrams from the Change. Those who learn to hear, see, and understand this language gain access to the power and riches of the universe within. This language appears in the pages that follow, and its message comes in a form not unlike parables and dreams. Its message describes God's thoughts and nature. The imagery and symbols appear to answer the questions in direct and literal ways, and may often illustrate a moral or religious principle. While I have presented interpretations of the visions and hexagram symbols, and what the meaning can be, I cannot give final meanings. Because symbols convey many meanings and applications for those who see to understand them on deeper personal levels, additional interpretations are encouraged.

Answering Questions

Seeking answers to "Either/or" questions is the oldest and most frequent type of guidance sought. These are two part questions where each option can be judged and compared to the other. If for example, a decision must be made on whether to take one path or another, or whether the outcome of a situation will be favorable or unfavorable, the question should be set up to address the outlook of each decision or outcome. The single question, "Which of the two paths before me should I take for the greatest fulfillment for all concerned parties?" will not give a clear answer. However, asking this question in two parts, as follows, gives you a better way of looking at the decision: "What can I expect by taking the first path?" and "What can I expect by taking the second path?"

On average "Either/or" questions give clear choices about two out of every three times these questions are asked. About one third of the time the answer to these questions will be in the middle, meaning neither yes or no or both yes and no. This makes perfect sense if you consider the Taoist symbol of the whole as representing mainly yang at one end, mainly yin at the other end, and a mixture of the two in the middle. Between the binary opposites of light and dark, masculine and feminine, heaven and earth lies a unity where all qualities or forces exist in a state of harmony.

Ultimately the answer to the question "to be or not to be" is not one or the other but both. Since most people like black and white outcomes shades of grey that claim neither tend to be frustrating. As already mentioned the seeds of this frustration came with the beginning of creation. They began with the pattern of binary opposites. Long story short, the search for "either/or" answers must be expanded to accept "both." This is not easy because it requires us to think and act in new ways. It requires that you shift from asking "either/or" questions to asking, "How can I embrace both possibilities?" This shift will allow you to look at ultimate reality in a different and more inclusive way.

When you know something about other people and real life situations, visioning will deepen your knowledge of them. From the perspective of psychic readings, a question asked by many newcomers is how accurate is my reading going to be? As in visioning, the answer to this question depends on the subject and your knowledge of it. Answers to questions such as what is going on with this situation or relationship and where are things going from here tend to make sense and be accurate. However answers to question such as what can you tell me that I don't know or what's coming up in my life that's not on the radar make less sense and have less accuracy. In the first case, we have a context and specific benchmarks but in the second case we have no way to validate the intuitive information.

The desire for certainty about the future is really a desire to control the future and live in the realms of hope and comfort. For example, questions such as, is this suspect telling the truth, where will I find my stolen possessions, or who did this behind my back, have no clear answers unless you have a context and some knowledge about the subject. With no real information or tips on what is going on, the answers to such question will be uncertain and rather useless.

The Dating Dilemma

After a year of separation, Linda and her partner decided to end their relationship of nearly twelve years. Now at the age of forty-three Linda found her self at another fork in the road regarding the dating scene. Before this relationship, she had mainly dated women but from time to time, she also dated men. She preferred the private company of women but felt better about being with men socially. While her family accepted that she was a woman who loved women, they always felt better about her male companions. Linda became a client about sixteen years ago and gets counseling about three times a year on average. This visit was her latest request for insight into how to think about the subject of being intimate with men or women and all things considered, what would give her the greatest fulfillment. Over the years, this topic had come up three other times.

The question she asked was, "Given my interest in dating women and men, what is God's idea of my dating future?" The visioning effort introduced the two images that follow.

> *-Two women hold hands as one looks over the fence at men and women hold hands*
> *-One person stands on two small boats floating side-by-side in an attempt to keep them balanced*

The first vision suggests that heterosexual relationship grabbed her attention because it implies a feeling that the grass was greener on the other side of the fence. As she said earlier, it was easier to socialize with men. As the only lesbian sibling in a large family, she felt constant pressure at family gatherings. She added that she was attracted to some men, but not at much as women.

The second reveals an undecided attitude about her future choice in dating men or women. The scene of standing on a two small boats in the second vision implies indecision on an emotional level. I added that the scene might raise the questions, "Are you rocking the boat with your indecision or is the boat rocking you?" Even though she agreed with this way of seeing her situation, she still felt the need for more of a decision. With that, I recommended the added perspective of hexagram judgments and text.

Regarding the outlook of her would-be experience in dating women she came up with the Change hexagrams titled *The Gentle (57)* which gave the *C+ Grade,* and *Opposition*

(38) dating for dating men, which gave the *C- Grade.* The two grades were in the average category, and neither gave a solid indication of what outcome would work best. I suggested that rather than think in terms of dating only women she would do well to begin using affirmations and prayer to ask for Divine guidance to set up the best outcome regarding her next love relationship.

The Gentle (57) implied that Linda's success with women would depend on patience and acceptance of her natural personal development. It tells us that the hallmarks of her relationships with women will be easygoingness and easy communications. In the parable about the Narrow Way Jesus gives an example of the central theme of *Opposition (38).* His parable refers to choosing between two conflicting paths and correctly judging which path is best. It tells us that Linda's situation is confusing because there is no agreement about what is going on and little understanding about the conflict at hand. Even though most people will prefer *The Gentle (57)* to *Opposition (38)* because of its "better grade," the potential for choosing the correct path as indicated in the text of Hexagram 38 and near average grade makes it an acceptable choice.

The Concerned Grandmother

Janet, a would-be grandmother, wanted to know why her daughter had a recent miscarriage and couldn't stop thinking about it. Although I told her that insights to her question could not be validated, she still wanted to know something that she hoped would make her accept what took place and that she might share with her daughter. This is one of those questions where the answer relies upon faith. I began the visioning by asking for the highest truth about what took place. What I saw was that the embryo-fetus had a problem with its spine and the entire left side of its body. While focused on this vision in words, the fetus spoke and said:

> *"I couldn't keep my intention to come into this life with severe handicaps as originally planned. As more time passed the reality of the burden I would be placing on my young parents, extended family and my self became unbearable."*

This spoken vision message gave me the impression that the would-be child bit off more than it could chew. It's as if the child or potential person concluded it needed far more assistance than initially thought and that the miscarriage was an act of compassion for the parents and all concerned parties.

Upon reporting what I received, Janet felt relieved. She said she didn't know if or when she would share this insight with her daughter but she felt much better hearing this simple report. Even though there was no physical evidence to bear out what I got she felt at peace about what we discussed. As usual, I had no idea of what vision would come up. I had a sense that the grandmother would be accepting of what I had to say as I had worked with her on many other issues. In this case, the visioned response made sense to both of us right away.

After writing out the vision, we consulted the Change to add an additional perspective to the vision. What came up with *Following (17)* delivered the message that an unexpected event must be understood before order can be restored. The trigram combinations that make up this hexagram suggest that the disturbing and unforeseen circumstance comes from hidden forces. It hints that the dreadful miscarriage was a call to have faith in the unseen power for good in the universe.

Relocation Decision-making

The company Wanda worked for gave her a 70-day notice that her job was moving from Tacoma, Washington to Salem, Oregon. They told her that if she wanted to continue her job as a computer programmer with the company she worked for the past seven years she needed to relocate. The decision she faced was whether to stay put and find work in the Tacoma area or relocate as the company requested. Her problem was complicated because she owned a home in Tacoma but couldn't sell it for any kind of profit in the tumbling 2008 real estate market. She was open to renting her home but wasn't sure if this was a good idea. She also wondered if the company was trying to get rid of her now or would be doing so later.

The initial question she asked was, "What is God's view of my relocation dilemma and the possibility that I might lose my job?" For this question, the visioned insights for this question were *a tree pruning,* followed by a *dizzy sensation.*

When I mentioned that the pruning image might mean her company was doing some downsizing she quickly agreed. This made sense to me as well even though she didn't tell my why the company was moving her job to another state or the basis of her fears about losing the job.

The dizzy sensation seemed to represent uncertainty. While darkness is also a sign of uncertainty, the dizzy sensation is a more pronounced version of ambiguity.

The single hexagram answer to this question was *Minor Restraints (9).* This hexagram raised the question "What is the hurry?" and served as a message to control anxious thoughts and wait for signs of sure success Central to the meaning of this hexagram is the meaning of Jesus parable of the Unrighteous Steward. The parable raised the question of whether Wanda's attitude toward this subject matter is just or unjust. While the hexagram as a whole implies that a fairly small issue is on the table, the parable points out that unjust attitudes are those where we disappoint another's expectations, neglect to keep our word and fall short of the listening to the Divine; just attitudes deals with keeping one's word or promise. The message of the parable offered an additional insight into her decision.

Given that she wanted to keep her job even if it meant relocating, we rephrased and limited her initial question to get the "best" or most likely hexagram outcomes between, "What grade represents the likelihood of continued employment?" and "What grade represents the likelihood of being terminated from my job?"

The answer to the continued employment question was *The Family (37) graded B.* The answer to the employment termination outlook was *Repair (18) graded C+.* The straightforward conclusion is that her employment with the company was more likely to continue than be terminated. It was more likely because the B grade for continued employment was higher than the C+ grade for termination.

Wanda's second question was, "All things considered, what is God's view of me staying put in Tacoma even if I don't find other employment by the time my company needs me to relocate?" The vision and Change hexagram for answering this question were:

> -*Someone driving a car with a fully opened parachute tied to the reap bumper*
> -*Yang in Excess (28)*

The first image hints at an effort to move forward in spite of resistance. Since the parachute slows the car, the suggestion is that she would experience a lot of resistance and work against her self by staying put to look for work in Tacoma.

The D Grade for the hexagram *Yang in Excess (28)* refers to barely passing and expands the meaning of the image. Like the vision, this hexagram tells us that staying put in Tacoma was not for her.

Wanda's third question was, "What is God's view of me relocating to Salem and renting out my house while I'm away?" The visioned insight and Change hexagram for this question showed up as follows.

> - *two people having a tug-of-war*
> -*Small Changes (62)*

As we talked how the tug-of-war image might apply, Wanda got in touch with the different ways that renting her house would be an unresolved conflict. She thought she might rent her place out as a furnished home but decided that was impractical. She worried about how well the house would be taken care of, whether she could move back if she found another job in Tacoma, and the list of potential conflicts went on.

The single hexagram grade of C+ for this question came from *Small Changes (62).* The presence of the C+ grade softens the appearance of the tug-of-war in the vision insight and the conflict is probably less difficult that it seems. While the better than the D grade for staying in the Tacoma is better than the C+ grade for renting out her house, neither option seemed good enough.

At this point, we brainstormed a bit to come up with better options and asked two additional hexagram only questions. The first was the rather long question, "What can I expect by taking the job in Salem, renting a small apartment in Salem, keeping my Tacoma house as it is, and driving back for my three off days per week?" The second question was, "What can I expect by looking for other options?"

The answer to the longer first question was *Seeking Nourishment (27)* with no moving lines. The answer to the second question was *Great Power (34)* followed by *Teamwork (7).* The *A- Grade* given for the first question (equivalent to two grades because of the non-moving lines), and the combined *A Grade* and *D Grade* given for the second question made this a clear choice. She took the first option because it was far better than the option of looking for other possibilities.

Asking one or more unplanned questions comes up with fair regularity. When there are no choices good enough to act upon you can often create other options that may lead to better results. However, in some cases there are no good choices or clear outcomes. For example, even though people expect one answer to emerge from their either/or questions or to choose one path or the other it often happens that there is no clear answer. Instead of a black or white result, the true result is a shade of grey. This may come about when the hexagram judgments for both options are equally bad or equally fair. When this happens potential solutions may come from looking into options beyond the fixation on either/or choices, accepting that you have not asked the right question, or that the outcome needs to remain unknown for a time in spite of your demand for an answer now.

The Care Giver Problem

Over the past five months, Sharon was unhappy with her caregiver of fifteen years. She really loves her caregiver Matt and had fantasies of having a romantic relationship with him, but knows he has a girlfriend. She defines herself as a shut in and only goes out when Matt takes her. She defines her illnesses as schizophrenia, panic attacks, agoraphobia, and posttraumatic stress disorder. Sharon is an elderly woman and has been my client for just over four years. She has a special needs trust administered by one of her sisters to take care of her financial needs. Her problem is that Matt has been spending less time with her over the past several months even though he continues to collect full payment for his services. She suspects he's spending more time with his girlfriend, but despite the reason for his absence her concern is that she is not getting her needs met. She was thinking about replacing Matt and wanted to know if this was a good idea to act upon.

Sharon's vision centered questions ask for God's idea of her relationship with Matt now and in the future and guidance on how to resolve her problems with him. The first part of her three part relationship question was, "Where are things at now in my relationship with Matt, how does it look and how do I think about things in a clear headed way?" The visions I caught to answer this question were:

> -*Sharon follows Matt on a path but as she reaches for his hand, he's not really there*

-Sharon's in her house waiting for Matt as he goes around and around in her entryway revolving door

Regarding the first image, I explained that what she thought was there was not, and that it implied that her desire to have Matt show more interest is unfulfilled. The vision points to her frustration and feeling that she counted for nothing based on Matt's lack of presence. It's as if Matt was invisible to her and as such she felt ignored and neglected.

I suggested the second image was telling her that by standing in the doorway, Matt was only half way in the relationship. It's as if he was partly committed and flexible enough to have it both ways. She agreed that Matt had been acting tentative about being in the relationship and that she was waiting for him to enter into it more fully. There were no surprises in these two images and they put into concise symbolic language her thoughts about Matt.

The second part of her relationship question was, "All things considered how does Matt think and feel about being my care giver, and what are his intentions?" The visions to answer this question were:

-Someone under a tree picking its fruit while another person on a fence does the same
-A man pushing a woman in a wheel barrel as he reads his book

I suggested that she was the fruit tree and that Matt has two thoughts about her. The Matt standing on the ground is certain about the fruitful nature of his relation with you and that his standing with you is solid. The Matt on the fence is uncertain about his commitment to you even though he is getting fulfillment from the relationship. As a whole, the scene hints that Matt will not work without compensation for his services, but half the time he is uncertain about his commitment to the relationship. The sense that Matt was not sure about his commitment, yet eager for compensated, struck a chord with Sharon. It strengthened her desire to correct the situation.

The scene of pushing a wheel barrel while reading a book in the second image suggests that Matt is preoccupied with other things while working to support Sharon. When I asked Sharon about the image she said it confirms her suspicions that he is preoccupied with his girlfriend. That makes sense I added, but he may have other reasons for being lost in his own thoughts.

Just to keep things honest, I suggested that it might be helpful to catch a vision to describe her thoughts and feeling about Matt. Sharon agreed. The visioned answer to this question was the image of *Sharon waiting for Matt to open her locked jail cell for her daily time out.*

This scene needed no interpretation. She fully agreed that it represents her feeling that Matt has complete control over her freedom, and her frustration with the prison like confinement. In addition to being physically limited, the experience of imprisonment is completely unacceptable to most people.

The visions for both Sharon and Matt's thoughts and feelings about the relationship suggest that each of them wants positive things from the relationship—freedom for Sharon and compensation for Matt. The visions also revealed to Sharon that Matt seems to feel better about the relationship than she does.

Sharon's relationship assessment continued with the question, "All things considered what is God's idea about my future with Matt, how does it look, what is my experience likely to be, and what can I do to improve it?" The visions and Change hexagrams I caught to answer this question were:

-S*omeone driving a car with the breaks on*
-S*omeone walking in a maze*
-Minor Restraints (9) moving to Limitations (60)

In the first image, the car represents the relationship and the breaks refer to a strained forward movement. Together they imply doubts and difficulty about going forward in the relationship. The good news is that the relationship continues to move forward; the bad news is significant hesitation about the relationship.

As in the first image, the maze represents feelings of being anxious, tied up, and lost. When hexagram perspectives were added to the vision insight, we got a better view of how the universe was answering her question.

The Change hexagrams for the relationship were *Minor Restraints (9)* moving to *Limitations (60).* Hexagram 9 serves as a message to control anxious thoughts and wait for signs of sure success before making changes. Jesus teaching about this hexagram suggests that Matt is not keeping his promise to Sharon and implies that this behavior did not come about overnight, but in a gradual way. At the highest level, Hexagram 60 advises Sharon to have faith in her intuitive insights. It recommends collecting more information about her relationship with Matt and suggests that her position in the relationship is one of a truth seeker gaining greater knowledge. The hexagrams expand the visioned answers to this question. They tell us that Sharon should avoid making quick changes in her relationship with Matt. Although more will be said about how Sharon is advised to deal with Matt in the next question, the hexagrams suggest that she collect more information and act with caution before replacing him with a new care giver.

With this insight, Sharon decided that she was not going to make any decision without Matt's input and agreement. To simplify the larger request for guidance this question was reduced to two either/or questions that would be answered by hexagram grades alone to assist Sharon in making clearheaded decisions about her problem with Matt.

The first either/or question was "Do I consider replacing Matt as my care giver in the near future or do I let go of this idea until things are clear?"

The first graded hexagram judgments for the first question were *Enthusiasm (16)* moving to *Youthful Folly (4)* (Graded A and C-) for considering the replacement of Matt. The second was *The Joyous (58)* moving to *Following (17)* (Graded B and C-) for letting go of this idea until things cleared up. Based on the higher-grade average for replacing Matt rather than not doing so until thing cleared up, the wiser choice for Sharon is to consider replacing him.

Sharon's next either/or question was, "Do I replace Matt completely or reduce his status from full-time to part-time?"

This question gave us the graded hexagram judgments of *The Creative (1)* moving to *Coming to Meet (44)* (Graded A and D) for replacing Matt completely, and *Holding Together (8) moving to The Abyss (29)* (Graded B and D) for reducing his employment from full-time to part-time. As in the first question, this response suggested that Sharon replace Matt. In spite of the graded results, she felt reluctant to make this decision. I understood this feeling and suggested that since the graded judgment for letting Matt go was not much better than the alternatives of reducing his hours or waiting a while until things cleared up she could take the middle path. In the end, they met and agreed to reduce Matt's hours in a way that worked for both of them. They agreed to do this on a trial option basis. Had the hexagram grades been much further apart, ignoring the higher judgment would be painful.

Healing My Knees

Dorothy, age 79, called to get a healing on her knees. She had operations to replace her left knee in 2007 and right knee in 2009. Almost two year after her second operation, walking was still painful and she wanted the healing to help her feel better. She wanted to eliminate the pain and walk without using her walker. When she asked if the healing would bring instant pain relief I told her it would bring some relief, but added what the healing would and would not do. I told her that the she would feel better in the short term, but that only when people truly change their thinking and life do conditions change for the better in fact, perception, or both. I added that most of the people healed by Jesus became sick again and that even though Jesus brought Lazarus back from the dead Lazarus died later. To set up the vision centered reading and healing for Dorothy I proposed that we answer two questions. First, what is the nature and origin of her knee problem? The vision insights about her knee problem were.

-Someone walks slowly upstream
-Someone shopping downtown on a windy day

I told her that the image of walking upstream suggests that her tendency to go against the grain stressed her legs and knees. It's as if she spent too much time going against the established flow of events in her environment instead of going with the flow.

While shopping refers to self-improvement, the windy day suggests confusion, interference, and indecision. This is not unlike the physical stress injuries experienced by athletes who push themselves beyond their comfort zone to get beyond obstacles. Like walking upstream, moving through wind resistance places additional stress on the knees. The images of opposing water and wind bring to mind the possibility that Dorothy's knee problem may be rooted in negative thoughts and feelings. I added that these contrary emotional patterns operate like unconscious habits and emotional addiction.

The follow-up question about her knees was, "What is the spiritual solution to healing my knee problem?" The two healing visions and Change hexagrams were.

-Someone using crutches to walk
-A balanced seesaw with a bowl of sugar at one end and a bowl of lemons at the other end
-Great Possession (14) moving to Small Changes (62)

In addition to pointing to her crutches and physical handicap, this vision implied that the walker is part of her healing. After discussing this image, she mentioned that she wanted to teach Art at a local Senior Center, but does not do so because her need for the walker is a little embarrassing, and dampens her enthusiasm. The image suggests that she should not use this as an excuse and implied that the walker is part of her healing. It reminds me of the adage, 'use it or lose it.' She agreed when I added that as long as she helps herself and serves others she would advance her own healing. .

The rather obvious meaning of the second image is that her healing calls for balance between the opposites depicted by sweetness and bitterness. This balance embraces what is easy and difficult, going with the grain and against the grain, and maintaining a balanced life in general. Even though no one likes pain, it usually comes with the healing process. In this sense, pain can be a very good thing.

The Change hexagrams *Great Possession (14)* moving to *Small Changes (62)* tell us that the gift indicated by the first hexagram is attained by the second hexagrams' step-by-step approach. As indicated by the vision-based solution to her knee problem this hexagram pair suggests that Dorothy can assist in her healing by serving others with her creative talents. The idea of making small changes is like taking little steps toward a destination. With time and patience, she will reach her destination. Although taking little steps may be unexciting, the healing potential and end result is worth the effort. I concluded this healing session by summarizing the three most important things to she could do to have an enduring healing: Thank God for what you already have, namely that you can get about with your walker; help others with the creative (artistic) gifts you have, and practice the attitude of peace of mind.

8

Well-known Personalities

Whatever is true of the Universe as a Whole
must also be true of the individual as part of this Whole.
—Ernest Holmes

This chapter applies visioning with the Change to three well-known public figures. While the people in your life are not necessarily famous personalities, they have at least one thing in common with these well-known figures. They are people with whom you know something about such as loved ones, relatives, villains, or heroes from your past. These individuals represent parts of who you are, and are presented here to answer questions you may have and give insights about the status of your life. Through visions and dreams, the deeper mind uses familiar objects, scenes, places, animals and experiences to impart their wisdom to you through its universal language of images and symbols. In the examples given in this chapter, the answers to questions appear as fragments of parables and dreams. While they are direct and appear as literal statements, their symbolic nature conveys additional meanings for those who look beyond my interpretations.

Visioning comes to life when it helps you to expand a limited understanding of answers to questions such as how am I living my life, who am I, where am I going, and where am I coming from? You might ask about the value of looking for spiritual perspectives when you already have biographies or information about a person. This is a valid question, as some individuals see little value in describing their inner nature. The biographies of accomplished people in this chapter and our own biographies are well understood and perhaps sexy, but they only give us a rear view. For people who seek self-knowledge visioning insights function like light shining in the darkness. As long as you have knowledge of the subject matter in question and of God's nature, there is no limit to the Divine wisdom available to you. Long story short, visioning insights can awaken you to many new possibilities and help you see that within every person is the signature of God.

While the questions raised and answered here can apply to anyone, I have selected these public figures because society as a whole knows many things about them. As such, the visioning insights gathered here offer new examples of how you might apply the process to other people or yourself. Although we know a lot about these public people from secular perspectives, we know little about their spiritual body, strengths, weaknesses, and purpose in life. After giving a mini biographical sketch of the person you will see insights from the rational intuition approach—visioning with the Change—to answer the questions, what is the aura of this person's personality, the inner nature of this person's assets, and lifetime goal or purpose. I believe that you can apply these methods to find enlightened answers to your questions.

Barack Obama

President Barack Hussein Obama was born August 4, 1961 in Hawaii. Obama was born to a white American mother, Ann Dunham, and a black Kenyan father, Barack Obama Sr., who were both young college students at the University of Hawaii. Obama's parents separated when he was two years old and divorced soon thereafter. Obama Sr. left for Harvard to pursue his PhD in Economics and then returned to Kenya in 1965 to work as a government economist. Barack Sr. wrote to his son regularly as he traveled around the world on official business for Kenya but only visited once when Barack was ten. Barack's mother remarried an Indonesian oil manager and moved to Jakarta when Barack was six. Several incidents in Indonesia left Barack's mother afraid for her son's safety and education so, at the age of ten, she sent Barack back to Hawaii to stay with his grandparents who lived in a small apartment. While living with his grandparents, Barack enrolled in Hawaii's top prep school the Punahou Academy. He excelled in basketball and graduated with academic honors in 1979. As one of the few black students at the Academy, Barack became aware of racism and what it meant to be African American and struggled to reconcile social perceptions of his multiracial heritage with his own sense of self.

After high school, Obama studied at Occidental College in Los Angeles for two years and then transferred to Columbia University in New York. In 1983, he received a degree in Political Science from Columbia. Upon graduating, he worked in Harlem as a community organizer for two years and then became a community organizer for a small Chicago church-based group for three years helping poor South Side residents. Barack then attended Harvard Law School, and in 1990 became the first African American editor of the Harvard Law Review. This position gained him national attention and gave Barack the platform that led to a publishing contract and advance for writing his personal memoir about race relations titled *Dreams from My Father,* published in1995.

During his summers, Obama returned to Chicago where he worked as a summer associate at the Sidley & Austin law firm where he met Michelle Robinson. After graduating *magna cum laude* from Harvard in 1991, he returned to Chicago. He declined the job offers from top Manhattan law firms with their starting salaries near $100,000 annually in order to practice as a civil rights lawyer, teach at the University of Chicago's Law School, and continue dating Michelle. Barack and Michelle were married in 1992, and welcomed two daughters—Malia in 1998 and Sasha in 2001. Obama's advocacy work set the stage for him to run for the Illinois State Senate as a Democrat. He won election in 1996. While he was unsuccessful in his run for the U.S. House of Representatives in 2000, he made a successful run in 2004 for the U.S. Senate. He became the Senate's only African American and just the third black U.S. Senator to serve there since the 1880s.

Obama's second book, *The Audacity of Hope* was published in 2006. In this book, he discusses his visions for the future of America, many of which became talking points for his upcoming presidential campaign. Shortly after its release, it hit number one on the New York Times and Amazon.com bestseller lists. In February 2007, Obama made headlines when he announced his candidacy for the 2008 Democratic presidential nomination. He had a hard fought battle to defeat Hilary Clinton to become the presumptive nominee in June 2008. On November 4 Barack Obama defeated Republican presidential nominee John McCain for the position of U.S. President and became the 44th president—and the first African American to hold this office.

When Obama took office, he inherited a global economic recession, two ongoing foreign wars, and the lowest international favorability rating for the U.S. ever. He campaigned on the ambitious agenda of financial reform, alternative energy, and reinventing education and health care—all while bringing down the national debt. Shortly after taking office, the Obama administration persuaded Congress to expand health care insurance for children, provide legal protection for women seeking equal pay, and pass the $787 billion stimulus bill to promote short-term economic growth. Loans were made to the failing auto industry, new regulations proposed for Wall Street and he cut taxes for working families, small businesses and first-time homebuyers. For his efforts and lifetime achievements, he received the 2009 Nobel Peace Price.

Obama took the lead in getting Congress to pass legislation to reform health care in the United States. Within a month after the 2010 midterm elections, in the lame duck period, he announced a compromise deal with the Congressional Republican leadership that included a temporary two-year extension of the Bush era tax cuts, a one-year payroll tax reduction, continuation of unemployment benefits, and a new lowered estate tax rate. His magical compromise overcame opposition from enough members of congress to result in a tax relief package and stimulus of $858 billion.

Divine Perspectives

Aura of personality—The intuitive insights that came up to describe the aura of President Obama's personality as a divine idea were the three visions followed by one hexagram given here.

-A *red, white and blue aura*
-A man surrounded by orange light as he speaks to a large crowd
-The sound of music
-Opposition (38)

The first vision of red, white and blue for Obama's aura brings to mind the American flag. As a symbol, flags represent pride, allegiance, and the celebration of new changes. The red suggests energy, passion and the emotion of anger. White represents truth, awareness and guidance; and blue hints at clarity of mind, peacefulness, and emotional control. The American symbolism of red, white and blue suggests as well that Obama personally identifies with America's core values and creed that all citizens have an opportunity to develop their potential.

The orange color in the second image is actually a blending of yellow and red, and brings to mind the warmth of the sun. In addition, this color is symbolic of the ability to heal with words. In some cases, orange is also a blending of peace and love.

The sound of music in the third vision is associated with the qualities of inner harmony and balance. Music is often easy to hear and soothes the emotions. This inner makeup shows itself in Obama's smooth approach to communicating his ideas, and suggests a receptive, sit back, and let things unfold approach to life.

The presence of *Opposition (38)* from the Change suggests that Obama is inclined to embrace different viewpoints and believes that each opposing perspective has just as much validity as the other. The idea is that as long as each group retains a healthy degree of independence each one can learn to compliment the other. This hexagram serves as an example of Obama's work with political opponents in the sense that his good intentions often contradict those who seek recognition from the community he shares with them.

Personal Assets—From the Divine perspective President Obama's assets are represented by the visions and hexagram that follows.

-A star player on a sports team
-A high jumper makes the winning leap over a high jump bar
-Someone lifting weights before a mirror
-Ascending (46)

The star player in the first image is a slang term for an important and well-recognized person. It implies that Obama's standing, as president, will depend on the team's success. The image of a sport team player further associates the Obama strength as working with professional and social groups. As a whole, this vision hints that he fully supports the team and gets approval from his peers.

The high jumper in the second image is symbolic of Obama's interest in competition and the attainment of high goals. It suggests that he is aggressive and has a need to compete, win, and live up to his potential.

The person lifting weights in front of a mirror in the last vision represents his need for self-improvement. It puts forward that Barack goes out of his way to make himself a better man. The idea of seeing himself in the mirror relates to introspection and his efforts to increase his self-esteem and see situations from different perspectives.

The hexagram *Ascending (46)* proposes that Obama seeks to advance his connections with people and works to gain a higher status or rank with others. It suggests that his growth in situations is greater than growth achieved by the rich because it comes from his heart more than his pocket. This hexagram also implies that people relate to Obama's open and communicative manner.

Lifetime goals—The Divine perspective of President Obama's lifetime goal shows up in the following visions and hexagrams from the Change.

> *-A mountain climber hikes to the summit of the world's tallest mountain*
> *-The first marathon runner to cross the finish line*
> *-Books on the top shelf*
> *-Keeping Still (52) moving into The Family (37)*

The mountain climber symbol is an indication that Obama seeks the highest of goals and that he aims to accomplish a record setting human feat that may pave the way for others to follow. The upward climb is a universal symbol of going the right way. An example of setting his sights on the summit of the world's tallest mountain shows itself in the title of Obama's book, *The Audacity of Hope.* Climbing uphill also implies going against the grain instead of seeking the quick and easy downhill goals. While everyone has goals, very few pursue world record setting goals.

The winning marathon runner in the second mental picture informs us that Obama is not only skilled at winning competitions but has great endurance as well. The long marathon race is a metaphor for persistence, strength and working toward goals over the long haul. The fact that Obama sees himself as a skinny fellow with a big psychological engine makes him well suited to win marathon competitions.

The picture of books on the top shelf in the third vision brings to mind his interest in helping people to learn about their higher purpose in life. Knowledge from the top implies that other ideas, less relevant to the highest ideas, have a lower status. The top shelf books may also represent the value Obama's places on higher education, and opportunities o acquire wisdom of the highest order.

More than any of the other sixty-four hexagrams *Keeping Still (52)* refers to straightforward connections to following the law and explains Obama's lifetime interest and background in constitutional law. It also stands as a symbol of being still, centered and focused regarding established traditions, authority and ways of life from both private and public perspectives. The second or future hexagram, *The Family (37),* represents order and harmony in the realm of ideas and suggests that Obama's lifetime goal embraces agreement and integration. Health organizations, families, social groups and even communities serve as examples of this hexagram in that they all stress the value of individuals coming together to work toward a common goal. Because this hexagram represents elected officials and other influential people who represent and guide people toward common goals, it implies that President Obama's job as US President qualifies as a way to pursue his life's purpose.

Warren Buffett

Warren Edward Buffett was born August 30, 1930 to his father Howard, a stock broker-turned-congressman and his wife Leila. In 2008 he was ranked by Forbes as the richest person in the world with an estimated net worth of approximately $62 billion. He was the second of three kids and the only boy. From an early age, he displayed an exceptional aptitude for both money and business. While other children his age were playing hopscotch and jacks,

Warren was making money and saving money by selling chewing gum, Coca-Cola, and weekly magazines.

After graduating from high school it was never Buffett's intention to go to college, but his father urged him to attend the Wharton Business School at the University of Pennsylvania. Buffett stayed two years and then returned home to Omaha where he transferred to the University of Nebraska-Lincoln to complete his studies for a B.S. in Economics. He soon applied to the Harvard Business School's MBA program but they rejected him for being too young. Slighted, Warren enrolled in the Columbia Business School where famed investors Ben Graham and David Dodd taught. He received his M.S. in Economics in 1951 and attended the New York Institute of Finance. Buffett married Susan Thompson in 1952 and they had three children Susie, Howard and Peter. In 1957, Buffett purchased a five-bedroom stucco house in Omaha, where he still lives today, for $31,500. The couple began living separately in 1977 although they remained married until her death in July 2004. After Susan's death, Warren married his longtime-companion Astrid Merks whom he lived with since his wife's departure in 1977.

In summarizing his learning from the business school and his investment philosophy, Buffett said, "The basic ideas of investing are to look at stocks as a business, use the market's fluctuations to your advantage, and seek a margin of safety. That's what Ben Graham taught us. A hundred years from now they will still be the cornerstones of investing." In 1962, Buffett became a millionaire through his various business partnerships. He invested in and eventually took control of a textile-manufacturing firm, Berkshire Hathaway as CEO. In 1988, Buffett began buying stocks in the Coca-Cola Company, eventually purchasing up to seven percent of the company for one billion dollars. It would turn out to be one of Berkshire's most lucrative investments, and one that still holds.

When Berkshire Hathaway began selling preferred shares of its stocks in 1990, Buffett became a billionaire on paper. Even though buying the company was a mistake due to the failure of the textile industry, Berkshire became one of the largest holding companies in the world as Buffett redirected the company's extra cash to acquire other businesses and stocks of public companies. A hallmark of Berkshire Hathaway has become that of buying whole companies rather than public stocks. It now owns a large number of businesses that are dominant players in their respective industries, various niche markets, or have other unique characteristics to separate them from their competitors.

Buffett has always given himself a low compensation for his work as a CEO. Compared to CEO's in comparable companies he has kept his salary low (it has always been less than $200,000 annually) and has a history of using more public transportation than other CEO's. Warren Buffett has written several times of his belief that the rich earn outsized rewards for their talents. He says he plans to give away virtually all of his wealth when he and his wife die. In 2006, he announced a plan to give away his fortunes to charity with over eighty percent going to the Bill and Melinda Gates Foundation. He opposes the transfer of great fortunes from one generation to the next and wants his kids to get just enough of his wealth to feel that they could do anything but not so much they would feel like doing nothing.

The socially progressive Buffett formally endorsed Barack Obama and made campaign contributions to his presidential campaign. In backing Obama for president instead of his opponent John McCain, he remarked that McCain's views on social justice were so far from his own that McCain would need a "lobotomy" for Buffett to change his endorsement.

Divine Perspectives

Aura of personality—As a divine idea, the key elements of Warren Buffett's aura and personality may be explained by the visions and Change hexagrams given here.

-A gold circle with a brown center
-Someone climbing a ladder
-People playing a chess game
-Biting Through (21)

The first vision of the gold circle with a brown center shows a difference between Buffett's outer and inner personality. While the gold outer circle represents his more noticeable traits of self-mastery, self worth and spiritual understanding, the brown center is symbolic of an inner personality driven by practicality, money management and material security.

The second ladder-climbing image points to his desire to get to the top and achieve success in his endeavors. Implicit in the climb is not only higher awareness but also the fact that the climber will have to come down with or without the knowledge of how to do so. In spite of his many successful investments and great wealth, Buffett had his share of losses. He pledged to give away nearly all of his wealth to charity upon his death. This pronouncement may mean that he is aware of the need to manage the journey down as well as up the ladder.

Playing chess in the third vision is symbolic of mastery, achievement, and the intricacies of competition in the game of life. It hints that Buffett views life as a game, "plays" to win, and continues to move toward his goals in spite of setbacks along the way.

The presence of Biting Through (21) from the Change speaks to Buffett's ability to fix problems sooner rather than latter and to take decisive action to correct his idea of injustice. It also refers to his talent for introducing far-reaching ideas to others even though they may want to keep things as they are.

Personal Assets—From the Divine viewpoint, Warren Buffett's main assets are described by the visions and change hexagrams given here.

-An archer shooting arrows at a distant target
-A passenger on a train with his motorcycle
-Someone on a mountaintop looks over the city with a telescope
-Relatedness (30)

The archer vision is symbolic of Buffett's competitive spirit and intention to achieve his goals through good marksmanship. The distant target points to future or long-term goals. It suggests that he has long-range plans and the self-discipline needed to hit the bull's-eye when his target is in sight.

The second vision of the passenger on a train with his motorcycle tells us that one of Buffett's strengths is his ability to align himself with an established order or business while retaining his independence and unique approach. An example of the meaning conveyed in this vision shows up in Buffett's investment philosophy of looking at individual stocks as a business. The train passenger with the motorcycle suggests that Buffett moves forward both as an investor in the stocks of established businesses such as Coca-Cola, and as the outright buyer of unique businesses. In each case he functions both as an individual and as a member of the established order.

The third mental picture of someone on a mountaintop refers to his innate desire to accomplish great things. The person on the hilltop suggests that Buffett identifies with playing the role of "king of the mountain." The telescope modifies this vision by adding the assets of clarity and vision that come from his elevated perspective.

Getting Relatedness (30) from the Change hints that Buffett is a recognized authority figure and that he receives admiration and respect from the people under his influence. It also tells us that he takes the lead when it comes to the collection of facts, practical problem solving, and the use of reason in his approach to life in general.

George "W" Bush

Conversationally known as "W" to distinguish himself from his father, George Walker Bush was the 43rd President of the United States. Born on July 6, 1946, in New Haven, Connecticut were his father and future president George H. W. Bush was attending Yale College. In 1948, His father moved to Odessa, Texas and went to work in the oil business. "W" grew up mainly in Midland, Texas and Houston and later attended ended Yale where he received a degree in History in 1968.

Even though W came from a prominent political family and was immersed in politics since childhood, his prospects of living up to his pedigree were dim until he turned forty. Possibly limited by dyslexia, Bush proved an uninspired student in high school, had a "C+" average at Yale, and the University of Texas law school would not admit him. However, he was able to start and graduate from the Harvard business school after a stint in the Texas Air National Guard as a commissioned second lieutenant. His late marriage to Laura Welch and rebirth as a believing Christian brought stability to his floundering life. Luck plays an important role in much of W's life including his eventual election to the nation's highest office.

Bush was discounted many times in his life and career for being clumsy and unintelligent due to his fractured speaking style. After nearly losing his oil and gas business and a failed attempt at running for the U.S. congress in his hometown of Midland, Bush assembled a group of investors to buy the Texas Rangers. Prior to entering politics again to run for the Texas governorship his most notable achievement in private life was becoming president and chief operating partner of the Rangers baseball team. Even though being governor of Texas is mainly a ceremonial position, Bush worked out a power sharing deal with the powerful lieutenant governor; a Democrat named Rick Perry, and established his reputation as a person able to cross party lines. This reputation served as a springboard to his presidential bid as a traditional conservative favoring small government, tax cuts, a strong military, and opposing gun control and abortion. His race against Vice President Al Gore was the closest election in a century and in the end he won the presidency with 271 electoral votes, just one more than needed, even though he lost the popular vote by half a million. The divided five to four Supreme Court decision generated enormous controversy, with critics asserting that the Court, and not the electorate, had determined the outcome of the election.

The main accomplishment of Bush's domestic agenda was a quickly enacted $1.35 trillion tax cut in June 2001. His early foreign policy was defined by the rejection of many international treaties that the White House felt were bad for American interest including the Kyoto Treaty on global warming, the biological weapons convention banning germ warfare, and 1972 Antiballistic Missile Treaty. The terrorist attacks on the World Trade Center and Pentagon on September 11, 2001 that killed 3,000 people was the most significant event of President Bush's tenure. This event altered and established the direction of his presidency. Many critics of his administration's policy in Iraq described it as a distraction from the war on terror, effectively preventing the United States from battling war on its genuine front in Afghanistan. While W failed to restructure Social Security despite months of campaigning for his second term, he signed into law the largest expansion of Medicare since its creation—a prescription drug coverage program.

Beginning in 2007, the nation's long-running housing boom collapsed. As the problems continued into 2008, the Bush administration sought to counter the economic crisis but despite their efforts, the financial conditions continued to worsen, and in October 2008, the financial system seemed on the verge of collapse. The final major act of his administration was the passage of a $700 billion financial rescue package to recapitalize the banking system.

Divine Perspectives

Aura of personality—Through Visioning and the Change we can understand the Divine's idea of President Bush's personality. The aura of his personality shows up in the following visions and hexagram from the Change.

-A dark blue aura with golden brown beneath
-An individual building a house out of bricks
-Someone adds water to a half-full glass
-Limitations (60)

The colors in the Bush aura suggest a deeply traditional and religious outer-personality, and business oriented inner-personality. Dark blue is often associated with conventional values and with careers such as law enforcement, the military, and well-defined hands on professions. In addition to representing mastery, the golden brown inner layer also points to Bush's interests in self-mastery, material security, and stability.

The mental picture of building a house with bricks expands upon the solid earthy theme of the golden brown color. As a symbol, the house represents how we view ourselves both as individual personalities and in relation to society. The brick exterior suggests an extra layer of strength, protection, and endurance.

The scene of someone adding water to a glass that is already half full tells us that inherent in the Bush personality is the tendency to see the glass as half-full rather than half empty. Although his optimism is not apparent in the previous two images, the color gold mixed with brown implies confidence and mastery (qualities associated with practical optimism).

The addition of hexagram Limitations (60) tells us that Bush is aware of the limits to what he can and cannot do, what he should and should not do, and that he has learned to live within them. It further suggests that he tends to put too much attention on matters that don't deserve the focus and too little on important topics.

Personal assets—In the language of the Divine, Bush's main assets show up in the visions and Change hexagram given here.

-Someone shaking a fruit tree
-A horse wearing blinders jumps over hurdles on an obstacle course
-Fulfillment (2)

As a symbol, the first vision represents a hurried and perhaps aggressive attempt to attain payment for one's labor. It implies that Bush is not shy about reaching for fulfillment. This approach to reaping what he has sown is perhaps a no nonsense asset in the business world.

As a symbol of power and freedom, the horse represents a key aspect of the W's character. Because the horse wears blinders to prevent being distracted by objects at its side this image also tells us that Bush is able to get the assistance he needs to keep his focus on the paths he chooses. The act of jumping over hurdles suggests that while Bush tends to face many obstacles, he has the discipline to get beyond them. These obstacles may be mental, emotional or physical in nature.

The appearance of *Fulfillment (2)* expands and grounds the visions of President Bush's assets. This hexagram tells us that among his main assets are acceptance of the established order. It suggests that his success and recognition are the result of both following the path laid out for him and sticking with the tried and true.

Lifetime goals—According to the Divine, Bush's lifetime goal and purpose appear in the visions and Change hexagrams that follow.

-Someone climbing the world's tallest mountaintop
-Someone repairing wires on top of a telephone pole

-Someone picking fruit from trees planted in the town business district
-Standstill (12) moving to Development (53)

The first vision of the President's purpose needs little interpretation. As a symbol, the mountain climber scene tells us that his ultimate lifetime goal is one of achievement. It also suggests that his path is one of an achiever who needs to aspire to the peak of his chosen profession. It is interesting to note that this image is the same one that came up to describe President Obama's purpose. In this sense, it tells us that the two men had the highest of goals in common.

The second image implies that Bush's purpose in life is to learn how to communicate with others and cultivate long distance relationships. His position on top of the telephone pole puts forward the idea that he seeks to stay in touch with people in both high and far away places.

The vision of an individual picking fruit from trees in the town business district is symbolic of financial abundance and fruit bearing business deals. Collecting fruit in this way implies an expectation that fulfillment grows on trees, and that it may be natural and easy to come by. This vision may help to understand the apparent fact that Bush's success was in large measure based on his family's social position and his father's business and political connections.

The Change describes his lifetime goal and purpose are with *Standstill (12)* moving to *Development (53).* The first hexagram tells us that Bush is often misunderstood, and not seen or heard by other people. It also suggests his new ideas have the best chance to develop when he remains open to what others have to say. *Development (53)* hints that he can get the results he seeks by taking a sensible yet, bit-by-bit approach to direct people who generally agree with him. Along with the first vision, this hexagram pair gives a plausible answer for why Bush had an indirect path to the presidency and why he attained it as a late bloomer.

9

Spiritual Solutions for Social Problems

In the quest for social justice, one's vision of society never conforms to some external pattern, but is modeled and shaped in accordance to the innermost transformation that is going on in his or her spirit.
—Howard Thurman

In discussing the purpose of spirituality and social transformation Thurman taught that "modern society is a wounded body." This chapter uses visioning and the Change to catch the Divine perspective on the nature and solution to three eminent society problems. Through its ancient universal language of imagery and symbols, ideas from the deeper mind are given here for interested members of society to view these problems. While spiritual solutions exist for every issue, I have used the examples of unemployment, illegal immigration, and fighting terrorism because there is enough public awareness of their existence to appreciate divine thoughts about the subject. Experts have proposed many solutions but few solutions represent direct revelations from the deeper mind on such matters.

In the previous two chapters, the visioning process with the Change provided insights to answer questions asked by some of my counseling clients and to assess the personalities and goals of well-known public figures. Here the subject matter and questions are different but the approach to catching Divine ideas is identical. Rather than being irrelevant to behavior, information from the deeper mind is the source of all behavior that is uniquely human.

As seen in previous chapters the methods of visioning and the Change have ancient histories. Both of these intuitive methods help us to understand God's answers to the questions we ask. Even though both methods predate all world religions, the insights derived by them provide the foundation for every religion. In addition to religion, other disciplines for understanding the human soul include philosophy, science, psychology and the occult. People from all lifestyles have drawn heavily upon some form of visioning to catch and understand God's thoughts. In this chapter, answers to questions about the universal problems and their solutions appear as interpretations of the visions, symbols and Change hexagrams.

By integrating the Change into the visioning process, people unfamiliar with the I Ching can make use of its rational wisdom. Those already familiar with the I Ching can relax into the great intuitive powers of visions and dreams. This integrated approach is well suited to addressing group as well as individual interests, and personal as well as social concerns. In the end, spiritual consciousness is transformed as the social order is being transformed into the ultimate reality of community.

As in the previous chapters, I have presented interpretations of the information contained in the visions, images and hexagram symbols. These interpretations give indications of how to think about their meanings from the perspective of the Divine and how you may participate in the process of transforming our society. It is impossible to give final interpretations because this information, as with the symbolic information contained in dreams and parables, contains additional meanings and applications for those who seek to understand them on deeper levels. As already mentioned, a picture is a thousand words.

Searching for spiritual solutions to social problems is a means to a greater end. As in the work of assisting to transform individuals, transformation of the social order requires an understanding of the realities of the environment. Transformation requires courage to accept that suffering is a consequence of seeking change. As Thurman once said, "The person concerned about social change must understand the material being dealt with and expose the roots of his or her mind to the truth that is the unseen model of the facts."

Underemployment

Americans are underemployed if they are unemployed or working part-time but wanting full-time work. The problem of underemployment and unemployment is a worldwide reality. It is one of the major causes of our poverty, backwardness, crimes, and frustration in society. Underemployment is a situation in which a worker is employed, but not in the desired capacity, whether in terms of compensation, hours, or level of skill and experience. All underemployment, unlike unemployment, occurs in circumstances where a person who is searching for work cannot find a job. Underemployment usually means the employment of workers with high skill levels in low-wage jobs that do not require such abilities, and involuntary part-time workers who would like to be working full-time but can only get part-time work. It also refers to the hidden underemployment practice of underutilization where employers employ workers with legal or social restrictions or work that is highly seasonal.

The unemployed refers to people who do not have a job, are available for work, and are actively looking for work. People who cannot either join an enterprise or create a job are unemployed. Most of the people who become unemployed remain without work for very short periods. However, many of the unemployed remain without work for long periods. The adverse consequences of unemployment are much more acute for this group. Prior to the invention of unemployment compensation people unable to find work had a stark choice: starve or break the law. Because some unemployment goes unacknowledged, there are limited historical records.

Unemployment falls into one of two categories that are often hard to distinguish: voluntary or involuntary. Voluntary unemployment is a person's decision, whereas involuntary unemployment exists because of the social and economic environment in which the person operates. Voluntary unemployment includes workers who reject low wage jobs whereas involuntary unemployment included workers fired due to an economic crisis, industrial declines, company bankruptcy, or organizational restructuring. The clearest cases of involuntary unemployment exist where there are fewer job vacancies so that even if vacancies were filled, some unemployment would remain.

There are limits to what policy makers can do to improve unemployment levels. Experts often suggest that a growth in part-time and temporary jobs may indicate future growth in full-time work because employers hire these workers before committing to hiring new full-time employees. Regardless of how society interprets the shifts taking place between part-time, temporary and full-time jobs, it is important that policy makers focus on the broader goal of reducing underemployment, not just unemployment. Part-time and temporary jobs like those associated with census-taking or large one-time projects are far better than no job and many reduce the unemployment rate, but they do not represent the kind of job creation needed for a sustainable economic recovery. Higher employment ultimately depends upon getting people back to work in private-sector jobs, which will not only take them off the dole and generate short-term income, but will also set them on the path toward increasing skills, developing better habits, and creating wealth. If society truly wants to create jobs it must address the dynamics that keep employers from offering jobs and that keep people from accepting jobs.

Divine Perspectives

The Problem—The nature of underemployment and unemployment problems are represented by the following visions and hexagrams from the Change.

-People in line waiting to board a ferryboat
-A landslide caused by a rainstorm
-A firestorm destroys many homes
-The Wander (56) moving into Abundance (55)

Waiting in line to board a ferryboat suggests that the way is blocked and that it will take time to connect the different sides or forces—jobs and the jobless. Taken as a symbol, the people in line represent the unemployed who have no control over the number of position available on the employment boat. To be effective as a means for reducing unemployment many people must accept the limits of the ferryboat.

The landslide caused by the rainstorm in the second image is emblematic of a natural breakdown of old ways and an opportunity for major reorganization to take place. While this vision shows destruction it hints that after the damage comes rebirth. The need for rebuilding after the landslide suggest that dealing with the unemployment problem calls for mending the broken connection between job providers and seekers.

As a symbol of devastation, the home destroying fire-storm in the third vision tells us that the unemployment problem is associated with society's loss of safety and security. As seen in the first two visions it is symbolic of upheaval and people overwhelmed by circumstances beyond their control.

The Change hexagrams offer another perspective to expand our understanding of the underemployment and unemployment problems. The *Wander (56)* informs us that this social problem brings up many different feelings and views without resolving anything. It tells us that it's best to look beyond appearances and seek the comfort of divine ideas without rushing to any conclusions. Since the desires to go forward, do nothing, and retreat all vie for attention at the same time, the problem is one of competing interests. The second hexagram, *Abundance (55),* tells us that the unemployment problem is the natural economic response of coming back into balance after reaching the highest possible point of economic expansion and wealth. Simply put, what goes up must come down. It's as if too many people in society received financial gains that were not merited—gains resulting from circumstances beyond their control.

Releasing—The Divine insights on what society must release or change to deal with the problem of unemployment show up in the following mental pictures and hexagram from the Change.

-Baggage removed helps an airplane to take off
-Traffic lights modified to control the flow of traffic
-Mail delivery is delayed due to bad weather
-The Gentle (57)

The vision of removing the luggage from the airplane to make it light enough for take off hints that society can improve its unemployment status by reducing the fat that prevents it from taking off. The image implies that society cannot lift itself up because it is carrying more weight than it needs. Because flying aircraft represent spiritual awakening and soaring to new heights, the luggage that prevents the plane from lift off is symbolic of attachments to things that block our openness to greater awareness about how the solve the problem of not getting off the ground.

The second vision of traffic lights to control the flow of traffic is symbolic of societies need to manage the course of its members. It implies that the lack of regulation is a reflection of a time of crisis that demands changes in order to restore order.

The third mental picture of delayed mail delivery due to bad weather has to do with an overdue message about pending unemployment issues from the unconscious. Because storms often represent confusion, and peace comes after storms, this scene is a message for society to change directions when the bad weather passes. This adjustment activity should release tensions and increase the opportunity for spiritual awareness that follows the storm.

The *Gentle (57)* advises that society can make progress in dealing with the unemployment problem through skillful communication and patience. It proposes that changes be made by building upon gradual effort to expand, and that plans for quick results should be abandoned.

Solution—In the language of the Divine, solutions to the unemployment problems are presented through the visions and Change hexagrams that follow.

-Passengers on a bus ride
-Students in school
-Standstill (12) moving into Contemplation (20)

The busload of passengers is symbolic of society taking the lead to move its great potential for self-expression in a new direction. The bus full of people represents the unemployed as a collective movement of energy from one place or endeavor to another. It suggests that society should be in the driver's seat to move its unemployed citizens in a new direction.

The students taking classes in the second mental picture hints that the solution to the problem calls for new learning among the unemployed and the need for the unemployed to take a new course toward employment. Painful as they may appear, we can see this image as a reminder that life is a school and that we are all here only to learn and grow. Personal and collective lessons never change until we learn them, so we might as well work on solving the problem now.

The first of two hexagrams, *Standstill (12),* suggests that society can begin to solve the problem of unemployment by dealing with misunderstandings and seeking common ground among the differing viewpoints on the problem. It points to resolving the conflicts between material concerns or the costs of supporting those in need, and the moral concerns or costs of ignoring their plight. The second hexagram, *Contemplation (20),* proposes that society needs to investigate the facts at hand and observe the whole unemployment environment before acting to resolve the problem. It informs us that the mistakes of nearsightedness decrease when we are clear about available options regarding needs and wants.

Illegal Immigration

With over ten million undocumented immigrants in the US as of 2009, the issue of illegal immigration continued to divide Americans. The term illegal immigrant refers to all non-US nationals and to all non-US citizens who have entered the US without authorization and who are deportable if detained, or who entered the US legally but who have fallen "out of status" and are deportable. Other terms that are commonly used include undocumented immigrants, undocumented aliens, unauthorized immigrants, illegal migrants, illegal aliens, migrants, or undocumented workers.

Illegal immigration continues to be a controversial and divisive topic, not only in the US, but also throughout the world. Illegal immigrants compromise a diverse category. Some undocumented immigrants entered the country illegally and others entered legally but overstayed the time allowed on their visa or violated the terms of their permanent resident permit. The net flow of the illegal immigration pattern is almost entirely from countries of lower socioeconomic levels. Most illegal immigrants move to find opportunities for greater economic growth and a better quality of life. Many leave loved ones and valuable possessions behind. Some move to foreign countries to give their children a better life. From the perspective of the costs and benefits potential immigrants believe the probability of benefits and successfully migrating to the destination country are greater than the costs.

Throughout history there continues to be many ways that migrants cross the border to get into the US. Some cross the border by boats, with the assistance of smugglers, and in shipping containers, trucks or boxcars. Many find a way to get to their destination even though it may involve deadly risks. Unfortunately, some immigrants enter the country on an involuntary basis. During the 19th century, many came into Europe and the United States during the slave trade. Over time, the importation of slaves diminished. It has thankfully become almost non-existent. It still exists in the common emerging trend of smuggling young girls and women into the sex-slave trade.

Some people say that illegal immigration benefits the US economy through additional tax revenue, expansion of the low-cost labor pool, and increased money in circulation. They contend that immigrants bring good values that are consistent with the American dream, and that the opposition to migrants stems from racism. Many undocumented immigrants find employment in low skilled, labor-intensive jobs such as landscaping, construction, restaurants, hospitality, domestic services and agriculture. Some argue that illegal immigrants tend to take on jobs that residents or citizens refuse while others argue that illegal immigrants take away jobs in general.

Opponents of illegal immigration want to deport aliens who break the law by crossing the US border without proper documentation or who overstay their visas. They do not want to reward them with a path to citizenship, or give them access to social services. They argue that illegal migrants are criminals and social and economic burdens to law-abiding, tax-paying Americans. While work regulations in the US prohibit employers from hiring migrants, this does not deter many employers. In fact, many employers even take advantage of an employee's undocumented status by paying wages below what the federal law requires and allowing an employee to work in unsafe conditions. Some employers feel they can get away with these human rights violations will illegal immigrants because they won't report their employer out of fear of deportation.

Divine Perspectives

The Problem—The visions and hexagrams I caught for representing the Divine's ideas about the illegal immigration problem were.

> *-Many people line up for dinner at a table with no more space*
> *-Tug-of-war between groups invisible to one another*
> *-Many people line up to cross a bridge full of people*
> *-Innocence (25) moving into Following (17)*

The first vision of people in line to eat is symbolic of migrants expressing their need for nourishment and waiting their turn in the face of limited supply while those at the table represent US citizens. The difficulty in getting a seat at the table suggest that aliens have an additional need for family and group connections, and feel rejected by American society.

The second image of a tug-of-war between two groups is a sign of fighting and being at odds with aspects of oneself. It tells us that society can deal with illegal immigration when it learns to take itself out of the battle of opposites so that its differences with the undocumented migrants can be reconciled. When opponents are visible to one another, neither side sees, hears, or understands the other side as desired and each remains frustrated.

The third vision of people attempting to cross a bridge is symbolic of seeking to change from an old to a new direction in life. This scene implies that the illegal immigration problem arises out of the need to overcome obstacles and make the transition from poor conditions of the past to conditions of opportunity in the present. The large crowd attempting to cross the bridge represents limitations imposed by the ideas and needs of others and the possibility of a collapsing bridge.

The presence of *Innocence (25)* tells us that the illegal immigrants are blameless spectators who were born into social circumstances beyond their control. It hints that people tend to view the important matters of illegal immigration through feelings more than logic. The movement of this hexagram into *Following (17)* recommends that an attitude of flexibility is needed to overcome resistance, and that the migrant problem will not improve until both parties, led by US society, can take a step back, get centered and ask for spiritual help. As society learns to receive visions from the same source, and understand them in the same way, the visions become manifest.

Solution—From the Divine perspective, the visions and hexagrams that tell us what society can do to assist in solving the illegal immigration problem were.

> *-Illegal migrants hold a ladder steady for citizens to climb*
> *-Many migrants working on a plantation*
> *-A surveyor makes plans for a new road*
> *-Destroying the Old (49) moving to Modesty (15)*

The image of people holding a ladder steady suggests US society can put itself in a position to resolve the illegal immigration problem by accepting the support of migrants. Climbing upward in general is a sign of moving in the right direction and the individual steps taken by American society represent growing levels of achievement in accepting the help offered by undocumented migrants.

The second vision of plantation workers is symbolic of illegal immigrants supporting US plantation owners to advance goals. Viewing migrants as plantation workers suggests the capacity to offer employment and to assist in their fulfillment. As a symbol, workers on the plantation also suggest doing what is needed to meet the requirements for growth and gathering the harvest.

The surveyor image in the third vision is symbolic of making plans for a new direction, expansion and opportunity. As a solution to the immigration problem, it recommends that US society take the lead to provide the groundwork needed to pave the way for making constructive changes. The design of new roads is symbolic of a course correction and represents a new way to get from where we are to where we want to go.

The presence of the hexagram *Destroying the Old (49)* advises US society to accept new information and make a major shift toward the "better" outcomes in its policies toward illegal immigrants. It implies that the benefits of migrants outweigh the costs and that letting go of old approaches will open the door to learning what is new and right. The future hexagram *Modesty (15)* is about the Golden Rule that says, "Treat others only in ways that you're willing to be treated in the same situation." This rule is arguably the most universally ethical principle in history. It suggests that American society can apply the Golden Rule by placing itself in the place of those on the receiving end of their actions. As a whole, it hints that it is wise to view the illegal immigrant problem as an opportunity to shape the destiny of US society in a positive way by choosing the path of inner strength rather than outer conquest.

Fighting Terrorism

A terrorist is one who advocates, creates, or practices the use of terror as a means of coercion. The meaning of the word terrorist will differ from person to person because the characteristics and traits of each terrorist may differ. Terrorism is a political act, the goal of which is to make an impact on society and create change. In most cases, the terrorist motivation is neither personal desire nor ambition. Because military power cannot stop terrorism, there is no winning the War on Terrorism.

The intent of terrorist attacks fit into three categories: 1) attacks that cause mass casualties, 2) attacks that involve weapons of mass destruction, and 3) attacks that cause mass disruption. The use of biological and chemical weapons of mass casualty cause enormous levels of sickness and death. Weapons of mass destruction are weapons that cause damage to buildings, dams, bridges, computer systems and other structures of society. Mass disruption weapons cause social, political, and economic danger to society. These disruption weapons may be of the agro type aimed at disrupting the food supply or manufacturing, or the cyber type aimed at hacking into bank and government records, or the eco type such as arson and perhaps oil spills aimed at destroying the environment.

While terrorism is goal centered in creating fear in a society to achieve political goals, terrorist acts create terror to achieve certain objectives. Terrorism aimed at causing fear in society is indiscriminate in that it does not specifically target the people it kills and wounds. The nature of modern terrorism is that anyone can be a victim, but terrorism is not random. Examples of objective driven terrorist acts include hostage-taking, acts committed as retaliation for perceived injustice and as warnings of future acts of terror if the government does not change its policies.

In most cases, terrorism is a political act to achieve a desired goal through violence. It is not an act committed by the irrational and insane. The terrorist is not a criminal in the traditional sense because he or she does not act for personal gain or gratification. In some cases, the terrorist believes the objective is worth the life of the terrorist and the lives of the people taken. Even though death is often the result, the intent is not to kill those who die in the attack, but to affect the larger society as a whole.

Until the fighting and terror attacks stop, it is difficult to shift the fight against terrorism back to law, diplomacy and the justice system. According to experts only when the fighting stops can society focus on solving the problems of neglect, human rights abuses, and dedicating more aid resources.

Divine Perspectives

The Problem—From the Divine viewpoint, representative visions and Change hexagrams on the terrorism problem showed up as given here.

> *-Protesters locked out of a meeting of officials*
> *-Rats in the basement of a house*
> *-Contemplation (20) moving to Return of the Light (24)*

As a symbol, the first mental picture hints that there are no lines of communication between the society represented by the officials and the terrorists represented by the protesters. When the lines of communication are down the feelings of alienation grow stronger and in addition, neither side sees, hears, or understands the other. As long the wall stands, people cannot meet face-to-face. The meaning of the second vision showing two invisible people unable to converse or see one another is a variation of the first vision. It points to being misunderstood and the frustration of not getting recognition from the other. It's as if the terrorist and society count for nothing in the others eyes.

To be invisible to another means being overlooked, unacknowledged and unappreciated.

The second mental picture of rats in the basement conveys the degrading message that US society as a whole views terrorists as filth and associates them with poverty. The presence of rats in the foundation further suggests that terrorists are unwanted irritants and annoying people that eat away at society. Because rats are also symbolic of bad habits, they also represent inner traits to be acknowledged and eliminated. On a deeper level, they are messengers here to tell us that the whole of society is broken and needs healing.

The first hexagram *Contemplation (20)* tells us that the dilemma of terrorism is one of not having enough understanding of the terrorist and terrorism. This lack of understanding is a message to investigate the differences that separate the terrorist from society that they seek to terrorize, and to withhold taking corrective action until the facts are at hand. The change from the first hexagram to the second titled *Return of the Light (24)* announces that the problem of terrorism is a natural occurrence within the larger cycle of life. It suggests that violence marks the beginning of an awakening whose ultimate goal is both a return to the inner light of wholeness and the beginning of a new cycle of growth. The 24th hexagram also reminds us that the seeds of unwanted behaviors always find a place to grow and that we are obliged to cooperate with them.

Releasing—Through visioning and Change hexagrams the Divine tells us that society can release its old ways in order to heal terrorism as shown here.

-People encircle a lake by holding hands around it
-Several people cooperate in painting a mural
-A hillside gathering of people
-Biting Through (21)

The first vision of people holding hands around the lake represents the giving and receiving of loving energy. Like all bodies of water, the lake can symbolize reflection that leads to awareness. The people who make the circle represent a society seeking inner growth and changes to move toward wholeness.

The scene of people painting a mural suggests co-creativity and teamwork. Figuratively speaking, a community mural is symbolic of new creative ways of expressing unconscious potentials and attitudes about who we are. It stands for the beginning of a changing mindset, perspective and potential solution toward terrorism.

The third vision of a hillside gathering represents people coming together to unite for a higher purpose and shared vision. The mountain assembly is a symbol of society's aspiration to communicate and work together.

The hexagram *Biting Through (21)* is about conflict resolution. It tells us that society can support the Universe and the problem of terrorism by taking action to learn about and correct injustice. It serves as a reminder that if we deal with problems when they are little, we will not have to deal with big problems. When we learn to deal with problematic situations early on, we won't continue to meet them in a new guise at every turn.

Solution—In the language of visions and the Change, God ideas about the solution to the dilemma of terrorism appears are shown here.

-Meals served to passengers on a train
-A motorcyclist riding across the countryside
-People working together to build a house
Progress (35) moving to Shocking (51)

The vision of meals served to passengers on a train gives a glimpse of the Divine idea about solving the problem of terrorism. We can understand the passengers pulled along on the ride as people representing the terrorists and US society. The vision also tells us that many people need to be on board and nurtured for progress to take place. Serving meals refers to the need to care for the mental, emotional, physical and spiritual needs of both groups who agree to learn new ways of being. In addition, the meals served symbolize providing 'food for thought' and assistance to terrorists in the development of their potential.

Unlike the train that offers little flexibility of direction, the motorcycle in the second vision gives us a different perspective. The image of the cross-country motorcyclist is symbolic of freedom and independence in one's chosen direction or course in life. This scene suggests that in addition to efforts to move forward, the solution to the problem must also include ways to honor the need for autonomy. While the train implies power and focus in one direction, the motorcycle suggests that we embark on an open-ended journey.

The third image of people working to build a house is emblematic of the teamwork required to create something new. It represents an opportunity to expand our awareness in a way that helps terrorists to build a foundation and structure to support their needs, and helps society to create an appreciation of what the terrorists have to offer life. When viewed as a home the house represents the values, feeling and heart of the people who live in it.

From the hexagram *Progress (35),* we can understand that the solution to terrorism needs to include a clear vision of growth and expansion. It requires steady development and hints that success will depend upon people willing to work toward the same goals. The movement of the first hexagram into *Shocking (51)* implies that the way out of terrorism will have much to do with friendly yet unanticipated circumstances that act to shape what takes place. It also tells us that neither society nor the terrorists are in control of the forces working through them to create the ultimate solution. This hexagram points to the force of the universe itself, and suggests that the solution demands seeing ourselves as both one with and part of the world rather than separate from it.

10

Consulting the Change

The method of the I Ching does indeed take
into account the hidden individual quality
in things and people, and in one's own
unconscious self as well.
C.G. Jung

Consulting the Change is like visioning in that it's an intuitive attempt to catch and understand God's thinking for the questions you ask. The process begins with the knowledge that you can contemplate the divine to gain insights into the questions you want the Divine to answer. The Change starts from the premise that the Universe always knows more than you know and has better ideas than you do. When you approach the Change believing or knowing that you are one with the Divine, and have access to its wisdom and blessings, you transcend your ego and gain direct access to God's thoughts. If, on the other hand, you believe you are separate from the Divine, the insights you get will be ego-based and reflect ego-beliefs.

As in visioning, the first step in a successful consultation calls for being centered. Centering calls for taking a few moments to relax, quiet your mind, and contemplate your oneness with the Divine. There is no need to make anything happen as you are simply recognizing that the answer you seek is already in the mind of God. Your job is to let go of any expectations, hopes or fears and open to receive what the divine has to offer.

One and Two Hexagram Answers

There are three ways to create hexagram lines needed to answer your question. The methods you use will depend on the questions you ask and the amount of insight needed to answer your question. The first and easiest way makes use of one coin to create a single hexagram. The coin is tossed or flipped once for each of the six lines to create the hexagram. The second way makes use of three coins cupped in your hands, shaken and then dropped to create each of the six lines of the hexagram. This method creates the possibility to two hexagrams. Here, the first hexagram created may contain moving or changing lines so that the first hexagram represents the present and the second hexagram the future. The third way is a shorthand version of the traditional yarrow-stalk method and which makes use of sixteen colored marbles or beads of equal size to produce a present and potentially future hexagram.

When the insight from a single hexagram will provide enough guidance there is no need for visioning or a second hexagram. This method is simple because it only requires a single coin to create one hexagram. You will probably use it a great deal because most of the time you won't have very important questions and don't need in-depth insights. The likelihood of receiving any particular hexagram is one out of sixty-four. Although you may have no plans for more insight with this method, you can add visioning to expand upon the insight given by the lone hexagram. If you are like me, you will use the single hexagram method much more than the two hexagram methods.

The first or single coin method for producing hexagrams calls for flipping one coin and recording the landing pattern of the six Heads or Tails to build the six lines of the hexagram starting with line one on the bottom and moving upward line by line to line six. You begin by letting the head side of the coin represent a yang line and a tail side a yin line. This is the most elementary and direct way of creating Change hexagrams. Since you are not in control, the Universe will determine whether the coin lands head side up or tail side up as shown below. If for some reason, you think you can predict in advance whether the coin will land head or tails, choose another method to ensure that you're not in control.

Coin face		**Type of line**	**Probability**
Head	=	——— Yang	½
Tail	=	— — Yin	½

The bottom, second and third lines make up the lower trigram; the fourth, fifth and sixth lines make up the upper trigram; and the six lines together represent the complete hexagram in the following example (Hexagram 27 titled *Nourishment).*

Line	**One Coin Toss**	**Draw This**
		Nourishment (Title)
6	Head	———
5	Tail	— —
4	Tail	— —
3	Tail	— —
2	Tail	— —
1	Head	———
		27 (Number)

Two hexagrams are appropriate when you ask big questions and need greater depth. You can create two hexagrams at the same time by using three coins. When you do this the first hexagram is for the present and the potential second hexagram represents the future. While the Chinese method in the Book of Changes creates the two hexagrams in one step by using three coins or yarrow-stalks (also the equivalent of sixteen marbles), and place the final emphasis of interpretation on moving lines, moving lines are not used in this book. Here as in the traditional Book of Changes, there are 4,096 (64x64) combined hexagram outcomes (1/64th for the first or present hexagram times 1/64th for the future or second hexagram). The likelihood of receiving any particular hexagram combination is 1/4,096. With no moving lines, interpretation is simplified, and there is no need to study the meaning of up to six moving lines. As in the single coin method, you can add visioning, if needed, to expand upon the insight given by the hexagrams.

Any three coins of the same size can be used to create the possibility of two hexagrams at the same time. Cup the three coins in both hands, shake them, and let them drop on a flat surface in a random fashion. The first drop of the coins represents the bottom line of the hexagram, the second drop represents the second line, and so forth as follows:

3-Coins			**Line Type & Symbol**		**Probability**
Head	Head	Head	Changing Yang	———————— –	3/8ths
Head	Head	Tail	Yang	————————	1/8th
Head	Tail	Tail	Yin	——— ———	3/8ths
Tail	Tail	Tail	Changing Yin	——— ——— –	1/8th

After you drop the coins and record the line type or symbol, you need to repeat the process five more times. The sequence or pattern of the six lines (one, two, three, four, five, and six) gives your hexagram. The bottom three lines make up the lower trigram; the top three lines make up the upper trigram; and the six lines together represent the complete hexagram. The following example will illustrate how this works:

Line	Coin Toss Result			Draw This	Then This
6	Head	Tail	Tail	___ ___	___ ___
5	Head	Head	Head	_______ _	___ ___
4	Head	Head	Tail	_______	_______
3	Head	Head	Head	_______ _	___ ___
2	Head	Tail	Tail	___ ___	___ ___
1	Head	Head	Tail	_______	_______

Lines 3 and 5 are changing yang lines and become yin lines in the second hexagram. When the first hexagram contains a changing yin line it becomes a yang line in the second hexagram. The non-changing lines in the first hexagram remain the same in the second hexagram. In the example above the non-changing lines are one, two, four, and six.

A New Approach to Ancient Divination

As mentioned above the use of three-coins to produce hexagrams reflects the probabilities of one-fourth for changing yin, one-fourth for changing yang, three-eights for yang and three-eights for yin lines. The probabilities for lines in the marble and yarrow-stalk methods is one-sixteenth for changing yin, three-sixteenths for changing yang, five-sixteenths for yang, and seven-sixteenths for yin lines. In the method based on marbles, yang lines are three times as likely to change as yin lines. There is little difference in the frequency or pattern of hexagrams created by the three coin or sixteen marble method of creating hexagrams in the short-run, but the use of sixteen marbles is more consistent with how the Universe works and should be the method of choice over the long run.

Creating hexagrams with marbles is a shorthand version of the ancient yarrow-stalk way of creating hexagrams in that the probabilities are identical. To use this method you need sixteen colored marbles, beads, or equal-size objects in four different hues, reflecting the ratios just mentioned. These objects are selected at random from a container such as a pouch, bag, or purse. After you select and record the line represented by the first marble you place it back in the pouch with the other marbles. This process if repeated five more times until you build a complete hexagram bottom to top. The marble group sizes and meanings follow.

Marble Group	Line Type & Symbol		Probability
Group 1 (5 marbles)	Changing Yang	__________ _	5/16ths
Group 2 (3 marbles)	Yang	__________	3/16th
Group 3 (7 marbles)	Yin	____ ____	7/16ths
Group 4 (1 marble)	Changing Yin	____ ____ _	1/16th

You can use any four hues for the marbles or other objects. The colors I use are black (one), white (three), dark blue (seven) and yellow (five). As already mentioned the marbles or other objects must be the same size so your finger can't tell the difference. If you use small objects, you may want to try thirty-two, which means doubling the probability ratios given above.

By looking up the upper and low trigram patterns in the table following this section titled "Matrix of Trigrams and Hexagram Numbers" you can determine the sixty-four hexagram numbers and names, and then begin to discern their meaning to you. To find the hexagram number you created, find the lower trigram pattern of your hexagram (the first three hexagram lines) along the left hand side of the table and the upper trigram patterns of your hexagram (the top three hexagram lines) along the top of the table. Now take note of the number where the two meet in the central part of the table and write it below your hexagram. If, for example, the lower trigram is Thunder and the upper trigram is Mountain the intersection of the two trigrams is number 27 and the name is *Nourishment.*

Finding Your Hexagram Number

You can find all 64 hexagrams in the table titled "Matrix of Trigrams and Hexagram Numbers." To do so you'll need to find the lower and upper trigram patterns on the left hand side and top side of the table, and then fin the number at the place where the two intersect. For example, if the lower trigram is Fire and the upper trigram is Wind the intersection gives Hexagram 37. You can find all of the hexagram names and meanings in the pages that follow.

The moving or changing lines may produce two hexagrams as seen in the example 3-Coin Method. The process of finding the hexagram numbers when moving lines are involved is the same for hexagrams when there are no moving lines but for these trigrams ignore the small mark next to the changing line. The mark is only there to indicate that the line is a changing line. After you select and record each of the six lines, you have created your hexagram. Check out the following example of the using the sixteen marbles.

Line	**Marble**	**Draw This**	**Then This**
		Gathering Together	Deliverance
6	Yin	___ ___	___ ___
5	Changing Yang	_______ _	___ ___
4	Yang	_______	_______
3	Yin	___ ___	___ ___
2	Changing Yin	___ ___ _	_______
1	Yin	___ ___	___ ___
		45	40

In this example, the first hexagram number based on the intersection between Earth in the lower trigram and Lake in the upper trigram is 45 and represents *Gathering Together (45).* The second hexagram number comes from the intersection between the lower trigram Water and the upper trigram Thunder is 40 and represents *Deliverance (40).*

Matrix of Trigrams and Hexagram Numbers

UPPER TRIGRAM ▷ / LOWER TRIGRAM ▽	Heaven ☰	Thunder ☳	Water ☵	Mountain ☶	Earth ☷	Wind ☴	Fire ☲	Lake ☱
Heaven ☰	1	34	5	26	11	9	14	43
Thunder ☳	25	51	3	27	24	42	21	17
Water ☵	6	40	29	4	7	59	64	47
Mountain ☶	33	62	39	52	15	53	56	31
Earth ☷	12	16	8	23	2	20	35	45
Wind ☴	44	32	48	18	46	57	50	28
Fire ☲	13	55	63	22	36	37	30	49
Lake ☱	10	54	60	41	19	61	38	58

Table of Hexagram Numbers, Titles and Grades

	Hexagram Titles	***Judgments Grades***
1,	The Creative	A *excellent*
2,	The Receptive	A *excellent*
3,	Beginning in Difficulty	C- *average*
4,	Youthful Folly	C- average
5,	Waiting	C- *average*
6,	Conflict	F *failure*
7,	Teamwork	D below average
8,	Holding Together	B *above average*
9,	Minor Restraints	C+ *average*
10,	Conduct	C *average*
11,	Prospering	A excellent
12,	Standstill	C- *average*
13,	Fellowship	B above average
14,	Great Possession	A excellent
15,	Modesty	A *excellent*
16,	Enthusiasm	A *excellent*
17,	Following	C- *average*
18,	Repair	C+ *average*
19,	Approach	A *excellent*
20,	Contemplation	C+ *average*
21,	Biting Through	D below *average*
22,	Grace	C+ *average*
23,	Splitting Apart	D below *average*
24,	Return of the Light	B above *average*
25,	Innocence	C+ *average*
26,	Accumulating Wisdom	C- *average*
27,	Seeking Nourishment	A- *excellent*
28,	Yang in Excess	D *average*
29,	The Abyss	D *below average*
30,	Attachments	C+ *average*
31,	Influence	C- *average*
32,	Duration	B *above average*

Table of Hexagram Numbers, Titles and Grades (Continued)

	Hexagram Title	***Judgments Grades***
33,	Retreat	D below *average*
34,	Great Power	A *excellent*
35,	Progress	B above *average*
36,	Darkening of the Light	C+ *average*
37,	The Family	B above *average*
38,	Opposition	C- *average*
39,	Obstacles	F *failure*
40,	Deliverance	B above *average*
41,	Decrease	D below *average*
42,	Increase	A *excellent*
43,	Breakthrough	C+ *average*
44,	Coming to Meet	D below *average*
45,	Gathering Together	A *excellent*
46,	Ascending	A *excellent*
47,	Adversity	F *failure*
48,	The Well	A- *excellent*
49,	Destroying the Old	B above *average*
50,	Building the New	B above *average*
51,	Shocking	C+ *average*
52,	Keeping Still	C- *average*
53,	Development	B *above average*
54,	The Outside Partner	C- *average*
55,	Abundance	B *above average*
56,	The Wander	C- *average*
57,	The Gentle	C+ below *average*
58,	The Joyous	B above *average*
59,	Releasing	C- *average*
60,	Limitations	C- *average*
61,	Inner Truth	C+ *average*
62,	Small Changes	C+ *average*
63,	Partial Completion	C+ *average*
64,	Before Completion	C- *average*

The Sixty-Four Hexagrams

The Ancient Chinese Book of Change purports to teach a method for relating individual affairs to the stages and processes most closely affecting them, thus fashioning a key whereby future generations could unlock the secrets of the future and determine the surest way to live in harmony with the circumstances prevailing.

—John Blofeld

1
THE CREATIVE

Above: Heaven *(Jesus, Extroverted Intuition)*

Below: Heaven *(Jesus, Extroverted Intuition)*

Summary: Yang; Expansion; Promoting new ideas; Outer-directed creativity; Easy self-expression; Emerging potential; Conception; Inspiration, Imagination. A Grade

Of all 64 hexagrams, THE CREATIVE represents the greatest potential and personifies the preexistence and purpose of Jesus Christ. This story begins in the Gospel of John who writes, *"In the beginning was the Word, and the Word was with God, and the Word was God. He was in the beginning with God; and all things were made through Him, and without Him was not anything made that was made. In Him was life, and the life was the light of men. The light shines in the darkness, and the darkness cannot overcome it [1]."*

The biblical image of darkness suggests that all difficulties in life emerge when the lights go out, such as confused perceptions, impaired functioning, and danger. Many people struggle to find any meaning in life at all, and it's difficult living up to our potential when we aren't sure what our potential really is. It is not that we don't want to know rather the darkness makes it hard to find answers. Like the prophets of the ages who waited for the arrival of God's light and received the promise of spiritual solutions to every problem, the presence of this hexagram suggests that you are receiving Divine ideas and have an opportunity to manifest divinity. The circumstances symbolized by this hexagram give life and youth and have dominion over the powers of darkness. Your new ideas bring opportunities to release limitations, expand awareness, and move toward the manifestation of new forms.

THE CREATIVE represents the kind of strength that remains conscious and masters the obstacles present in working from above downward. It refers to ease in self-expression and practical, outer-directed approaches to using intuition. Seeking and receiving new ideas, insight, and intuitive understanding are at the heart of its meaning. Moving in the direction implied by this hexagram is life giving and youthful because it brings new thinking and amazing feelings. Your association with the events at hand is not born out of schooling or significant preparation or even karma, but of imagination and an act of grace. The situation at hand is an example of the inner world at work in bringing forth ideas that can benefit the lives of many people.

Getting THE CREATIVE is a sign that your desire to inspire others has come together with people interested in what you have to offer. It often points to inventors, promoters, artists, and those having no taste for life as it is. You can now share your innovative ideas with others who appreciate and understand them. The Heaven trigrams above and below, within and without suggests that even though you may be impatient with the demands of the physical world and find it difficult to see things through to completion your faith in intuitive insights will serve to inspire others. The events of this hexagram point you in the right direction, and give you the right opinions and ways to think about things.

2
THE RECEPTIVE

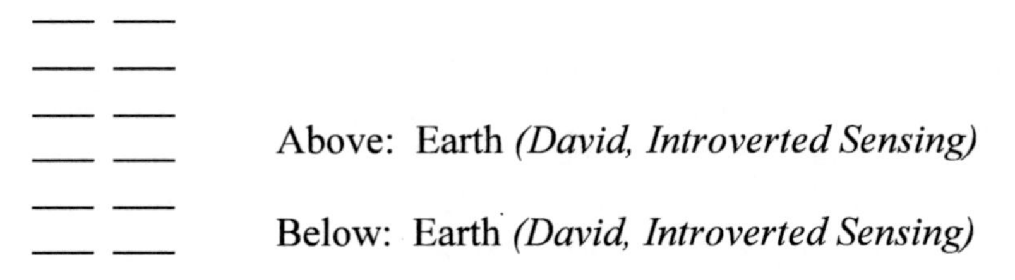

Summary: Yin; Ground; Devotion; Yielding; Fulfillment; Subjective view of physical reality; Accepting; Ego-centered impressions; Supporting what is; Inner-directed approach to world; Service. A Grade

Of all 64 hexagrams, THE RECEPTIVE stands as a symbol of the greatest devotion. It represents simplicity and an awareness of the obstacles involved in upward manifestation that works from Earth toward Heaven. The life story of King David, the last Old Testament patriarch, personifies this hexagram. He was the second king of the United Kingdom of Israel (1007BC – 970BC) and successor to King Saul. God selected David to be king because of his modesty, childlike obedience and simplicity [2]. God favored David because David placed a higher value on religious devotion than on attachments to the physical world. In his famous battle with the irreverent Goliath, a symbol of brute human force, he refuses the physical protection of the king's armor and instead uses prayer to call upon Divine intervention to help him defeat the giant. Although he had his faults, he is depicted as the most honorable of all the ancient kings of Israel, as well as an acclaimed warrior, founder of Jerusalem, great singer and poet credited with the authorship of nearly half of the one-hundred and fifty Psalms. Like the psalms or

"Book of Praises," this hexagram serves as a message to have confidence in God's presence, guidance and provisions in the situation at hand. As biblical history records, God was so pleased with David that He promised him that his descendants would endure forever. Like Abraham and Moses, David reinforces God's ongoing preference for the unseen over the seen, the lesser over the greater and inner faith over external matters. He represents the heart, desires and love as the ruling intelligence, or king through which Spirit rules on earth. At the highest level, your role in the current situation bears some resemblance to that of God's humble servant David.

THE RECEPTIVE represents conditions where conscious devotion brings mastery over obstructions inherent in working from below upward. It refers to helping others and working with the established order rather than taking the lead. It calls for going behind others, or following their course rather than taking the lead. While the first hexagram implies acts in the world of the invisible with spirit, here the focus is upon matter and bringing material things to completion. When following others you can see where things are going and decide whether its beneficial to continue, however this is not as easy when you the lead. Here, success comes from seeking the tried and true and accepting the known and established.

THE RECEPTIVE serves as a sign of both success and recognition as you work to serve the established group or community. You can attain your goals when you follow and support others. While the first Hexagram 1 represents possibilities, Hexagram 2 represents actualities. By working as the "servant" to your community, you can attain personal success. The existence of the Earth below and above suggests that your effort to serve others is modest and uncomplicated, and aims to bring fulfillment to the established order. This paring of trigrams is associated with helping the people around you to understand that they are part of a larger whole whose outcome depends upon your support.

3
BEGINNING IN DIFFICULTY

Above: Water *(Joseph, Introverted Feeling)*

Below: Thunder *(Isaac, Extroverted Feeling)*

Summary: Sprouting; Starting as an underdog; Going against the grain; Fresh growth and development surrounded by obstacles; Great effort needed for advancement. C- Grade

An illustration of BEGINNING IN DIFFICULTY can be seen in Jesus' warning against fear and hypocrisy being revealed when he says, *"for there is nothing covered, that shall not be revealed; and hid that shall not be known. What I tell you in the dark, utter in the light; and what you hear whispered, proclaim upon the housetops [3]."*

Here Jesus tells us that God always knows what is going on and that nothing escapes notice. This implies that hypocrisy and incongruity between what we are on the inside and how we behave on the outside will be fully exposed and judged. The existence of shadow like elements implied by the lower trigram tells us that our brightest light can only shine when we accept our deepest darkness. We are generally unaware that the beauty of our inner darkness is far more attractive and will make us attractive long after our physical attractiveness has worn away. The soul's inner beauty grows deeper and stronger with spiritual awareness so that the more aware you become, the more beauty you manifest. The words, "Proclaim upon the housetops" mean that Jesus' message is available to all. At the highest level, your position resembles the role of Jesus and his disciples attempting to introduce spiritual knowledge to an audience with little openness to what you have to say. Since efforts to move at a rapid pace are beyond your control it is best to adapt to surrounding circumstances and proceed with caution. Although the task ahead is not impossible, it will require skill, perseverance and patience to advance. Do you have the patience? Are you willing to express your true nature instead of becoming a hypocrite in the face of outside pressures?

BEGINNING IN DIFFICULTY refers to the unexpected start of a new endeavor in the midst of limited opportunities for growth. The journey ahead resembles that of driving a car at night without headlights. The lighting is limited and the way is unclear, but progress is possible through small steps. Your position is like the new little tree attempting to grow under the shade of taller trees. The new tree that finds itself rooted beneath relatives that take up the direct sunlight must accept this reality as no one is a fault.

BEGINNING IN DIFFICULTY points to the emergence of new growth in the midst of inherited trouble and unfamiliar territory. The combination of Thunder under Water suggests that others may not accept your unexpected presence and chosen course. Your desire to accept the ideals, conventions, and customs of your environment (represented by extroverted feeling below) has come fact-to-face with circumstances that are subjective, cool, and misunderstood (represented by introverted feeling above). Even though your intention to expand into new territory is spontaneous, warm and accepting as suggested by Thunder below you can only make real progress by turning within to know the mysterious nature of things represented by Water above.

4
YOUTHFUL FOLLY

———
— —　Above: Mountain *(Moses, Extroverted Sensing)*
— —
———
— —　Below: Water *(Joseph, Introverted Feeling)*

Summary: Close-minded; Inexperience; Lacking in faith and consciousness; Ignorance; Uneducated; Mistrust; Stupidity; Overconfident; Resistant to new learning. C-Grade

An example of YOUTHFUL FOLLY can be seen in Jesus' teaching about Treasures in Heaven when he spoke to a large crowd saying, *"Do not store up for yourselves treasures on earth, where moth and dust destroy, and where thieves break in and steal. But store up for your selves treasures in heaven, where moth and rust do not destroy, and where thieves do not break in and steal. For where your treasure is, there your heart will be also [4]."*

In this teaching, Jesus tells us that deeply divided people attach themselves to earthly treasures. His message implies that decisions people make with their pocket book reveal the nature of the heart. He counsels against building up desires for treasures on earth. To store up treasures means to think highly of, and to believe that things, whatever they are, are crucial to your livelihood and happiness. While material treasures can be a good reason for happiness, the possession of spiritual treasures brings far greater happiness and sustains it at a permanent level. You can know what you treasure by writing down what you think about, hope for, dream of, and spend time working to own or keep. We treasure material wealth, power, physical beauty, etc. because we think it holds some key to what is deeper or will guarantee that we won't suffer or die. Of the many things you can treasure the most important is your connection with the Divine. At the highest, level Jesus' words are intended to remind you that your real source of security and fulfillment are inside, rather than in outer forms or activities.

Getting YOUTHFUL FOLLY serves as a message that you are attempting to pursue a goal based on material appearances, even though your preparation and knowledge on how to bring about your wishes is lacking. The situation here is like that of an individual trying to get out of the woods with no compass or roadmap. It is likely that you are making an effort toward material gain without understanding what is required or the consequences of failure. Although you have specialized knowledge in some area of your life getting this hexagram suggests that unless you find the right teacher your potential for success is limited.

YOUTHFUL FOLLY is a sign that you are in the dark about what is required. You are eager for success but don't have sufficient knowledge on how to achieve it. The combination of Water under Mountain suggests that even though you may understand the result based on your internal perspective, you are looking through rose-colored glasses when it comes to manifesting this result. This comes about because you lack the required knowledge and commitment to reach the goal you seek. It is also likely that you are not really open to learning what you need to know.

5
WAITING

___ ___
____
___ ___ Above: Water *(Joseph, Introverted Feeling)*
____
____
_______ Below: Heaven *(Jesus, Extroverted Intuition)*

Summary: Waiting for now; Anticipation while expecting a result; Waiting for nourishment; Circumstances that require faith and patience; Letting the dust settling; A conclusion in the making. C- Grade

An illustration of WAITING appears in the story of Thomas' unbelief. As the story goes, Thomas did not witness the resurrected Jesus and had his doubts. He would not believe what the other disciples said they saw unless he saw Jesus first hand and felt his wounds. After eight days Jesus appeared to the disciples, including Thomas. After Thomas feels Jesus wounds he becomes a true believer. Jesus then says, *"Because you have seen me you believe: Blessed are those who have not seen and yet believe [5]."*

Thomas wanted to believe but had his doubts. He is an example of people who will not be satisfied until they get the evidence or facts. Although he a pessimist, he is also honest and down to earth. Unlike the other disciples he was absent from the first sighting of the risen Jesus, and as a result his unknowing and grief were prolonged. This story serves as a reminder that your surroundings, like the surroundings faced by Thomas, includes unknowns beyond your control. Instead of growing impatient with Thomas, Jesus invites him to put his finger into his hands and side to give him the necessary evidence for his belief. At the highest level, your position resembles the role played by the disciples who saw the resurrected Jesus before Thomas. They were excited and convinced of Jesus new existence but could only wait for Thomas to gain the conscious acceptance and belief they already had.

WAITING refers to anticipating an outcome whose timing and form is out of your control. It points to situations where people are excited and moved by new potential, but those they want to influence don't yet share their enthusiasm. Getting this hexagram calls for tolerance and faith that things will unfold. Since the desired effect will make itself known in its own time it is better to pause and accept the current mystery than push forward into the unknown.

As seen in the lower trigram Heaven, WAITING is a sign of hope and inner certainty about a new beginning in the midst of unknown characteristics represented by Water in the upper trigram. Your situation is like that of the inspired mountain climber facing bad weather; he sees the goal but can't continue until the storm passes. You are standing by for an opening to advance your position, yet held up due to mysterious and natural circumstances. The presence of extroverted intuition below suggests that in spite of your excitement you feel imprisoned by the uncertainties presented by introverted feeling above. Even though you are ready to advance, significant unknowns are ahead.

6
CONFLICT

———
———
——— Above: Heaven *(Jesus, Extroverted Intuition)*
— —
———
— — Below: Water *(Joseph Introverted Feeling)*

Summary: Irreconcilable differences; Arguing; Unresolved; Litigation; No-win situations; Outright opposition; Major disagreement; Obstruction despite sincerity. F Grade

The first verse in Jesus' teaching to put God's Kingdom first serves as an example of CONFLICT. In this verse from the Sermon on the Mount he says, *"No one can serve two masters; for either he will hate the one and love the other, or he will be devoted to the one and despise the other. You cannot serve God and mammon [6]."*

The difference between serving material wealth and serving God is found in contentment. The benefit of lasting inner contentment comes only to those who serve God. Getting blessing from the craving for material possessions is always uncertain and never brings a sustaining contentment with what we have. In the situation represented by this hexagram, people defend their positions with limited knowledge, complete confidence, and little regard for the prospect of peace. From experience we know that we can entrust ourselves to only one expert source at a time, who has skill in meeting one set of our needs such as a doctor for health problems or one lawyer for legal counsel. As patients, we serve doctors by following their prescribed health regiments because good health is so desirable, yet patients employ doctors to provide needed health services. This situation may present an unresolved conflict. Like a doctor or lawyer, God loves by serving scores of believers, hating none and seeking the welfare of all, yet God's love is unconditional. In relation to this parable, your position resembles the person who serves but desires something tangible in return. You are in CONFLICT with the upper trigram, a symbol of conscious alignment with the Divine. The spiritual solution to this problem is not easy as it calls for both catching God's ideas and releasing your ideas.

CONFLICT refers to a state of affairs in which you feel that your position is right while at the same time others have an opposing stance of equal force. It represents a clash between perspectives or egos that has come about because of an over-emphasis on external factors or appearances that are in fact a small part of the whole. In most cases, both sides in the clash automatically see the other party as wrong and justify themselves. When this hexagram comes up agreement is impossible; things are settled only when both parties can look beyond their differences to areas of agreement.

The presence of CONFLICT suggests that you feel limited by new developments that are completely unfamiliar to you and not under your control. Even though you have a great deal of knowledge about your position, you have nothing in common with the ideas opposing it. This is a classic struggle between your identity, and a stance contrary to your way of thinking. The situation represented by this pair of trigrams is the polar opposite of the one described by Hexagram 5. Here your misunderstood inner nature, represented by introverted feeling, must operate in an environment that demands confidence and creative action—namely defined by extroverted intuition. This combination of Water below Heaven suggests that you are not ready to suspend what you know, turn within, and embrace what the Divine wants to reveal. Although it is not apparent in the midst of the battle, the presence of hostility is an opportunity for growth. A resolution is possible for all parties only when the differences are dissolved into unity.

7
TEAMWORK

Above: Earth *(David, Introverted Sensing)*

Below: Water *(Joseph, Introverted Feeling)*

Summary: A Team; The Army; Parts working together as a whole; Collective force; Bringing together; Group goals trump Self-expression; Discipline and cooperation. D Grade

At the highest level, an example of TEAMWORK comes to mind in the second of two parables (more like analogies), where Jesus talks about the Conditions of Discipleship. In explaining that those who follow him to need to love him more than themselves he says, *"What king, going out to encounter another king in war, will not sit down first and deliberate whether he is able with ten thousand to meet him who comes against him with twenty thousand? And if not, while the other is yet a great way off, he sends a delegation and asks for terms of peace. So therefore, anyone of you who does not renounce all that he has cannot be my disciple [7]."*

Here Jesus is chiding the many people who were following him for not having a clue as to what they were getting in to with such behavior. They were like people going to war against a superior opponent without doing advance work as to the strength of the enemy. He is telling us that being committed to the Divine is a major endeavor and one needs to be prepared to see it through to the finish. When Jesus says we cannot be his disciples unless we give up our possessions, he means we must be willing to release our attachments and ideas if need be. If it comes down to a choice between being faithful to the Inner Light, on the one hand and keeping our possession on the other, followers must be willing to give up their possessions. The parable suggests that believers or team players must be ready to release what they have to in order to support the Divine team and its mission to serve humanity.

TEAMWORK refers to members in established groups, communities or collectives activity such as an army, well-defined organization, sports teams, etc. In addition to putting the group first, success depends upon every member's role and participation. In general, the team rises or falls with its members. If any member fails to do his or her part all fail, and if anyone is injured or removed the whole squad is weakened. If on the other hand any team member does well the entire team benefits. Unless all drivers, for instance, support the rules of the road breakdowns, congestion and accidents show up. At the collective level, the need for cooperation between individuals is necessary.

The presence of introverted feeling in the lower position and introverted sensation above implies that your misunderstood ideas have come face-to-face with an outer environment that calls upon you to support its established order. Getting TEAMWORK is a sign that group objectives should have a higher priority than individual goals. Your position is like a team member who works with and serves an organized body or collective linked by inherited circumstances or choice. The combination of Water below Earth suggests that the group cannot achieve its mission without your contribution. The situation here also resembles what we see in many species such as among a colony of ants or bees held together by shared missions. While you have limited opportunity for self-expression without the team, you will share in its success if the team is successful.

8
HOLDING TOGETHER

___ ___
____
___ ___ Above: Water *(Joseph, Introverted Feeling)*
___ ___
___ ___
___ ___ Below: Earth *(David, Introverted Sensing)*

Summary: An educational group; Sticking together; Union; Grouping; Close associations; Students learning from teacher(s); Individuals following a tour guide or mentor; Coming together; Cooperation and coordination. B Grade

An example of HOLDING TOGETHER appears in Jesus parable of The Watchful Servant when he says, *"Be dressed ready for service and keep your lamps burning, like men waiting for their master to return... [8]"*

This parable deals with the Second Coming or judgment after ego or bodily death. It compares laziness and self-indulgency to diligence and focus on the kingdom. Believers should be ready for judgment at all times as their encounter with the Divine can happen without notice and suddenly. Being dressed and ready means getting regular help such as daily prayer, meditation, study, and fellowship with others to maintain our spiritual health. When we neglect spiritual practices, the problem of not being ready grows larger. While the words "keep your lamp burning" is wasteful in the material world, it means being awake and alert in the world of spirit. The more you focus on spiritual matters the more conscious you become about such matters. While staying awake takes effort, nothing is more fulfilling and joy producing than serving the Divine. When you wonder whether you have the time, energy, and ability to serve the Divine should know that its strength and wisdom is available to support you at all times. At the highest level, your role in the parable is like the watchful servant or individual committed to their spiritual practice. The message of this teaching and the hexagram tells listeners to keep their spiritual practice alive and ask for help on a regular basis.

HOLDING TOGETHER refers to situations where people are aligning themselves with a group or practice in which they have an interest. While it represents leadership based on having specialized knowledge, this role depends upon the willingness of followers who desire this knowledge. It is like GATHERING TOGETHER (45) but differs in that this hexagram refers to learning within secular organizations where as Hexagram 45 deals with learning inside spiritual organizations. Your success in the circumstance at hand will come about through supporting those in possession of the information you seek. Your role is analogous to being one of several individuals following the beat of a single drummer. You are in an excellent position to support and learn from those with specialized training, and may want to share your good fortune with others.

HOLDING TOGETHER suggests that your public role is like the central character of an organized body or philosophy. If for example you are a licensed medical doctor, attorney, or member of the clergy, you may choose to play a leading role to advance the mission of your profession or work as the center of your small group. While it is unlikely that you will seek to lead others and you are not obligated to play a management role in your profession, from time to time you may do so. The combination of Earth under Water points to cooperating with others and serving the established community so that everyone moves in the same direction. You may become a center of influence by simply supporting the center or take it upon your self to see to it that every member finds a way to get his or her interests served.

9
MINOR RESTRAINTS

____
____
___ ___ Above: Wind *(Aaron, Introverted Thinking)*
____
____
________ Below: Heaven *(Jesus, Extroverted Intuition)*

Summary: Accumulating Resources; A minor education; A small collection of energy; Improving; Small refinements; Adaptability; Cultivating knowledge. C+ Grade

At the highest level, an example of MINOR RESTRAINTS appears in Jesus' Parable of The Unrighteous Steward where he says, *"He that is faithful in that which is least is faithful also in much: and he that is unjust in the least is unjust also in much [9]."*

In addition to being a believer, to be faithful is to·be trustworthy, just, observant of and steadfast to one's word or promises. The unjust are the opposite of the faithful and dependable. They are people who disappoint our expectations, neglect to keep their word and fall short of the mark required by divine laws. The millions of little decisions you make day to day determine the kind of person you are. This includes, for instance, those little thoughts you choose not to dwell on or simply knowing that you cannot forge character in an overnight foundry. For instance, no one got fat over one hamburger. It takes hundreds of meals made up of thousands of little bites to eat too much of the wrong food. When an artist paints a masterpiece, the finished work did not come about over night. It took several little thoughts, decision, and brush strokes. In this parable, your position resembles that of the faithful or just person addressed by Jesus. The message is one of simple spiritual law: what ever you do with small amounts and responsibilities accumulates, gets refined, and shows what you will do with large amounts and greater responsibilities.

Getting MINOR RESTRAINTS serves as a reminder and question about the impact of your decisions on the future. It serves as a message to examine your thoughts and make adjustments as needed. An example of this hexagram appears in the case of an author overly anxious for his or her book to be bought by potential readers. Since those who buy the book will do so when they are ready, there is no need for the high anxiety. If you are willing to hold back and proceed with care, you can avoid difficulties, and in time make the connections you need to make. If you attempt to push new ideas too quickly or take others by surprise, there is little hope of success.

MINOR RESTRAINTS refers to situations where you are excited about introducing new ideas to people who generally agree with you. Even though your audience may be responsive and open to what you have to present, you should not expect the group to embrace wholly what you present. You would do well not to give more information than the mind of the recipient can hold. The combination of Heaven under Wind also represents an opportunity in which you are enthusiastic about sharing your original thoughts to a friendly and accepting assembly of people. However, because the assembly will probably not understand or be ready to act on what you have to say, your ultimate success will depend on being patient and adaptable.

10
CONDUCT

Above: Heaven *(Jesus, Extroverted Intuition)*

Below: Lake *(Abraham, Introverted Intuition)*

Summary: Knowing when to speak and when to keep silent; Manifesting God's ideas; Treading; Watchfulness; Following the Divine; Acting with vigilance and awareness; Making the correct appearance. C- Grade

An illustration of CONDUCT can be taken from Jesus' teaching about the responsibility of his followers to pay taxes when he is he cornered by religious leaders and tempted by a trap question. He says, *"Render to Caesar the things that are Caesar's, and to God the things that are God's [10]."*

When Jesus tells those who question him to pay the tax and honor God as well, his response is not expected. He breaks the either/or, yes/no pattern of the answer imposed by traditional religious leaders, by changing it to the "both/and" pattern. He explains that the government is entitled to collect the tax and the masses need to pay the tax. His simple wisdom is that if the law of the land requires that everyone must pay taxes, then that is what you must do. We may resist paying taxes, but the fact is that by our lifestyles we've run up a debt to the government who feels obligated to support the interests that support our lifestyles. The government wants to be paid back, and it's a little late to say you don't owe anything. As a part within the whole you must do your part to follow its rules. By not cooperating with the whole you may do harm to yourself and others. In this verse, Jesus says pay the tax, rather than be upset over having to give it up and covet the money, since doing so is an earthly distraction. Your position resembles the role played by those who want an either/or response from Jesus on the tax issue. His simple response implies that serving the state and honoring God are not in conflict. He settles the dilemma by allowing both positions and sees compliance to earthly responsibilities as a part of being submissive to the Divine.

CONDUCT refers to the challenge of expressing your faith and inspired awareness in the midst of others who have their own agenda. As seen in the teaching by Jesus, the difficulty is the result of real differences in beliefs, thinking, and goals between people who don't share the same understanding about what needs to happen. This hexagram calls to mind an identity crisis in which those in power question one's knowledge and trust in his or her spiritual insights. Here the person of faith sees those in control as having ideas contrary to their own. Since the difficulties here are the result of your faith in the unseen, which is not shared by others, it is best to express your position only when others are receptive to hearing what you have to offer.

CONDUCT suggests that you are about to act on your urge to present knowledge to others without regard to its appropriateness, e.g., presenting dream interpretation methods to an engineering audience or spiritual principles to a military unit. At the highest level, this hexagram suggests that your awareness and reliance upon the Divine may be the foundation of a new design or concept. In the situation at hand, your faith may allow you to co-create with others. The combination of Lake under Heaven represents your intention to project your vision and confidence into the minds of others. In general, you can influence the people you need to reach with your visions and intuition only when you embrace and demonstrate their meaning as your personal experience of the world.

11
PROSPERING

___ ___
___ ___
___ ___ Above: Earth *(David, Introverted Sensing)*
____
____
_______ Below: Heaven *(Jesus, Extroverted Intuition)*

Summary: A change for the better; Inner strength and outer acceptance; The right time to manifest an idea; Potential for great achievement; Ideal conditions for prosperity. A Grade

Jesus gives an example and way to understand his message about the subject of prosperity in his parable of The Sower. In it, he tells of a sower who went out to sow his seeds and illustrates the fate of the seed. Some seed fell by the way side; some on stony ground without much earth; some fell among thorns; and other seeds fell on good ground [11].

This parable tells us that knowledge of the Divine does not produce uniform results for all. The seeds that fall by the way side and upon stony ground represent those hearers who never really grasp the truth; others will get the truth but lose it to discouragement or neglect represented by seeds falling on stony ground or among thorns; but many will respond, bringing excellent results from the Sower when seeds fall on good ground. In today's terms, it sounds like a story about why you only get a few good responses to sending out a mass email. The parable starts with an outrageous beginning of indiscriminate sowing and ends with an outrageous ending where the harvest is great. Instead of the sower going bankrupt by investing many seeds where they are least likely to grow, he makes a fortune. While this sounds like something foolish, he advises believers to do the same thing. Long story short, this parable is an explanation of how God's life operates through us. At the highest level, your position is that of the Sower who sows Divine seeds to people of all levels of consciousness. The parable suggests that the present situation contains prosperity as the result of your inspired thinking (lower trigram) and the diverse receptive community (upper trigram) of receptive individuals before you.

PROSPERING refers to occasions where new ideas have an opportunity to prosper. It represents situations where your ideas come into view because they agree with the Inner Light. The environment, like the beginning of spring, signals new growth and conditions that will continue to expand and be of benefit. In the circumstances represented by this hexagram, the creative elements are in power and the devoted receptive elements respond to their influence and change for the better. Even though this hexagram points to abundance, it is often associated with insensitivity because many creative people are caught up in the excitement of the moment and neither reflective about themselves nor careful about who or what is shoved about in the demonstration process.

PROSPERING brings together the power of inspiration and people ready to support inspired ideas. It refers to environments where the potential for fulfillment in form is the natural outcome of divinely centered thoughts. In the situation at hand, you are excited about producing something new and your enthusiasm has the enough support and assistance from others to bring it to fruition. The existence of Heaven below Earth points to circumstances where the people you need to work with follow your lead and help to manifest your thoughts. Here we see that eggs begin to hatch, plants spring up from the earth, ideas take form, things happen and the world is different. It represents the universal creative process where new possibilities become visible.

12
STANDSTILL

———
———
——— Above: Heaven *(Jesus, Extroverted Intuition)*
— —
— —
— — Below: Earth *(David, Introverted Sensing)*

Summary: Stagnation; Obstruction; Misunderstandings; Not seen or heard as desired; Stuck, or blocked; Weakness in faith; Confusion, disharmony; Communication breakdowns; Unable to reach another. C- Grade

At the highest level, an illustration of STANDSTILL comes into view in Jesus' pronouncement that He is the True Light when he says, *"I am the light of the world: he that follows me shall not walk in darkness but shall have the light of life [12]."*

Jesus calls Himself the light of the world because he knows he manifests the brilliance of the being and nature of God. Catching God's ideas through our intuitive and spiritual nature also bestows the power to give life to the lightless and lifeless. While many have glimmerings of spiritual light and a few are bright with knowledge, most people are blind to the truth and ignorant of the Light Within. Light has the power to blind and cause resistance among people who prefer to live in ignorance. Thieves and lawbreakers, for instance, prefer the darkness and run from the light. If a police officer comes in the night and shines his or her spotlight as the thief is breaking into a house, the thief runs off, preferring the darkness. Those who follow the light without getting to know its true nature will end up in darkness as well. To walk in the fullness of the promised light you must believe in the light, follow the light, and trust that it will deliver you from darkness. In relation to the situation at hand, your place resembles the person who seeks to follow the true light represented by catching Divine ideas. Even though this hexagram suggests that you are not in the light, a sincere effort to follow the light will help you see the light.

Getting STANDSTILL suggests that the people you are trying to reach do not share your perspectives about the physical and social universe. This difference in viewpoints results in a misunderstanding between you and others. It's as if your position about the established order is opposed by ideas that challenge your sensibilities. The effect of this divide is a tug-of-war between your wish to follow conventional precedents on the one hand and the call to create something completely new on the other hand. Whether the conflict is within you or between you and another person, your tendency to focus on appearances and forms makes it difficult to seek or accept spiritual solutions to your problem.

The presence of STANDSTILL serves as a message that remaining open to what others have to say is necessary if you want new beginnings to have a chance to develop. By setting down-to-earth requirements aside for now you can gain access to your creative potential. The combination of Earth below Heaven implies that the more you open the door for new light and spiritual development the better you can serve the world around you. Until you first learn to accept your limitations with the material universe, you will find it difficult to experience the creative world. Even though the spiritual teachings that lie ahead may be beyond your current understanding, they will lead to inspiration and in time assist you in supporting your environment.

13
FELLOWSHIP

———————
———————
———————   Above: Heaven *(Jesus, Extroverted Intuition)*
———————
——— ———
———————   Below: Fire *(Jacob, Extroverted, Thinking)*

Summary: Community; Partnership; Pursuing common interests; Gathering of like-minded people; Relatives; A physical or spiritual family; Agreements; Friendships; Association. B Grade

An example of FELLOWSHIP emerges in the brief story about Jesus True Family where someone said to Jesus, *"Your mother and your brothers are standing outside. They want to see you." Jesus answered them "My mother and my brothers are those people that listen to God's teaching and obey it! [13]"*

Through this story, Jesus redefines family as a spiritual bond with those who share his desire to do the will of God. While physical family members may not have the same interest or accept the truth, the spiritual family binds its members together with the same purpose, goals and desires. When you acknowledge God as the source, God's family becomes your family, and your loyalty to God comes before all earthly commitments. Jesus stresses the priority of spiritual family here because he hopes to be able to count on his disciples. The character you reveal ultimately shows your acceptance into the Divine family. From the spiritual perspective, this story suggests that your position in the situation represented by this hexagram resembles the leader of a group or community of individuals seeking to know the Divine. As a spiritual family member, you are in a partnership with many others who share the same purpose, goals and desires.

FELLOWSHIP refers to associations based on creative ideas, where common interests rather than inherited or private goals define the connection between individuals. It represents gatherings between people on the same wave length where participants understand and support the learning of others in the group without losing sight of their learning. The situation at hand suggests feelings of warmth in connecting with others to build upon group goals. When this hexagram comes up you are in a position to direct activities and events that inspire others. Through relationships based on the exchange of creative and perhaps spiritual ideas, individuals get to know themselves better than at most times and find that they are able to make the compromises necessary to get along with others.

In FELLOWSHIP, the existence of Fire under Heaven favors inspiration and mental stimulation rather than dealing with responsibilities and practical details. It implies that your desire to lead comes into view by simply bringing people together to share their thoughts. This is an excellent combination for gaining clarity about existing ideas and getting fresh insights about new ideas, but it's not a good sign for getting things done. Your position is at both the center of influence and the person who learns about new ideas with others. In the situation at hand, you may take the lead to work with and learn from people who generally agree with you. You have an interest in leading the way to gathering with people who are enthusiastic about the same proposals. In general, this hexagram points to an opportunity to direct others to share their thoughts and inspired ideas with like minds.

14
GREAT POSSESSION

———
— —
———　　Above: Fire *(Jacob, Extroverted Thinking)*
———
———
———　　Below: Heaven *(Jesus, Extroverted Intuition)*

Summary: Heightened clarity and understanding; Great wisdom and discernment; Independence and freedom; High inner worth; Meeting the Divine; Large-scale spiritual insight. A Grade

A biblical illustration of GREAT POSSESSION appears in the account where Jesus appeared before his eleven disciples, after his resurrection, to give The Great Commission. Here he says, *"All authority in heaven and on earth has been given to me. Go therefore and makes disciples of all nations .... Teaching them to observe all that I have commanded you; and I am with you always even to the end of the world [14]."*

From this narrative, we can infer that Jesus' top priority for his disciples is making other disciples. For disciple making to be a first priority you need to look for opportunities in all areas of daily living and step into the life of absolute acceptance of spiritual authority in all things. Every thing we do in life, individually or organizationally, at all times has the potential for influencing others toward the Divine, in verbal and non-verbal communications. Jesus sees education as an important component of disciple making. There is potential teaching within the bounds of work, friendships, and in physical families. Those who commit to make disciples will receive help in the midst of their struggles and suffering. In the situation at hand, your position is like the spiritual teacher or disciple who has an audience with another's ego. As implied by the hexagram and Jesus' words, you now have an opportunity to learn, teach and influence others in spiritual matters.

GREAT POSSESSION suggests that people with novel ideas and inspired thoughts are in a position to attract the attention of those in power. The presence of this hexagram is an opening for gaining significant respect from others by sharing your original ideas with people in leadership positions. It also implies that your thoughts about the circumstances at hand are gaining recognition and clarity. This hexagram is the reverse of the preceding one. It is more favorable than Hexagram (13) because here one's inner worth and faith accords with those in control. In the preceding hexagram, the people in charge are uplifted by simply affiliating with other like-minded people.

GREAT POSSESSION refers to situations in which your inspired thoughts have an audience with the leaders of an organization or community. In general, you have a unique opportunity to bring something new and original to people in positions of influence and as a result, your creative thoughts may be recognized, understood and shared with many. Your position resembles that of the specialists presenting a new design, concept, or invention to central figures or other persons in charge. Heaven under Fire suggests that the people in charge are open to your ideas and see their potential, even if they offer a novel approach to their problems. As such, your personal life and thoughts may be on public display more than usual.

15
MODESTY

___ ___
___ ___
___ ___ Above: Earth *(David, Introverted Sensing)*
____
___ ___
___ ___ Below: Mountain *(Moses, Extroverted Sensing)*

Summary: Moderation despite merit; Humility and concern for others; Reticent and reserved in manner; A spirit of fairness leading to good fortune; Ego transcendence; Leading and serving an established community. A Grade

An illustration of MODESTY emerges in the Golden Rule endorsed by all world religions and is the most popular universal ethical principle in history. The golden rule says, *"Treat others only in ways that you're willing to be treated in the same exact situation [15]."*

In many ways, the concept of doing for others what we would want done for ourselves is a summary of Jesus' teaching about how to live for others. It also captures the spirit of the Old Testament Law and teaching of the prophets: living to bless others is God's will for us in all of our relationships. The Golden Rule appears in numerous cultures, religions, ethical systems, secular philosophies, indigenous (Native) traditions, and even in the mathematical sciences, e.g., the golden mean. It crosses many traditions and philosophies, and reveals a profound unity underlying the diversity of human experience. This rule is the principle practice of the family of God, and it means relating with other people through expressions of human kinship and as brother or sister. Your role in the situation at hand is that of a community leader charged with serving your community. You can apply the Golden Rule with consistency by taking the lead to put yourself in the place of those on the receiving end of your actions.

The situations represented by MODESTY offer an opportunity to shape your fate by choosing the path of inner strength rather than outer conquest. Under its influence, gains are not by a stroke of luck, but rather by established time-honored traditions and solid bit-by-bit progress. The path of events put forward by this hexagram is unassuming and seen as well defined and non-threatening. Like a slow train moving across the countryside, your leadership at this point is powerful, yet modest, controlled and conventional. Even though you are required to attend to practical details such as performing tasks and following established guidelines in order to serve group needs, this does not imply a lack of vision or forethought.

The presence of MODESTY implies that you are likely to succeed in influencing the individuals in your circle. In the circumstance at hand, your community will likely recognize and support your leadership. The combination of Mountain below Earth suggests that you are in a position to persuade and command the people around you to follow time-honored guidelines. Your influence resembles that of the humble, but strong Moses who gently led his people to a new way of life. The success of your guidance will depend on group members willing to both accept your controls and serve the demands of the established collective. Even though individuals may accept your authority, you will need patience to build a consensus for decisions that affect the entire group. While the initiative is yours, success depends on how you treat the people you lead and the extent of their support for your authority.

16
ENTHUSIASM

— —
— —
——— Above: Thunder *(Isaac, Extroverted Feeling)*
— —
— —
— — Below: Earth *(David, Introverted Sensing)*

Summary: Providing-For; Inducement, New stimulus; Passion; Recognition; Movement free of restraint; Encounter with the Divine; Feeling inspired and energized; Aliveness. A Grade

A biblical example of ENTHUSIASM is present in the story of Jesus Cleansing the Temple. After finding moneychangers seated at tables and the temple used for crass commercial reasons Jesus found it intolerable, overturned their tables, and drove them out of the temple with a whip chord as he said, *"Take these things out of here! Stop making my Father's home a marketplace [16]."*

Cleansing of the temple has to do with the replacement of the old way of worshiping God with a new ways that are open to all. There is no evidence that Jesus planned to take this surprising action. While no gospel writer actually says that Jesus was angry it is implied. This story is one of a handful that reveals the shadow or darkness in Jesus personality and shows his way of dealing with the shadow. Instead of repressing his upset so that it became part of his dark side, he was able to integrate his capacity to express it in his conscious personality. The story also illustrates that your own immoral shadow can let you in on how people act in corrupt ways toward one another. In this story your position resembles the people who accepted the Temple before Jesus arrived, but whose experience was transformed by his unanticipated cleansing. In this sense, the hexagram is a symbol of the liberation and recognition that comes through a sudden, yet natural shift in your recognition of an inspired new way.

ENTHUSIASM refers to correcting an unsettling situation that has manifested in the normal course of life. In spite of being out of the limelight and supporting others in the background, you are now taking over the direction of a task or project in which you may have considerable power and strength. This unexpected state of affairs takes its form and content from what you can and cannot do. You will need to get a realistic assessment of needed elements and responsibilities. The truth about startling new developments will eventually come out. Your efforts to help others adjust to new conditions will likely bear fruit because you are willing to assist a community that favors new growth.

ENTHUSIASM refers to individuals bound to earthly interests who are willing to support new conditions. When it comes up you have an opportunity to help shape unanticipated events in the physical and social realities before you. As Jungian types, introverted earth below suggests that your desire to serve an organized group or collective is taking place in the accepting environment represented by extroverted feeling. The combination of Earth under Thunder points to your interest in helping a community or group deal with far-reaching circumstances. Examples of this hexagram are present in events such as the coordinated cleanup or rebuilding effort required after a disaster, the sudden need to create new solutions or take immediate action to deal with a positive or negative development. In all cases, it represents broad changes in the physical or social universe and the need to serve new circumstances.

17
FOLLOWING

— —
———
——— Above: Lake *(Abraham, Introverted Intuition)*
— —
— —
——— Below: Thunder *(Isaac, Extroverted Feeling)*

Summary: Preparing for rest and recuperation; Flexibility; Adapting to winter-like conditions; Adjusting to another; Compliance; Overcoming resistance; Going after. C- Grade

An example of FOLLOWING can be understood in Jesus teaching about Father and Son when he answers his disciples by saying, *"Truly, truly, I say to you, the Son can do nothing of Himself, unless it is something He seen the Father doing; for whatever the Father does, these things the Son also does in like manner. For the Father loves the Son, and shows Him all things that He Himself is doing [17]."*

Being a son or daughter of the Divine involves identity with its will and co-creating with the Divine. The joys and appearances of the outer world have enabled many people to ignore the Divine. Most people make their decisions without seeking help from Spirit. Many people only turn to God when they have some particular need that they can't meet on their own. When you depend on Spirit to point the way, you are its subservient son or daughter. Those who maintain a spiritual practice such as meditation, sacred education, prayer or visioning, will always have a strong connection with the Divine. If you have not had a positive relationship with the Divine, you have a trust problem, lack faith in the Divine, and probably don't have a spiritual practice. When you are aware of your constant dependence upon Spirit, you will seek its guidance daily. As you release your opinions to catch God's ideas you will manifest the Divine and in the process find personal fulfillment. In relation to this teaching, your position resembles the Son who follows the uncertain and often troubling Christ path with faith.

FOLLOWING serves as a message to learn about the needs of your environment in order to deal with the sweeping changes in your personal life. Its presence is often associated with powerful yet unexpected events that rely on knowledge and trust in God. Even though this hexagram points to unexpected yet far-reaching shifts, great achievements are possible with faith and an open-minded attitude toward getting help from spiritual sources. In general, uninvited situations will not improve until you ask for spiritual help, and then let Spirit take the lead.

FOLLOWING serves as a message to rely upon your intuitive and spiritual nature to provide answers to the questions you ask. Its existence describes the presence of 'out of the blue' events that call for having faith in the unseen powers of the Universe. In the situation at hand, you are likely facing feared and unwanted shadow events that must become conscious and accepted. The combination of Thunder under Lake suggests that you can only overcome disturbing and unforeseen circumstances by understanding the hidden forces at work. Even though you have disconcerting fears and a fight-or-flight reaction, a few deep breaths and moment of meditation should work wonders to create peace of mind. If this doesn't bring peace continue doing so until or whenever your fears no longer dominate your thinking.

18
REPAIR

———
— —
— — Above: Mountain *(Moses, Extroverted Sensing)*
———
———
— — Below: Wind *(Aaron, Introverted Thinking)*

Summary: Restructuring; Correcting decay or corruption; Restoring the proper order; Mending, renovation, and putting something into a correct and conclusive form; Fixing a mistake. C+ Grade

An example of REPAIR is present in the story of Jesus going into a synagogue on the Sabbath day and healing a man with a withered hand. When confronted by the religious authorities as to why he broke the law by working responded with questions by saying, *"Is it lawful to do good on the Sabbath days or to do evil, to save life or to kill?"* He added, *"The Sabbath was made for man and not man for the Sabbath [18]."*

The Sabbath is a celebration of life and creation. It is one of the main things to set the Jewish people apart from everyone else. This story makes two important points. First, Jesus tells us that taking care of the hurting person before you should take precedence over traditional laws. In the end, what really defines us isn't so much what we believe, but whether and how we love. Second, by ignoring the letter of the law Jesus was able to integrate his annoyance into his conscious personality and become a stronger, more resolute person. Had he repressed his irritation to go along with the rigid view of the law his anger would become a part of his shadow. In this story, your position resembles the role of friendly healer played by Jesus who does healing work in an environment that had a law against working so. At the highest level, this hexagram suggests that communicating with an attitude of friendship and good intentions will be effective in adjusting and perhaps changing out-dated rules, systems or structures. It tells us to heal and do good to fix what needs fixing.

Getting REPAIR comes as a message that in order to overcome failures you need to talk openly about problems with those in charge. It refers to the psychological decay resulting from small yet persistent patterns of indifference. This has come about because of bad habits such as ignoring one's self or others, ignoring what needs to be changed, not searching for new meaning, and in short, not adapting to new realities. This hexagram serves as a reminder to reappraise and discuss what is taking place, and then introduce changes where necessary. Here, your success will depend upon being agreeable and helpful in working to correct mistakes.

REPAIR comes as a sign that your pleasant manner of speech can assist the people in power in changing their intentions. The combination of Wind under Earth points to an open and sociable approach to explaining policies, rules and making realistic modifications. It serves as a message for you to reexamine the rules and way of life put forward by the established leadership. With your assistance those in charge can transform the laws and systems they follow in a sensible manner. In the situation at hand, your position also resembles that of an observer who understands the community and knows how to converse with its leaders about their problems and solutions.

19
APPROACH

___ ___
___ ___
___ ___ Above: Earth *(David, Introverted Sensing)*
___ ___
____
_______ Below: Lake *(Abraham, Introverted Intuition)*

Summary: Promotion; Beginning of upward movement; Becoming great; Approaching a goal; Notably above average in size; Advancement; Spring-like conditions. A Grade

An illustration of APPROACH shows up in Jesus teaching about the Greatness of Humility when an argument started among the disciples as to which of them was the greatest. In knowing their thoughts Jesus says, *"If any man desires to be first, the same shall be last of all, and servant of all." And he took a child, and when he had taken him in his arms, he said unto them, "Who ever shall receive one of such children in my name, receives me: and whosoever shall receive me, receives not me, but him that sent me [19]."*

To the self-important disciples arguing about their own greatness, Jesus asks a young child to stand in a place of honor next to him. The disciples are so eager to protect Jesus, that they exclude little children because they consider them a bother. The idea is that in the Kingdom of God humility, servanthood, and seeing Christ in a child are signs of greatness. Because children are symbolic of our underdeveloped and vulnerable personality aspects, they represent enormous potential. To receive someone in God's name is to believe in him or her, to accept their credentials as valid and true, and to honor them as a guest. Jesus message is that things are not as they seem and that the Kingdom honors humbleness rather than self-importance. As mother Teresa said, “Don’t seek to do great things, seek to do small things with great lives.” Instead of trying to be a great man and woman of God, you should try to be someone who serves a great God. Your position in this teaching and in the situations represented by this hexagram is one of having faith in the unseen power of spirit to manifest itself in the world.

APPROACH implies that confidence in your intuitive and spiritual nature is beginning to manifest in practical ways. The presence of this hexagram is a sign that there is less ego involvement in the growth of new endeavors. Because your community respects your inner knowledge, it is likely that your knowledge will serve many. Here your knowledge of the Divine has an opportunity to rise to the occasion and find expression in the material world. The opportunity for rapid present because you have continued to recognize the divine by taking the proper steps to make your personal interests secondary to the expression of Spirit.

The presence of introverted intuition below and introverted sensation above suggests that your interests and understanding exist in an environment receptive to following inner-directed interests. In the situation at hand, success comes about because people value subjective impressions of physical reality more than physical reality itself. APPROACH suggests that people in your community are receptive to acting in accord with your inner knowledge and confidence in unseen forces. Your role in the situation at hand is one of providing insight to people willing to follow your spiritual advice. You can now manifest what you know because it is clearly understood and useful to others. This hexagram and PROSPERING (11) are similar in that both find an audience ready to recognize and follow inspired ideas. The difference is that here new ideas are based on inner-directed understanding and faith where as with (11) the new ideas are based on outer-directed creative designs.

20
CONTEMPLATION

Above: Wind *(Aaron, Introverted Thinking)*

Below: Earth *(David, Introverted Sensing)*

Summary: Viewing; Withholding action; A need to collect more information and study; Observation; Meditation; Introspection; Careful reflection and inspection. <u>C+ Grade</u>

An illustration of CONTEMPLATION comes to mind in the verse at the heart of Jesus preparation for his last supper with his disciples. When asked where it will take place he says, *"Go into the city, and there you will meet a man bearing a picture of water; follow him into the house where he enters [20]."*

The presence of the unnamed man carrying the jar of water has symbolic meaning. It is likely that his assistance was agreed upon in advance and hints that Jesus' last act was to direct his disciples to follow the way of the Aquarian Age myth. The hostility of the authorities no doubt called for a certain amount of secrecy regarding the last supper. Just as water flows from the heights to generate electricity to create physical light, water carried in the jar of the Aquarian person seeks a less aware consciousness to generate greater insight. The Aquarian Archetypal Era that follows the Piscean Era actualized by Jesus makes possible the development of conscious maturity and moves us toward new spiritual grounding as well as intellectual pursuits. Throughout the 2,100-year Piscean Age, we have depended for leadership on the few but in the Aquarian Age the message of Jesus and others is available to all through the mass media. Beginning with the new 21st century Aquarian Age, each individual must integrate the spiritual power in Jesus message and use his or her own talent for the service of others. In this story your position resembles the disciple seeking to follow those who help you develop a greater connection to and awareness of the world—namely, the one bearing the water jar. At the highest level, this hexagram points to clarity and spiritual understanding.

CONTEMPLATION advises you to withhold action until you can investigate the facts at hand. It suggests that any attempts to act on current plans or make gains in the sphere of material concerns without involving others are likely to end in disaster. By stepping back, being patient and collecting more information, you can get beyond surface appearances and simply wait for new possibilities to emerge. Additional study will lead to a closer involvement and understanding of the community and realities at hand. This hexagram also points to an opportunity to gain practical understanding about events in the situation at hand.

CONTEMPLATION describes a circumstance where you need to take things apart, use logic and experience to analyze the components, and then follow an established method or procedure to get an objective understanding. The use of a research method or systematic procedure to advance your awareness is suggested when this hexagram comes up. It calls for the universal step-by-step process of defining what you want to know, finding what is already known about it, and then reaching out to collect enough facts to answer your question. The paring of Earth below Wind identifies your position as one of needing to understand what is going on. Before going forward you would do will to accept the physical and social realities as they are and then learn how to work with them.

21
BITING THROUGH

———
— —
———   Above: Fire *(Jacob, Extroverted Thinking)*
— —
— —
———   Below: Thunder *(Isaac, Extroverted Feeling)*

Summary: Reform; Dealing with difficulty; Conflict resolution; Taking decisive action to correct injustice; Separating innocence from guilt; Imposing penalties for wrongdoing. D Grade

An illustration of BITING THROUGH is present in Jesus parable about Bearing Fruit when he says, *"For a good tree does not bear bad fruit, nor does a bad tree bear good fruit. For every tree is known by its own fruit [21]."*

The teaching suggests that you are what you say you are. It is easy to look at your persona, but difficult to look at the darkness of your being. We are experts at seeing the good actions in our lives, and excusing the bad. Becoming honest with yourself begins with looking to the mistakes in your own life before pointing the finger at somebody else. To judge another's character and the condition of their heart you must look beyond their behavior, and listen to how they speak. The things you say, and how you say them quickly expose and unveil the condition and attitudes of your shadow, which is another way of saying the core of your being and heart. As a symbol, the ultimate test of a good fruit-bearing tree is one that helps people to align their lives to the character of their heart, to sacred education, and to God's ideas as revealed through their intuitive and spiritual nature. It is out of the overflow of the heart that the mouth speaks troubling or flowery words. Just as a full and lush tree does not necessarily produce the best fruit someone who looks great and behaves as if they are spiritually rich, may in fact be the worst person to follow. Your position in this parable resembles the fruit tree whose quality is uncertain. Because the intentions of your heart are unfamiliar to others, yet judged by them, the narrative asks, "What kind of fruit are you producing?" If you are honest with your self, in accord with God's nature and thoughts, you are producing good fruit.

BITING THROUGH refers to a state of affairs where wrongdoing has taken place, or is about to take place. You should take swift and decisive action to fix the problem, otherwise the result of negative deeds or words will be penalized over the long term. By taking the time to correct troubling thoughts before they expand, you can avoid major troubles. If you deal with problems when they are little, you will never have big problems. You can eliminate many doubts from the minds of those who judge you by taking the time to get in touch with the shortcomings and behaviors that undermine your efforts.

BITTING THROUGH suggests that your desire to make changes may be unwanted by the people in charge of judging your intentions. It's as if you are the person who brings far-reaching ideas to others who want to keep things as they are. The state of affairs between Isaac's and his second son Jacob personifies the trigram combination of Thunder under Fire. Jacob stole his father's blessings and God's covenant from his older brother by tricking his blind father Isaac into believing he was his older brother. Like attitudes toward Jacob, people may admire and despise your action in the end. Because your ideas may threaten the established order it may be difficult to reach the people you need to contact by the direct approach. You ideas may be rejected if you speak the truth openly, and if you get your way by trickery, you'll have to take responsibility for your actions.

22
GRACE

———
— —　Above: Mountain *(Moses, Extroverted Sensing)*
— —
———
— —
———　Below: Fire *(Jacob, Extroverted Thinking)*

Summary: Embellishing; Elegance; Adornment; Pleasant; Decoration; One-dimensional thinking; Focus on outer form; An appearance of beauty in form and style. C+ Grade

An example of GRACE is present in the story of the public baptism of Jesus by John the Baptist before he started his ministry [22]. We can begin to look at this event by asking, why did Jesus, Son of God want John to baptize him? The sacred ritual of baptism, like all sacred rituals, is humanities way of declaring heaven on earth. A baptism is really a commissioning service, and reminds us that we are who God says we are. The main reason Jesus chose to receive the same baptism as others is to show them that he was united with all believers and that all believers might have this in common with him. Even though John recognized who he was, Jesus did not want to reveal his rank above John to others, but rather focus on their mission and service to God. Through the outer ritual of baptism, he identifies with the problems of humanity. At the highest level your status is like the humble role played by Jesus if getting baptized. His baptism by John was a right of passage that opened vistas of greater spiritual leadership in his community and served as a clear visible sign to connect with those he planned to reach.

The presence of GRACE for the situation at hand implies that you are reaching people by appealing to their senses in a form that they recognize. You are dealing with the aesthetics of an external form that, while desired, may not be the essential element. For instance, having money, status, material ownership or even good looks often inclines people to assume that God blesses them for being righteous. Unless you look beyond appearances, you will miss the realization that God is the true source of fulfillment. Even though we measure financial status by outer material wealth, we measure inner wealth by one's relationship with the Divine.

Getting the hexagram GRACE is a sign that you are about to take the lead in manifesting a form that is pleasing to the eye. The Jungian perspective on extroverted thinking within and extroverted sensation without suggest that your apparent interest in the external world of facts, planning, and problem solving is being expressed in an environment which values concrete reality rather than the subjective impressions of concrete reality. Here, your attachment to appearances is the source of your dependence upon objective data and intellectual conclusions. The combination of Fire under Mountain points to your intention to take charge of producing a striking physical appearance in the world of material forms. This trigram pair suggests that People respect both your creative leadership and commitment to traditional requirements. In general, it hints that your role is one of directing and cooperating with others to produce an attractive and functional form.

23
SPLITTING APART

———
— —
— — Above: Mountain *(Moses, Extroverted Sensing)*
— —
— —
— — Below: Earth *(David, Introverted Sensing)*

Summary: Stripping away; A focus on inferior people and ideas; Fears and lack of faith; Breaking-up; Decline; Gradual Undermining; Wasted potential; Deterioration. D Grade

An example of SPLITTING APART comes into view in the story of Jesus walking on a lake tossed with waves and inviting Peter to leave the ship and walk on the water to him [23]. Peter walks out on the water to meet Jesus, but when he focused on the contrary wind he began to sink and needed help to avoid drowning. It is only when the other disciple's panic, thinking that Jesus is a ghost, does he step into the boat with them and calms the wind. Before this, he tried to encourage them to have faith.

This story is a dramatic illustration of how fear can get in the way and keep us from our destiny. Peter stands out from the other disciples because he was one whose flaws and weaknesses were visible. He was far from perfect, yet Jesus called him a rock because he was dependable. Peter had to leave the safety of the ship and risk his life on the sea in order to learn both his own weaknesses and about having faith in God. Your position in this story resembles the role played by Peter who faithfully followed Jesus by walking on the sea. At the highest level, getting this hexagram represents an opportunity to follow Spirit's call to do things that you have never dreams of, having complete faith in God's support.

SPLITTING APART represents a circumstance where your ability to grow is limited by your beliefs and lack of faith in new ways. The implication is that you are in a situation where inferior ideas and even fears make little or no room for superior ideas. Things are depressing, options don't make sense and your ability to improve the situation seems inadequate. Since it may be impossible to get beyond limiting beliefs, it is better to keep still rather than making things worse by acting with no vision. If, for instance, you are lost and have no clue on where to go or how to find what you are looking for it is wise to stay put until you learn more about what is going on. Long story short, it is better to admit what you don't know than take action without faith in the outcome.

In SPLITTING APART, Earth below hints that you are accepting things as they appear even though the upper Mountain trigram suggests that a greater knowledge and way of life is available. Your limited awareness may make significant progress impossible, but you can avoid real losses by remaining devoted to your community and following the inner world of spirit. Illustrations of this hexagram come to life in personal and social activities where people truly want to be of service and help maintain the security of others. Even though your position calls for accepting the world around you with all its culturally defined behaviors it helps to know that all life depends upon the same Divine Source. Through a step-by-step approach to serving others and confidence in the Divine you can get beyond the current limitations.

24
RETURN OF THE LIGHT

___ ___
___ ___
___ ___ Above: Earth *(David, Introverted Sensing)*
___ ___
___ ___
_______ Below: Thunder *(Isaac, Extroverted Feeling)*

Summary: Renewal; Resurrection; Rebirth; Going from rest to activity; Making new again; Turning away from external confusion and back to the Light Within. B Grade

An illustration of RETURN OF THE LIGHT can be understood in Jesus parable of Weeds growing in the Wheat when he says, *"The kingdom of heaven may be compared to a man who sowed good seed in his field; but while men were sleeping, his enemy came and sowed weeds among the wheat, and went away. So when the plants came up and bore grain, then the weeds appeared also [24]."*

As the parable goes, the weeds and the wheat grow together but do not stay together. The weeds are pulled when the wheat is mature, gathered together in bundles, and destroyed by fire. Just like true believers, many who are not fully committed, go to church, pray, read the Bible or other sacred text, and even meditate, but they are only spiritual hobbyists. The weeds are not originally from the unenlightened, but they develop as such according to their strong influence. This parable exposes the problem of evil intermingled with good within spiritual communities, just as the same mix confront nations, groups, and homes. No matter how society tries to legislate or separate out lawbreakers from the rest of society, the seeds of wrongdoing and crime find a place to grow. In relation to this hexagram and the message of the parable, your position is like that of the healthy wheat separated from the weeds at harvest time. This parable implies that the spiritual family on earth, like the wheat, will be imperfect because its members who are dedicated and loyal must learn to accept the surroundings, even though many elements may be flawed.

Getting RETURN OF THE LIGHT refers to a sudden awakening after a period of gradual growth. It marks the beginning of a new cycle in which things shift from hibernation to activity and begin to grow. Natural growth, improvement, and fulfillment will take place, but these futures changes will come about at their own pace. Until the time of renewal arrives and unexpected changes take place, you must accept the slow hidden process of expanding human awareness. The promise of success comes to life in accordance with the natural order. A sobering effect of this hexagram is that even though you may want the perfect environment for growth you are obliged to accept and work with imperfect conditions as well.

The lower trigram Thunder signifies that your position within the larger community is akin to that of a future volcanic-like event that in time will change the landscape of the material universe around you. RETURN OF THE LIGHT suggest that you are about to experience a powerful new beginning that resembles the call of Moses or coming of Jesus Christ who served a people stricken with problems. In time, they had to deal with the major problems recorded through out the Old and New Testaments. In the situation at hand you have the urge to express something new and creative to the people you need to reach. Generally, what you have to present may be opposed in the short run but changes for the better are on the way as the people in your environment will experience the same renewal.

25
INNOCENCE

———
———
——— Above: Heaven *(Jesus, Extroverted Intuition)*
— —
— —
——— Below: Thunder *(Isaac, Extroverted Feeling)*

Summary: Influence from without; Entangled, but lacking evil intent or rashness; Action devoid of flaws; Purity of motive; Unexpected; Faultless; Astounding; Something remarkable. C+ Grade

The story about the birth of Jesus is an illustration of INNOCENCE. This story is found in the Gospel of Matthew at the beginning of the New Testament and starts with three miracles. First, God took human form as a baby in a manger. Second, a virgin conceived. Third, Joseph believed the angel. Mary was married to Joseph but before they began to live together and consummate their marriage sexually, he found out that she was pregnant with the child of the Holy Spirit [25]. As Joseph thought about secretly divorcing her, an angel of the Lord appears to him in a dream and commands him to take Mary home as his wife. The angel explains that she is still a virgin, not to be afraid, to name the child Jesus, and that he will save his people from their sins. For modern dream interpreters this prophetic dream adds to the realism of the story since it is easier for people today to believe in dreams of angels than in angels themselves. There is really no way to resolve the literal issue of the virginal conception on medical grounds because miracles by their nature are outside the normal laws of nature. Any rejection of Christ's supernatural origins leaves his supernatural life, death, and resurrection inexplicable as well. At the highest level, your position in this story and in the situation represented by this hexagram resembles the role played by Joseph. Like Joseph, your unexpected fate in the lower trigram meets the creative power of spirit in the upper trigram.

INNOCENCE points to unforeseen and sudden events that often result in creative and inspired outcomes. Although potential rewards are associated with this hexagram, your reaction to them will depend upon your relation to the Divine. While an inventive consequence is implied, events that are spontaneous, simple, and non-threatening tend to succeed, where as those which are troubling tend to fail. The current conditions are ideal for expressing heartfelt opinions, but not so favorable for reasoned communications. In evaluating the situation at hand, feelings will play a larger role than logic. New perspectives about the Divine are indicated when your intuitions and feelings work together to understand the answers to your questions.

INNOCENCE refers to outcomes made up of elements that are both uncertain and creative. In the situation at hand, you are trying to initiate a major event that others are not ready to embrace and may even fear. As you attempt to move forward, you may find that the people you want to reach have their own ideas and possibilities that differ from the ones that you have. The paring of Thunder under Heaven implies an innate yet creative conflict between your emotional and intuitive nature. Because lower trigram represents an effort to express something that others are not expecting, the appearance of Heaven in the upper position suggests that the audience who hears it is likely to respond in a creative manner.

26
ACCUMULATING WISDOM

Above: Mountain *(Moses, Extroverted Sensing)*

Below: Heaven *(Jesus, Extroverted Intuition)*

Summary: Building-up; Big energy, small channel for expression; Taming Power of The Great; Major restraint; A Great accumulation of energy within a limited area; Restricted strength. C- Grade

The meaning of ACCUMULATING WISDOM is present in the story of a scribe who asks Jesus the question: Which is the first (greatest) commandment of all? Jesus replied, *"The first of all commandments is, Hear, O Israel; the Lord our God is one Lord; and you shall love the lord God with all your heart, soul and mind, and with all your strength: This is the first commandment. And the second is like it, namely this: You shall love your neighbor as your self. There is no other commandment greater than these [26]."*

Learning to live by these two commandments is no easy task and doing so may take more than a lifetime. It is not enough to say I love you God, Creator, Universe, or Spirit. You Love by doing what it tells you is right, and doing it promptly, cheerfully, and without forethought. You can demonstrate love by catching and becoming God's ideas through your intuition and spiritual education. There are as many different ways of loving as there are right things to do. The commandment that says we should love God with all our heart, soul, mind, and strength means feeling and thinking lovingly and gratefully about our creator, the Universe, Unknown, or God and doing all the things required. The commandment that says you should love your neighbor as yourself means to love and pray for everybody. In addition to understanding the bad things in the world and the nature of darkness, you must love the good things and the Light Within. Your position in this teaching resembles the roles played by both Jesus and the scribe in giving and receiving the new mandates for living. This hexagram reminds us that ideas develop only when they are consistent with the manifestation of this great commandment.

ACCUMULATING WISDOM refers to a state of mind where you are more committed to creative ideas and designs than matter-of-fact plans. It serves as a message to aim your ideas toward one objective. Your success in the situation at hand will depend on being patient and holding steady to nurture the same goal. Your task is nothing less than remaining focused and following a fixed plan to complete the necessary steps to manifest your vision. The situation at hand can be understood as a sign to be careful not to get so caught up in your imagination till it is impossible to see what is essential and what is not.

ACCUMULATING WISDOM suggests that you are passionate about an ingenious idea or the beginning of something new, but must accept the realistic limits imposed on your circumstances and express your light within them. For example, if you are starting to write a new book or commit to beginning a new journey you must operate within culturally defined guidelines and take one-step at a time. The combination of Heaven under Mountain refers to a situation where something creative is stirring in you. The introduction of the new laws by Jesus to replace the numerous existing laws from Moses is represented by this trigram pair. Here, as in other cases, the introduction new concepts must be consistent with the ways of time-honored traditions.

27
SEEKING NOURISHMENT

Above: Mountain *(Moses, Extroverted Sensing)*

Below: Thunder *(Isaac, Extroverted Feeling)*

Summary: Giving and receiving nourishment; Ingesting; Following that which sustains the mind and spirit; Observation and evaluation; Knowing oneself. A- Grade

An illustration of SEEKING NOURISHMENT emerges in the New Testament parable of the Barren Fig Tree [27]. The parable deals with a man planting a fig tree in the good soil of his vineyard. After three years had passed and the tree yielded no fruit the owner wanted the chop down the tree rather than have this tree continue to take up good earth. However his gardener requested one more year so he could fertilize the tree and see it if yielded fruit. If not he agreed it should be cut down. The parable ends with the words from the gardener that are unexpected from the owner's view, yet the owner does not reject the gardener's request. The tree is not just useless but the owner's expectations have been let down. Were the tree to remain, there would be no particular benefit to the gardener and he would only be doing the extra work of digging around the tree and giving it fertilizer. The surprising thing said in this parable really takes place in us. It is common sense to throw way stuff that is useless, serves no purpose, and unwise to keep. In this parable, the destruction of the barren tree bear clears the way for the return of universal order and correct nourishment. As suggested in the parable you must decide on which path of nourishment will get the best result for your situation.

SEEKING NOURISHMENT refers to activities that may bring spiritual development and peace of mind. It suggests that your success will depend on making appropriate changes to get the results you seek. In the situation at hand your plans can be manifested when your activities are executed with repetition and control. You will accomplish the best outcome by working with new possibilities and guidelines for getting things done. After these considerations are accepted, you can integrate them into the recognized order. While your situation may challenge some of your basic beliefs, it also brings an opportunity to make positive adjustments.

When the sudden momentum and promotion of events represented by Thunder below meets the authority and established guidelines of Mountain above, fulfillment takes place. An example of SEEKING NOURISHMENT is present in the story about events following the birth of Isaac to his parents of extreme age. His unexpected existence required major family changes to fulfill God's promise to his father, and life-altering adjustments based on God's conversations with his father Abraham. This trigram pair suggests that your position is one of introducing a significant change to restore order and fulfill existing laws. You will get the best results by both accepting the new and aligning yourself with the established order.

28
YANG IN EXCESS

__ __
_____
_____ Above: Lake *(Abraham, Introverted Intuition)*
_____
_____
__ __ Below: Wind *(Aaron, Introverted Thinking)*

Summary: Excess yang; A loss of balance; Too many possibilities; A condition of going beyond what is desired or appropriate; Overindulgence; An over-abundance of information not yet digested. D Grade

An illustration of YANG IN EXCESS comes to life in the story of the Magi that God warned in a dream not to return to King Herod even though he had ordered them to let him know where he could find Jesus [28]. This dream came to the Magi after their visit to see the newborn Jesus. While Herod met privately with the wise men saying he wanted to worship the infant Jesus as they were planning to do, nothing was further from the truth. Just as the wise men ignored his orders and departed to their own country by another road, Mary and Joseph take another path. Their path included leaving Bethlehem and going into exile in Egypt to escape Herod.

This story clearly connects the story of Jesus with the story of Moses. Both Joseph, the son of Jacob, and Joseph the adoptive father of Jesus, were in Egypt as exiles. Both Moses and Jesus escaped death threats as baby boys. This story outlines the perennial battle represented by the hexagram—the Kingdom of Ego versus the Kingdom of God. Who or what is your ultimate concern. Do you answer to Herod? Do you search for Christ like the Magi, or wait for Christ to find you? In this story, your position resembles the roles played by the Joseph and the Magi. In their own ways both characters were aware of the greatness of what took place and the signs of danger associated with this event.

Getting YANG IN EXCESS suggests that your desire to socialize with others is a learning opportunity that calls for greater awareness and demands your full attention. Even though some information is available from the ordinary ways of interacting with others, you can learn a great deal on your own. By gathering with other like-minded people or catching God's ideas through your intuitive and spiritual nature, you can deepen your understanding in new ways. In addition to communicating with others and learning about new possibilities, an abundance of educational avenues offer knowledge and resources to enhance your growth. Because this profusion of information comes to you from many sides, you will need to make choices about the actions you should and should not take.

YANG IN EXCESS refers to situations where your connections to others on a person-to-person basis may be limited because the demands of your environment require greater knowledge than you can offer. The presence of Wind below and Lake above suggests that because you are interested in routine interactions with others, you may find it difficult to express ideas that reach beyond these ordinary concerns. An example of this hexagram shows up in the relationship between dream interpreters and dreamers. Even though the interpreter must listen to the dream and learn something about the dreamer, their understanding of the dream and ability to explain its meaning is often limited. In the events represented by this hexagram, your position is like the dream interpreter. You can only offer a partial perspective about the dream to the dreamer, even though the dreamer may want a deeper understanding.

29
THE ABYSS

___ ___
____
___ ___ Above: Water *(Joseph, Introverted Feeling)*
___ ___
____
___ ___ Below: Water *(Joseph, Introverted Feeling)*

Summary: The Abysmal; Water; Darkness; Mystery; Inner emotional life; The moon as a symbol; Habits, desires; Danger; Hardship; Difficulty; Unfathomable. <u>D Grade</u>

Psychologically THE ABYSS represents our habits, emotional tendencies, and historical ways of behaving. The Old Testament character of Joseph, the eleventh and favorite son of his father Jacob, personifies this hexagram [29]. As the story goes, his ten older brothers are jealous of his father's favoritism and sell Joseph into slavery to a high-ranking official in Egypt, telling their father that he is dead. This official throws Joseph in jail when the official's flirtatious wife wrongly accuses him of trying to sleep with her. Ever faithful to God, Joseph earns a reputation as an interpreter of dreams while in jail. Years pass until the Pharaoh of Egypt bothered by two troublesome dreams, hears of Joseph and his abilities. The Pharaoh summons Joseph, who successfully interprets the dreams, warning the Pharaoh that a great famine will strike Egypt after seven years. Impressed, the Pharaoh elects Joseph to be his highest official, and appoints Joseph to lead a campaign throughout Egypt to set aside food in preparation for the famine.

Getting this hexagram serves as a reminder that your experience in the current situation is marked by hardship and the problem of being misunderstood in spite of your knowledge and good intentions. In this story, your position resembles the private role played by Joseph, the skilled dream interpreter, and his public role as the Pharaoh's advisor. The situation you face now implies but does not demand the example of leadership demonstrated by Joseph. At the highest level, it is presumed that your knowledge, like Joseph's, can be used to assist others in their progress and that their connections will advance the standing of all.

THE ABYSS represents environments of potential harm, distress or annoyance. It serves as a message that your situation contains external or internal difficulties and opposing forces that will require effort to overcome. Even though the troubling circumstances will not go away, and there is nowhere to go, you can still seek the comfort of inner knowledge about what lies ahead. Just about any advancement will be difficult because other people such as associates, partners or relatives mat not agree with your direction and principles. To be effective with the dangers and mystery represented by this hexagram it is necessary to gain self-understanding, and if possible, use your skills to help other people with their concerns.

The ABYSS refers to a state of affairs where you are a knowledgeable member of a group whose skills have yet to be recognized. Even though you possess special education or experience, most people do not see it. The existence of Water above and below suggests that your unique talents will only be useful to those who recognize and seek them. Once you understand the natural character of circumstances for yourself and the needs of others your actions will succeed. An illustration would be the case of two or more specialists or trained professionals who gather with one another but neither is aware of the others background. While both or either party may assume the role of leader over the meeting it is also possible, that no leader will emerge or that the parties will compete or go their separate ways.

30
ATTACHMENTS

———
— —
——— Above: Fire *(Jacob, Extroverted Thinking)*
———
— —
——— Below: Fire *(Jacob, Extroverted Thinking)*

Summary: Radiance; Clinging; Ego-centered; Reliance on tangible forms and reason; Clarity; Connection; Interest in facts, practical problem solving; Leading or controlling others; Recognition; Strength. <u>C+ Grade</u>

Psychologically, ATTACHMENTS represents the ego, personal desires and will power. The Old Testament character of Jacob, son of Isaac and Rebecca, and the younger brother of Esau, personifies this hexagram. Esau was a hunter, brash, and found pleasure in the realm of the senses, whereas Jacob was soft-spoken, mental, and found pleasure in developing his spiritual and intuitive nature [30]. They were opposites in everything. As the story goes, Jacob steals his brother's inheritance right and eventually wrestles with God who renames him "Israel," meaning "struggles with God." Rebecca favors Jacob and helps him deceive his blind father Isaac into giving him the blessings that should have gone to his older brother Esau. Rebecca supported these immoral acts, set the stage for Jacob to become the third patriarch of the Israelite people, and for spirituality to continue its supremacy over the senses. His well-known vision commonly referred to as Jacob's ladder represents his systematic realization of truth. Jacob had twelve sons whom he blessed and inspired with his spiritual wisdom. His sons form the twelve tribes and nation of Israel, and their struggles, like Jacob's, are symbolic of the tumultuous story of the nation of Israel. In this story your position is like the competitive role played by Jacob who became leader of the nation of Israel. As represented in this story your experience of taking the lead, as Jacob did, comes about through your character or talent and by assistance from others.

The presence of ATTACHMENTS refers to a state of affairs in which your position in relation to others is that of leader or head of household. It implies that success is the result of cooperation with each member and depends upon the degree to which others respect what you have to offer. Here all parties would do well to go out of their way to cooperate with one another. By examining the role played by each leader and making changes where needed, you can eliminate unworkable elements and support those that nurture the relationship. Although your situation may be less than ideal, you can achieve your goals if the opposing forces work together and support one another.

Getting ATTACHMENTS implies that the people you are reaching out to admire what you are doing and see your role as one of an authority. Fire above and below implies that because your desire to direct people to follow one another is mutual both parties gain benefit in leading the other. The idea is that just as the people under your influence admire and respect your leadership, you admire and respect their authority as well. An example of this hexagram comes to life in the case of a well-respected external consultant and leader hired by the president of an organization. Even though the outside leader delivers training to employees who look up to the president for hiring the consultant they also look up to the outside leader who in turn looks up to the president. Because you are sharing recognition in the company of others, your role as a leader and co-leader will depend upon your cooperation with others.

31
INFLUENCE

Above: Lake *(Abraham, Introverted Intuition)*

Below: Mountain *(Moses, Extroverted Sensing)*

Summary: Persuasion; Attraction; Interaction; Courtship; Making an impression; Producing an effect by indirect means; The act, or effect of exerting some degree of force. C- Grade

An example of INFLUENCE comes to mind in the meaning of Jesus Teaching about the Law when he says, *"Think not that I have come to destroy the law, or the prophets. I have not come to destroy, but to fulfill [31]."*

In declaring his complete accord with ancient laws, Jesus offered persuasive new insights and thoughts to fulfill all the laws of Moses, the prophets, and the psalms. Nowadays, most modern spiritual people discard the letter of the law in favor of the spirit of the law. Because one extreme is as bad as the other is we need both to keep things evenhanded. A healthy religious life comes about when there is balance between understanding the nature and will of God and Divine ideas received directly through your intuitive nature. Without the soothing character of music, for instance, many people don't come close enough to ever hear the gospel's message. When a focus on the law predominates, self-righteousness tends to outweigh the positive message; and when the positive message of the gospel or intuitive insights from God ignore requirements of the Law, we lose the backbone of religion and its power for goodness and healing. In this verse of scripture, your position accords with promoting the Letter or Spirit of the Law while the party you are attracted to takes the opposite position.

Getting INFLUENCE suggests that you have an interest in attracting others to join you in partnership. Even though you have the power to persuade others to join your point of view, this power is limited and may be put to better use by remaining centered to see what is going on. You can achieve your goals by allowing all concerned to share their knowledge about the relationship. At best, you should encourage the other party to join you because of genuine concerns for what is best for all. The hexagram also serves as a message for you to encourage those who depend upon you to get what they need so they can act in their own best interest.

INFLUENCE represents a state of affairs where you are hoping to exercise authority and sway in a relationship where others are passionate about their position and know as much as you know about where they want things to go. When Mountain within is surrounded by Lake on the outside your position is like that of Moses in the midst of leading the Israelites in crossing the Red Sea. At the highest level, you can both attract and direct others based on the power of your faith in them. Although you have an interest in taking on responsibilities and assuming authority in the situation before you, other people may be less compatible than you would like them to be. As a result, each party is likely to plead their case in hope that their side prevails or they at least convince the other side to understand their view as valid.

32
DURATION

___ ___
___ ___
_______ Above: Thunder *(Isaac, Extroverted Feeling)*
____
____
___ ___ Below: Wind *(Aaron, Introverted Thinking)*

Summary: Constancy; Endurance**;** Self-contained, self-renewing movement; Perseverance; Continuity; Permanence; Longevity; Uninterrupted existence or growth. B Grade

An illustration of DURATION is present in the New Testament parable of the unclean spirit returning [32]. Through this parable, Jesus tells us that when an unclean spirit is cast out it leaves for a time but periodically returns to see if the person has slipped up in any way in order to give it the right to come back, and perhaps invite some unclean spirit friends. To get unclean spirits to leave the individual's emotional body or "house as a symbol" an exorcism can be done to sweep the house clean. When unclean spirits, like addictions, bad behaviors, or demons return and find no spiritual truth in the clean house they re-enter and make the condition worse than when they left. To change behavior you need to put the demon out, keep the demon out, and understand the reason for putting it out. You should not leave the house empty by doing one healing and walking away, but rather fill it with ongoing spiritual study. In this way, the renewing and enduring power of spiritual understanding takes root, occupies the house with its presence, and the unclean spirit or gang of spirits are shut out for good. Your position in this parable resembles the role played by Jesus in speaking healing words to cast out unclean spirits. Since many demons, like emotional addictions, will not go easily, only persistent efforts to replace them by embracing the truth, e.g., a 12-step program, will keep them from returning.

DURATION denotes a condition in which the connection between people tends to be trusting and comfortable. At the same time, there is an atmosphere of powerful and unanticipated life changing events. Even though your intended course relies on good intentions, you will need continued attention to release old patterns and replace them new growth producing behaviors. By remaining flexible and open to new ways of dealing with what may be a troubling state of affairs you can keep abreast of the times and change with them. Because you are generally optimistic about the future now is a good time to act on your intuition. The ultimate intention of this hexagram is like that of the road builder whose task is to first present the plan and then get it manifested. While the current situation has roots that are not easy to pull up, the conditions exist for making improvements.

When DURATION comes up your ordinary attempts to communicate with others on a person-to-person basis may create surprising opportunities for change and growth. The combination of Wind below and Thunder above implies that your efforts to connect and associate with others, while simple and straightforward, have the effect of promoting significant long-term changes. In the situation at hand, your role is like Moses' brother Aaron who spoke for Moses because of his speech impediment. Although Aaron was only the messenger, the important task of changing the consciousness of the people of Israel could not have taken place without Aaron's commitment to continually present his brother's message.

33
RETREAT

____
____
________ Above: Heaven *(Jesus, Extroverted Intuition)*
____
___ ___
___ ___ Below: Mountain *(Moses, Extroverted Sensing)*

Summary: Withdrawing; Letting go and letting God; Remain in the background; Waiting to move at the right time; Additional knowledge needed before changing course; Yielding. D Grade

An illustration of RETREAT comes to life in the short parable by Jesus about a Buried Treasure. In it he says, *"The kingdom of heaven is like a treasure hidden in a field, which a man found and covered up; then in his joy he goes and sells all that he has and buys that field [33]."*

The message is that any price would be worth paying in order to own the field and thus obtain the treasure. Paying the price is not a sacrifice but an amazing investment and embrace of the most wonderful thing that could happen to a person. The man in the parable was willing to do whatever it takes to obtain the treasure for himself. Symbolically he was willing to release his possessions and attachment to his ideas in order to gain entry into the kingdom of Heaven. He was very captivated by the treasure and recognized its value in bringing purpose and fulfillment into his life. It's as if he recognized that the hidden treasure would give his life meaning, happiness, and the opportunity for a better relationship with the Divine. Your position in this parable resembles the man who gave up everything he had to get the treasure. In this situation, you can benefit by replacing the path before you to with a better course.

When RETREAT comes up you are in a situation that calls upon you to leave the main road and suspend your plans for now. It serves as a message to let go of the past and contemplate the will of God. By letting go of your plans, you can use your intuition to deepen your spiritual understanding and keep your distance from the dangers that lie ahead. Although your limited involvement may result in some loss of ground in the beginning, you can protect yourself by using the time to study the situation and then act when the timing is right. While it is likely that you will experience some loss associated with releasing your position, you can find success by delaying the gratification of perceived gains until you know how to create the best outcome.

In Jungian terminology, the combination of extroverted sensation within and extroverted intuition outside suggests that your interest in concrete reality has come face to face with an opportunity to create a different outcome. In the situation at hand, your intentions have nothing in common with the creative potential offered by your environment. RETREAT refers to situations where the creative powers of the universe can only be reached by seeking help from the inner world of spirit which implies letting go of your personal plans. Simply put, getting this hexagram implies that your position is like the person in an authority role who finds it wise to withdraw from what he or she has planned in order to wait for a better course.

34
GREAT POWER

Above: Thunder *(Isaac, Extroverted Feeling)*

Below: Heaven *(Jesus, Extroverted Intuition)*

Summary: Great strength, boldness; Excessive power, pride; Going beyond the mean; Large and right; Inspirational; State or quality of being strong; Effective means of forcing, compelling, or motivating others. A Grade

An example of GREAT POWER comes into view in the parable of The Lost Coin. In the parable Jesus says, *"What woman having ten pieces of silver, if she loses one piece does not light a candle, and sweep the house, and seek diligently till she finds it. And when she found it she calls her friends and neighbors to celebrate the return of the lost coin [34]."*

In commenting on the symbolism in the parable, Jesus tells us that heaven rejoices at the finding of lost souls. It is evident that while the place where she lives is both dark and dirty she relies on God's help to find the lost coin. This parable tells us that even though you may lose your way and your possessions for a time, you retain your identity and value to God. No matter how much trash covers the lost silver coin it is still valuable. Whether people have wandered away or got lost at home God longs for their recovery. Like the woman in the parable, you are responsible for finding what is missing. The parable illustrates the point that a lost part of the whole is always "richer" and more powerful when found. In this example, your position, represented by the lower trigram, resembles that of the woman searching for what was lost. In the situation at hand, your effort to enlist God's help in restoring wholeness will likely meet with success.

Getting GREAT POWER serves as a message that you are now, or soon will be in a position of great influence over others. It suggests that influence comes about because you are willing to trust divine insights about your relationships and other events in your environment. It points to receiving creative ideas that can help you bring about the right changes and perhaps swift progress. Impulsive moves to implement the ideas represented here will likely meet opposition if they go beyond what others expect. If you display arrogance and show off your strength, any success will result in failure. In this sense, the hexagram hints that your desire to act on new insights may be too extreme, and if unchecked, may cause unnecessary trouble.

Heaven below Thunder refers to situations where new inspiration or revelations are the source of an unexpected event in your affairs. An illustration of this hexagram comes to life in the story of God telling an extremely old Abraham and Sarah that they are going to have a child. This unsettling event fulfills God's promise made to Abraham years earlier. Sarah laughed in disbelief at the news, but God had the last laugh and soon after, she gave birth to Isaac, her first and only child. GREAT POWER is a sign that your desire to create is taking place in a circumstance where significant change is already taking place. Depending upon how you interact with others the creative outcome you receive may be welcomed or unwanted.

35
PROGRESS

———
— —
———
— —
— —
— —

Above: Fire *(Jacob, Extroverted Thinking)*

Below: Earth *(David, Introverted Sensing)*

Summary: External progress, expansion, or promotion; Social advantage; Growth; Stepping forward; Prosperity; Steady improvement, development; Victory. B Grade

In the Parable of the Talents Jesus provides us with an illustration of PROGRESS. In the story, a wealthy property owner entrusted his wealth to three men who become stewards of his talents while he takes a leave of absence [35]. One steward receives five talents, another two and a third one talent. When the property owner returns from his long absence, he finds that the first two stewards understood the spirit of his instructions and character well enough to expand the talents he left under their control. He congratulates them and allows them to handle more of his possessions. The third steward who received only one talent feared he would lose it, so he buried it in the ground. The landlord took it away, scolded him for his lack of faith in expanding the talent and explained that every one who has will be given more, but from those who have not even what they have will be taken away. This parable serves as a lesson that our talents such as the talent to write, speak, or lead others are on loan to us. The parable also serves as a message to deal with other people based on their starting position, and evaluate yourself by your own starting position. In this parable, your position is as the stewards given an opportunity to expand the talents entrusted to them. In the situation at hand it raises the question, "What will you do with the leadership opportunity you are given?"

PROGRESS refers to situations where people want to support groups directed by a leader with charisma and social prestige. Its presence often coincides with public exposure and getting credit for success associated with ordinary life events. When this hexagram comes up people often extend themselves to help others in some way, but their success is dependent upon people willing to follow the same course. The situation at hand is a message that you may be receiving more than you can manage or work with in positive ways. Unless you get the help you need to develop and expand the talents you have you may lose them. What matters is not what you're given but you do with it.

Getting PROGRESS implies that your circumstances and talents serve as a foundation for others to build upon. This comes about because the people around you perceive you as their source of support. Your position is one of the Good Steward who provides security for those who recognize and depend upon what you have to offer. From a psychological perspective, the people in your environment have a significant personal investment in their perception of you. The combination of Fire without and Earth within suggests that your accomplishments are both admired and praised. An example of the recognition given to you can be seen in the respect given to David after he killed Goliath.

36
DARKENING OF THE LIGHT

Above: Earth *(David, Introverted Sensing)*

Below: Fire *(Jacob, Extroverted Thinking)*

Summary: Hidden brightness; Censorship; Choosing matter before spirit; Limited ideas or knowledge of what is possible; Unconsciousness; Lacking in awareness. C+ Grade

An illustration of DARKENING OF THE LIGHT is present in a verse in the Sermon on the Mount when Jesus says, *"Seek first the kingdom of God and his righteousness and all these things shall be added as well [36]."*

In this saying, Jesus is concerned with the heart of our intentions and the state of affairs that effect the hearts expression. To seek first the kingdom of God means to turn to Spirit first for help, to fill your thoughts with its desires, to take its character for your pattern, and to serve Spirit in everything. A darkened light refers to the loss of faith that God is the source of all that is. If you focus on God and its greatness and love for you, then you will have inner peace even if the world around you goes mad. If on the other hand you focus mainly on worldly things your light will dim and you will have fears and worry. Getting this hexagram suggests that your position is one of being worried, anxious, troubled, or uneasy. Your peace of mind will end if you pursue goals for material gain alone. Given your somewhat worried state of mind you should answer the question, is your purpose in life governed by spiritual or material goals?

In addition, you can review your possessions and desires, and see which ones truly support your spiritual growth.

DARKENING OF THE LIGHT refers to situations where people want to be in charge of their affairs, but accept the need to support the world as it is when they cannot get what they want. Because perspectives about what is possible are limited to appearances, you have a dim view of the big picture and look down on your physical and social circumstances. While ego demands for taking the lead and getting respect will limit your clarity, your inner light will help you see beyond appearances. Examples of this hexagram can be seen in the individual working at a job they don't really like just to pay the bills, or the bright subordinate working under a dull superior. In general, this is not a good sign for trying to negotiate advances your position because you are likely to exercise poor judgment. It is useful to remember that seeking a spiritual solution is the antidote to counteract negative environmental influences.

Getting DARKENING OF THE LIGHT is a sign of "original sin" in that it points to a state of affairs where you have allowed your fulfillment to become dependent upon the material circumstances in your environment. Instead of recognizing that true happiness lies within and that God is the true source of your good, you have unwittingly given your power and attention to the world of appearances. You are suffering because of your attachment to someone or something that cannot fulfill your hearts desire. The central teaching from Buddha that says, "No desire, no problem," advises that your desire for things is the source of your problems and that replacing this desire with a focus on oneness with God is the remedy.

37
THE FAMILY

———
———
— — Above: Wind *(Aaron, Introverted Thinking)*
———
— —
——— Below: Fire *(Jacob, Extroverted Thinking)*

Summary: Unity and mutual respect between leader and follower; Order and harmony among people and ideas; A Satisfying arrangement or design; Agreement and integration. B Grade

The story of Jesus activities and ministry to the masses told just before his famous Sermon on the Mount offers an illustration of the FAMILY [37]. It summarizes what Jesus was like and how his teaching and healing ministry spread as he moved from town to town in the region of Galilee. Almost everybody in the world has heard of the man named Jesus who lived 2,000 years ago, and each has some mental picture of what he was like. He liked people and people liked him. He came to the people and the people came to him. Wherever he went, he confirmed his Divine mission by miracles, which were healing sickness or disease with words of truth, and the influences of the Spirit that accompanied it. He ministered to the needs of the people and went to where they were instead of waiting for them to come to him. He offered spiritual solutions to every problem by getting his hands dirty. People wanted to be with him and saw that he had an answer to their problems. His teachings gave understanding and direction to his community. At the highest level, the crowds who followed Jesus serve as an example of those who may follow your lead. Your position in this story resembles the role played by Jesus in that those who follow your lead are not disciples, but people interested in following you without commitment or sacrifice.

Getting THE FAMILY points to an increase in your confidence and serves as a message to take the lead in managing your personal and group relationships. This comes about because people recognize you as a central figure and leader in the situation at hand. It serves as a reminder that all influence, expansion and self-recognition works from within and then widens to include the outer world. The environment represented by this hexagram favors stepping forward to direct most personal and even group relationships by communicating with others about their wants and needs. Healthy organizations, families, social groups, and even communities provide examples of this hexagram in that they all stress the value of individuals coming together to work toward a common good.

THE FAMILY refers to situations where you are an admired figure or leader of a group of like-minded people whose association with one another is rather commonplace. Your role is like that of elected officials or other influential people who represent and guide others toward common goals. The combination of Fire surrounded by Wind gives us a symbolic picture that represents people gathering to manifest the big picture, think positive and even accomplish significant goals. The symbol of Fire in the lower trigram suggests that you want to expand and express your self through progress. The environments represented by the upper trigram Wind hints that you should take things lightly, and then organize your thoughts.

38
OPPOSITION

———
— —
——— Above: Fire *(Jacob, Extroverted Thinking)*
— —
———
——— Below: Lake *(Abraham, Introverted Intuition)*

Summary: Contradictions; Division; Divergence; Polarizing; Alienation; Feeling distant, hostile; Antithesis; Duality; Separation; Conflict; Diametrically opposed; Unsympathetic. C- Grade

An illustration of OPPOSITION appears in Jesus' parable at the close of the Sermon on the Mount, which concludes with three warnings, the first of which says, *"Enter the straight gate for wide is the gate and broad is the way that leads to destruction, and many will go through it. But strait is the gate, and narrow is the way which leads to life and few will find it [38]."*

The narrow way leads to life, heaven and transcendence, while the wide gate and broad way leads to suffering and death. While Jesus tells us not to judge throughout much of the New Testament here he goes on to instruct us on how to judge correctly after all. He adds that the narrow gate is difficult to enter and few people will go through it, while the wide gate is easy and many people will go through it. These words are a wake up call and remind us to keep our focus on Spirit so that we can we can walk the tough path to reunion which goes against the grain of culture. It's worth the effort to follow the narrow way because in the end is life abundant. In relation to the situation at hand, this teaching implies that you are standing in two places at the same time: At the crossroads before both gates. By stepping back from the crossroads, you can remain centered and avoid the conflict of these divergent paths. Your position in the parable is one of standing before the two gates: one path leading through the narrow gate, and the other leading through the wide gate.

OPPOSITION serves as a message that different viewpoints are on the table and each party wants credit and acknowledgement for their position. The situation at hand is contradictory and confusing because there is no agreement about what is going on and each person's preference means little to those who have different needs. It's as if you are tied together like an odd couple or people with different goals who simply want attention and recognition for their position. Whatever you believe and think about, its opposite has just as much validity for those you need to work with. To make any progress in the current situation it is necessary to remain centered and understand those who have a different agenda or view. Although it is wise to make an effort to understand others, you should not demand that they understand you.

OPPOSITION points out that your good intentions contradict those who seek recognition and attention from the environment you share with them. As you reach for greater divine wisdom, you will find yourself in the midst of other people who want your consideration and admiration as well. The combination of a Lake surrounded by Fire gives us an image of two dissimilar elements that must often co-exist just as you must do in the situation before you. As long as each party retains a healthy degree of independence, they can learn to compliment one another. An example of the conflict and need for balance here may be seen in the simple case of a pastor or teacher attempting to prepare for his audience as family demands compete for his for attention.

39
OBSTACLES

Above: Water *(Joseph, Introverted Feeling)*

Below: Mountain *(Moses, Extroverted Sensing)*

Summary: An Obstruction, hardship, trouble or difficulty; A Blockage or hindrance; A barrier; Impediment; Inconvenience; A state of uneasiness; Complications; Problems. <u>F Grade</u>

An example of OBSTACLES presents itself in the story of what took place when Jesus comes before the Roman governor Pontius Pilate for questioning after his arrest [39]. His "trial" by the Jewish religious authorities was unprecedented because, of all those involved, Jesus was the only innocent person there, and nearly everyone including the Roman governor who sentenced him to be crucified, knew it. In the story, Jesus personifies the inner world of ideas and knowledge while Pilate is the outer authority figure with the last word. Pilate realized that he was seeing the persecution of an innocent man and attempted to get his accusers to release Jesus. Pilate's wife had a nightmare about the Messiah being killed and pleaded the case for him as well. Despite it all, the Jewish people and religious leaders pushed Pilate to order the death of the innocent Christ. Even if Jesus wanted to help Pilate, he could not avoid the fact that Pilate had no interest in understanding his purpose. When Pilate saw that he was gaining nothing and that a riot was about to take place he surrendered to the mob's will to have

Jesus crucified, washed his hand before the crowd, and claimed himself to be innocent. In this story, your position resembles the role played by Pilate. Like Pilate, your position comes about because you are not aware of the spiritual meaning for the problem you face now.

The presence of OBSTACLES is a message that an unfamiliar environment or way of doing things appears to oppose your established activities. It serves as a test between the various components of your life such as relationships and professional interest, and new requirements imposed by others. In the present circumstance, success only comes when those involved can let go or change their intended goals instead of battling the complications. You have limited external power because your freedom to act is dependent upon skills possessed by people who don't agree with your intentions. In the situation at hand, restrictions seem to come from nowhere, and you can do little to avoid them or make improvements. Your success will come about by pulling back for a time even though things may be confusing and it is difficult to know when or whether to go backward or forward.

The appearance of OBSTACLES indicates that your desire to assume authority opposes another person or group that has their own priorities. Even though you have talent and perhaps great skill in commanding or guiding others, the individuals around you are in full command of their particular specialty and don't hold sway to your authority. The image of a Mountain surrounded by Water suggests that your position is recognized and grounded but limited like an island surrounded by an ocean. The King of Egypt, for instance, was ruler of the physical territory but Joseph's ability to interpret dreams guided the King's heart. Like the King, you will remain unfilled until you acquire additional knowledge or assistance from others.

40
DELIVERANCE

— —
— —
——— Above: Thunder *(Isaac, Extroverted Feeling)*
— —
———
— — Below: Water *(Joseph, Introverted Feeling)*

Summary: Solution; Liberation; Unknown outcome; Internal, private, mysterious; Submitting to a calling; Release; Emotional breakthrough; Penetrating insight; Renewed growth. B Grade

An illustration of DELIVERANCE comes to mind in the parable of the wise and foolish builders that follows the Sermon on the Mount. In the parable Jesus says, *"Every one who comes to me and hears my words and does them, I will show you what he is like. He is like a man building a house, who dug deep, and laid the foundation upon rock; and when a flood arose, the stream broke against that house, and could not shake it, because it had been well built. But he who hears and does not do them is a like a man who built a house on the ground without a foundation; against which the stream broke, and immediately it fell, and the ruin of that house was great [40]."*

In relation to this parable, your position in the situation at hand resembles the wise builder who has taken some thought and effort to acquire the appropriate knowledge for building his life on a solid foundation. The wise builder uses a foundation and the unwise builder neglects doing so. The houses people build symbolize their identity, personality and soul. The people who don't know who they are often listen to others and build in a hurry; those who understand their identity honor their intuitive and spiritual nature and plan more carefully. Since the storms always come, the strength of every house is tested. The difference between the wise and foolish builders is this: the wise embody inner enlightment from the deeper mind, and the foolish ignore this wisdom. In this parable, your position is similar to the house builder who must make a choice: develop things consistent with the foundation of your identity or duplicate others even if it means ignoring your foundation.

DELIVERANCE represents the quality of mind that enables you to face major hardships resolutely from a place of inner knowing and strength. It points to the power of insight to make choices and to act upon them in spite of unexpected troubles. It may be seen as a message to listen to the Divine even if the results are contrary to what you're thinking. Getting this hexagram is an opportunity to free your self from disturbing thoughts by drawing upon your inner wisdom through channels such as dreams, visioning and the I Ching. The current situation also serves as a message that everyone has the capacity to look beyond appearances, let go, transcend, and transform their nature.

DELIVERANCE refers to situations where your knowledge and inner character have the potential to create a breakthrough that others are not expecting. As your private thoughts and feelings take form and begin to manifest the impact on others may be disconcerting and unwanted. Your position is like the skilled professional whose knowledge has a disquieting effect. An example of Water surrounded by Thunder is present in the connection between Joseph's interpretations of troubling dreams and the dreamers who sought his insights. Once the dreamer understands the dream or vision his life may change in surprising ways. This comes about because what was unconscious has now broken through to the conscious mind.

41
DECREASE

Above: Mountain *(Moses, Extroverted Sensing)*

Below: Lake *(Abraham, Introverted Sensing)*

Summary: Diminishing; External loss; Limited options; Unfulfilled goals and desires; Decline; Withdrawing; Moving back; Cutting back; Dropping off; Letting go; Investment; Imprisonment. D Grade

An example of DECREASE comes into view in the story that begins just after the baptism of Jesus [41]. In it the Spirit immediately leads Jesus out into the wilderness for forty days of fasting, temptations by Satan and being with the wild beasts; after this the angels came and administered to him. The story implies that we fight some of our greatest battles when we are trying to go in the direction dictated by inner wisdom but encounter exhausting obstacles. When we are in the wilderness, we focus upon ourselves, and it's an opportunity to clarify what we really want. In the wilderness, Jesus was tempted to shift his attention away from the questions of identity and purpose to basic human needs and desires.

In modern times, we are often tempted to give our loyalty to people or situations that promise to give us riches or power. In this story, your position resembles the role played by Jesus in relying upon his faith in God while the Satan archetype represents the tester who offers another way to live. Your desire to find your way out of the wilderness is symbolic of a desire for clarity of purpose. Even though the limitations represented by temptations and the wild beasts hold you back, they are part of God: they are teachers from the dark side and potential students of the light side.

DECREASE refers to situations work at cross-purposes to the paths taken to fulfill your potential. This comes about due to limited thinking or inner distractions. It points to the difficulties we've all had in applying what we know to get our needs and wants met. Your success will depend on shifting and perhaps giving up some personal time and resources to deal with the distractions. Even though opportunities for progress are diminished, and others don't recognize your wisdom or purpose, the seeds of a new way are present as well. The good news is that the circumstances represented by this hexagram point to a natural phase of learning and there is much to be gained if you accept the challenge. It signals the end of an old cycle and the beginning of a new one that will further define and strengthen your character.

Getting DECREASE also represents a state of affairs where your intention to advance with wisdom and knowledge has come face-to-face with temptations that oppose you. It has come up now is to serve as a message that there is little or no understanding between your inner and outer worlds. It is a message that those in power will probably not support people who express their interests in spiritual matters. Your position resembles that of the spiritual seeker or teacher whose worth goes unnoticed by the other people. DECREASE (41) is similar to DARKENING OF THE LIGHT (36) in that the surrounding conditions in both cases is less than desired, but here the difficulty is greater and can only be dealt with by a change in perception. In nature and in human behavior the combination of Lake surrounded by Mountain is analogous to partially filled containers that limit the life within, e.g., reservoirs, prisons and existence within the womb.

42
INCREASE

———————
———————
——— ———   Above: Wind *(Aaron, Introverted Thinking)*
——— ———
——— ———
———————   Below: Thunder *(Isaac, Extroverted Feeling)*

Summary: Self-improvement, well-being; Character enhancement; Adding to inner worth; Unexpected improvement; Good luck; Gain or benefit; Prosperity and growth; Optimism. A Grade

An illustration of INCREASE emerges in the explanation Jesus gives on the subject of why he teaches through parables [42]. He explains that parables help listeners learn about the mysteries of the Kingdom of God. A parable is a story with a hidden message that only "spiritually opened" ears can fully hear. Ultimately, the purpose of parables is to get us out of duality thinking: they aim to expand our consciousness. In addition, if they are to have their effect on us, we need to do some careful listening and be ready for surprises. Our main calling is to listen to parables in such a way that we can allow them to challenge us. Parables like dreams have more than one meaning, and most people don't understand them when they come up. There is a surface meaning and a deeper layer. Parables like much of the bible provide us with deeper layers of meaning and spiritual growth as we open ourselves to receiving their wisdom. Simply put, you can't judge a book by its cover or circumstances by first impressions nor can you discern the meaning parables or most dreams by first impressions. The real value of parables is to raise questions that make us contemplate the answers that are not obvious rather than giving clear answers to questions implied by the parable. The benefits identified by this hexagram come from the gains in consciousness associated with getting multiple opinions and looking at things from different perspectives.

Getting INCREASE points to situations where new and unexpected ideas are presented to a group of likeminded people. It suggests that others are open to what you have to say and there's a good possibility of a breakthrough that helps everyone achieve something worthwhile. Your involvement in routine activities may come as a surprise and bring new learning opportunities to all concerned parties. This hexagram represents an opening to expand the awareness of others in ways that they have not encountered before. It also signals an excellent opportunity to broaden their understanding and gain new experience that will make everyone's life rewarding. Here, your effort to bring new understanding is taking root and this is one of the few times that can be described as lucky for all concerned.

INCREASE signals the start of new growth caused by breakthroughs in understanding. Depending on the circumstances, this new growth may be small or far-reaching, anticipated or unforeseen. You may be of service by initiating across-the-board changes to the conventional thoughts held by the people in your environment. The combination of Thunder surrounded by Wind advocates that new ways of thinking about usual opinions is on the rise. The pattern of INCREASE emerges in fields of study involving the development of new techniques that eventually touch the lives of millions of people. It brings emotional depth to ordinary viewpoints and this added dimension can expand what we know from the ordinary to the extraordinary. The events at hand make possible the widest expansion of awareness and the capacity to communicate this knowledge.

43
BREAKTHROUGH

Above: Lake *(Abraham, Introverted Intuition)*

Below: Heaven *(Jesus, Extroverted Intuition)*

Summary: Stepping Forward; Advancement through cooperation or teamwork; Getting through; Making a decision; Awakening or moving into consciousness; Speaking the truth openly. C+ Grade

The pattern of BREAKTHROUGH is seen in the last chapter of John about an event that took place just before Jesus shows himself to his disciples for the third and final time after his resurrection. Simon Peter goes out in his boat to fish with the other disciples but caught nothing that night. The next morning Jesus appears and says, *"Cast the net on the right side of the boat and you will find some [43]."*

Peter's statement about going fishing is significant because it shows a break in his service to Jesus to return to his old profession as a fisherman. His actions represent his conclusion about the state of affairs that took place regarding Jesus death. It also suggests that Peter and the other disciples had to have some form of livelihood until the power that Christ promised came to them. Even though Jesus' disciples did not recognize him when first appeared, they quickly discovered it was Jesus when they cast their net on the right side of the boat as requested and caught more fish than they could haul in. It took a demonstration of his power to awaken the disciples to his presence. The ultimate awakening symbolized by this hexagram appears in Jesus' return to give the power and authority he promised to his disciples so they could carry out his purpose. In this story, your position resembles the role played by Simon Peter in that he is the natural leader of the disciples who wait for Jesus to deliver the final rite of passage. When Jesus appears at sunrise the following morning he commands Peter to feed the other disciples and all of them dine together with Jesus.

BREAKTHROUGH serves as a message that people are now able to seek and find the answers to problems that have blocked their progress for some time. There is a potential for conflict with those who don't oppose your creative ideas, but have a different position. When this hexagram comes up you should look for the missing information that can add the needed credibility or solutions to what you are trying to manifest. It is wise to invite the participation of others to test the clarity of your thinking and prove the validity of what you are trying to say. Instead of assuming you have the answers, it is best to recruit the experience of others to help find ways to better express your creative thoughts.

Getting BREAKTHROUGH refers to a circumstance where your creative endeavor should be reviewed by someone else who has knowledge of your intentions. In general, one of two outcomes is likely. First, attempts to bring forth your vision will be completely understood, and accepted by those who know and appreciate what you are doing. Second, what you are attempting to create will not be understood or make sense. If your ideas pass peer review so-to-speak, success is likely but if your peers don't give them a pass you'll need to go back to the drawing board. The combination of Heaven surrounded by Lake represents moving your new ideas, visions or dreams from the unconscious to the conscious realm. In broad terms, this means the shifting of awareness that has been subjective and personal into the objective and collective realm.

44
COMING TO MEET

Above: Heaven *(Jesus, Extroverted Intuition)*

Below: Wind *(Aaron, Introverted Thinking)*

Summary: Temptation; Premature meeting, encounter, or coupling; A false appearance of reward; Excitement and potential confrontation; Attraction, enticement; A risk taking activity. D Grade

The famous parable of the Prodigal Son serves as an illustration of COMING TO MEET [38]. Simply put, it is the story of a man with two sons. The younger son asks his father for his inheritance now, rather than wait. His father agrees and this son quickly packs up everything, and moves out to a distant country. The son squanders his wealth in wild living and to make matters worse a famine came over the whole country. After spending all of his money, this son gets a job feeding pigs. While living in poverty he comes to himself. He then remembers his father's kindness, apologizes and asks if he can return home to work as a hired servant. The father has compassion, invites him back with open arms and throws big party to celebrate his homecoming. The elder son who never left his fathers home hated his younger brother's return and was angry at his father for accepting him back. It was legal to ask for his inheritance but up to the father whether to dispense it at the time or not. In rejecting his father's house, wisdom and love, the younger son demonstrated different priorities. The old saying, 'Be careful what you ask for, you may get it,' seems to apply here. Each of the characters has something to learn and let go. The expanded message of the parable appears in your answers to questions such as, why did the younger son really leave his father's house. Why does anyone want to leave home? What was his relationship to his father and his older brother? Why is the older brother upset with his return? What did each party learn? In the situation at hand, your position is similar to the younger son who wanted to branch out and experience the world. Like the younger son, you are acting on impulse in beginning the new experience before you and may well experience many unexpected surprises.

COMING TO MEET deals with eager attempts to teach and expand the awareness of other people. By acting before thinking things through, you run the risk of presenting confusion and lowering your credibility. Because your preparation has been shallow, attempts to enlighten others appear childish which can make your intended course unfortunate and even dangerous. As you push forward with half-baked knowledge your actions will may be resisted, and force significant changes in your life and the lives of others. Getting this hexagram may have the powerful effect of causing you to make big adjustments in your plans.

COMING TO MEET refers to a circumstance where you are unwittingly about to introduce rather commonplace thinking to highly evolved individuals. It's as if you've been living in another world and now find yourself transported to a world inhabited by unfamiliar people. Your aim for normal communications may appear to go well in the short-run but needed wisdom still remains invisible to you. In the situation at hand, actions you take to get ahead are likely to end with embarrassment. The combination of Wind surrounded by Heaven suggests that since you are not looking for or ready to accept the expertise to accomplish your purpose, you would do well to step back, let go of your opinions, and ask for help.

45
GATHERING TOGETHER

Above: Lake *(Abraham, Introverted Intuition)*

Below: Earth *(David, Introverted Sensing)*

Summary: An Assembly, reunion or association of like-minded people; A spiritual meeting, congregation or community; Coming together around moral and spiritual goals. <u>A Grade</u>

An illustration of GATHERING TOGETHER comes to mind in the story of the short, wealthy and hated tax collectors conversion. As the story goes a short, wealthy man, named Zaccaheus goes out of his way to see Jesus by running ahead on the path Jesus was heading, climbing into a tree, and waiting for him to pass by. When Jesus sees him up in the tree, he invites himself to dinner with the man and accepts his contrition. Jesus speaks to the audience by saying, *"I came to save those who were lost [45]."*

The evidence of the man's sincerity and purpose is the fact that he runs ahead to where he knows Jesus will pass. When Jesus meets the man and invites himself to dinner at his house he intuitively knows the man's longing and faith in spite of his wealth. In reaction to the shame and criticism his profession brings on Jesus for meeting with him, he offers to give half of his possessions to the poor and pay restitution to any he has wronged to the tune of four times the amount he cheated them. Jesus sees that his acts of repentance are both genuine and required in order to eliminate the shame from himself and from Jesus for associating with him. Jesus insists that Zaccaheus has received salvation, accepts him as a fledgling disciple, and calls on the neighbors to welcome and accept him. Your role in the situation represented by this hexagram resembles that of the wealthy tax collector who decides to pursue a higher calling. This story is an example of spiritual reunion and puts forward that no matter how bad things have been you can always seek God's help and choose the path of reunion.

GATHERING TOGETHER refers to situations where one or more individuals are inspired to follow the teachings of a spiritual philosophy and leader. It suggests that you are both pursuing and assisting others in the development of understanding and wisdom. While an opportunity to assist others and expand the consciousness of all concerned parties at the same time is likely, you will have to recognize and take it. You may now gather with and sustain others in the accomplishment of common spiritual growth goals. The state of affairs before you point to the presence of teachings about the human soul that can change your relationship to the Divine in all-encompassing ways. Your desire to support others may well increase your sensitivity and deepen your understanding of spiritual truths.

GATHERING TOGETHER corresponds to an environment where you are motivated to serve and support spiritual leaders whose wisdom has been acknowledge. Your position is that of the obedient servant who delights in serving his guru. It represents situations where people support organizations such as churches, synagogues, mosques, ashrams and other spiritual assemblies. In each case, we find individuals, groups, or collectives united behind the guidance of someone believed to have great spiritual knowledge. Both GATHERING TOGETHER (45) and HOLDING TOGETHER (8) refer to meetings where learning takes. The difference is that this hexagram refers to spirit centered meetings and learning whereas Hexagram 8 refers to secular meetings and learning environments.

46
ASCENDING

___ ___
___ ___
___ ___ Above: Earth *(David, Introverted Sensing)*
____
____
___ ___ Below: Wind *(Aaron, Introverted Thinking)*

Summary: Promoting; Pushing or growing upward; Practical everyday outreach or advancement; Advancing or rising in connections to others; Attaining a higher rank or status. A Grade

The story of a Widow's Offering provides us with an example of ASCENDING. In it Jesus sees rich men giving large offerings to the synagogue, and then a poor widow quietly giving two pennies. Upon seen this he says, *"Of a truth I say to you, that this poor widow has given more than all of the rich men. For they all contributed out of their abundance, but she out of her poverty put in all the living that she had [46]."*

On the surface, this destitute woman would be the last person you'd expect to be generous to God. By giving all she had, she gave a one-hundred percent tithe. Unlike the rich men, her gift was quiet without pomp, circumstance or show. The message is that divine economics is not measured by the face value of currency and that gifts don't measure how much we give, but how much we keep. The story tells us that those who give large gifts may make a small sacrifice while the person who makes a small gift may make a huge sacrifice. In relation to this pattern your position, like the poor widow's, has no pretension in that your gift of reaching out to others comes from the place of saying ‘have a nice day,’ rather than the loud place of saying, ‘notice what I am doing.’ Your effort to assist the community is an act of love to serve your neighbor and the presence of God that dwells in every one. Your growth and promotion in the situation at hand exceeds that achieved by those of greater means because it comes from the heart rather than the pocket.

The existence of ASCENDING serves as a message that you are stepping into the limelight, either on a small or large scale. It comes at a time when you do not have to be strong or competent to succeed because the natural flow of events around you is tolerant and helpful. Nevertheless, you should examine your actions as a whole to see if they are taking you the direction you want. In general, your open and communicative manner gives you an opportunity to connect with the right people through friendly associations.

ASCENDING corresponds to social gatherings or groups of like-minded individuals within a larger community. Your position resembles the friendly neighbor who connects with others while they go about their workday. Your desire to communicate with people such as neighbors, the working class, and professionals should bring affable, down-to-earth exchanges. The pattern of expansion represented by this hexagram appears in news reporting through the various media such as radio talk shows, broadcast news, and in the movie and entertainment industries that meet general public interest needs. Wind below Earth emerges in structures such as subways, buildings, plumbing pipes, and in conventional jobs such as bookkeeping, law enforcement and carpentry. From the perspective of Jungian types, introverted thinking below and introverted earth above suggests that your interest in getting insights that fit with your ideas will materialize in an environment that requires you to support its subjective impressions of objective reality more than objective reality itself.

47
ADVERSITY

___ ___
____
_______ Above: Lake *(Abraham, Introverted Intuition)*
___ ___
____
___ ___ Below: Water *(Joseph, Introverted Feeling)*

Summary: Exhaustion; Oppression; Mental tension, worry, anxiety; Weariness, destitution, fatigue; Calamity; Hard luck; Stifling situations; Trouble; Dilemmas. F Grade

The illustration of ADVERSITY comes into view in a verse from the Beatitudes that announce favor toward those who aspire to live under God's rule. In it Jesus says*, "Bless are those who hunger and thirst for righteousness, for they shall be satisfied [47]."*

It makes sense that those who desire righteousness would avoid actively what is not righteousness. When there is honesty and genuine acceptance of Divine ideas then all things will be in right relationship. To desire honesty in yourself is to desire that you are living in line with the person you are and not in rebellion to it. This means knowing your identity and living in close contact with your intuitive and spiritual nature. The blessing of righteousness is evident when the desire to do God's will is so deep and so intense, that you know you cannot live without it, even when faced with troubling emotions. The righteousness of God is present whenever you catch God's ideas and act upon them. In fact, the great message of the bible from beginning to end is this: to be happy you must truly seek righteousness. Your position in this verse is like those who follow their own nature but find the strength to release it in order to align it with Divine wisdom. The state of affairs represented by this hexagram always presents the dilemma: follow the course of your own nature or the path of inner wisdom.

ADVERSITY refers to having strong internal urges and feelings on a collision course with the equally strong spiritual truths and wisdom. It comes up at times when the direction you want to take is uncertain and your understanding of the action you need to take is limited. The anxiety represented by this hexagram may push you to walk away from a relationship, an oppressive job or your place of residence, without warning anyone. Despite every effort to free yourself, circumstances and duties seem to hold you back and keep you stuck. When it comes up it is likely that you are looking for answers to understand some of the difficult feelings you're having.

ADVERSITY often points to situations where your personal thoughts may be on display to the people around you. It refers to an environment where people around you understand the intentions of your heart. An example of Water below Lake can be seen in situations where people cautiously approach those they believe have the wisdom they seek, such as individuals who might help them to interpret their dreams, read their subconscious thoughts, or comprehend a troubling personal mystery. They want to hear the truth and at the same time they are not sure they believe it or will follow what it says. This trigram combination represents an opportunity to have your inner world and character assessed with the aim of thinking more clearly about it. While this is a good thing, it can be troubling. When you gain clarity about an unconscious pattern you will gain awareness, but instead of getting peace of mind, it may bring transformation, conflict and psychic turmoil.

48
THE WELL

___ ___
____
___ ___ Above: Water *(Joseph, Introverted Feeling)*
____
____
___ ___ Below: Wind *(Aaron, Introverted Thinking)*

Summary: Expanded consciousness; Renewal; Increasing awareness of your essential nature; Self-discovery; Source; Reservoir of knowledge available to help all users. A- Grade

An illustration of THE WELL is seen in the most popular New Testament prayer given by Jesus when he is asks by one of his disciples if will teach them how to pray. Jesus replies, *"Our Father who is in heaven, Hallowed be thy name. Thy kingdom come; thy will be done, as in heaven so in earth. Give us each day our daily bread; and forgive us our sins, for we forgive everyone who is indebted to us. And lead us not into temptation; but deliver us from evil [48]."*

This deceptively simple prayer begins by acknowledging that there is only one God, one Divine source, and one Life that is whole, perfect, complete and free of sin. The second sentence, like the first one, points to balance toward Divine rather than human actions. It is a request for the Divine to execute its purpose on earth. It is also teaches us to recognize that because we are one with God, we have access to all that God has. The last two sentences teach us that we have access to all that God has if we can truly accept it. Jesus tells us that God meets all of our needs such as giving knowledge, healing, the ability to earn a living and the gifs we have, and is the source of our daily bread. In addition to continual forgiveness, Jesus tells us to depend upon God to help us in times of temptation. In the circumstances represented by this hexagram your position resembles one whose affirmative prayers are received by God and will be answered in a way fitting for your request and according to God's will and timing.

Getting THE WELL is a message that the people in your environment are involved in personal growth efforts and learning from consciousness-raising teachings. It points to an opportunity to socialize with groups who can help you fulfill your dreams. Even though you may affirm and sense the truth, and trust the knowledge of well-schooled individuals, you should validate what they have to offer before acting on it. By being sociable and friendly toward others, those you encounter will aid in the growth and expansion your awareness. If you keep an open mind, you will receive beneficial opportunities for self-expression, learning, or teaching others. Through everyday social contacts with others the result tends to be character building that enriches your life and helps you attain self-understanding as well.

THE WELL comes as a reminder that your success in the situation at hand will rely upon your friendly manner of connecting with the people in your circle. It suggests that your desire to reach out and interact with others is taking place in a community of well-trained individuals. In nature and in human consciousness the combination of Wind below Water represents the unseen spirit that animates every living creature that moves upon land, within the waters, and dwells in the secret life of plants. In everyday life, this combination implies that your approach to the talented but unrecognized personalities in your world is open and responsive. It suggests that you are part of a community of individuals with great knowledge, such as unlimited internet connections, a faith community or association of professionals. Whatever gathering of talent it is, you are in the right place at the right time to ask for and receive what they have to offer.

49
DESTROYING THE OLD

Above: Lake *(Abraham, Introverted Intuition)*

Below: Fire *(Jacob, Extroverted Thinking)*

Summary: Changing, Revolution, Overturning; Letting go; Transformation; Upheaval; A significant change in content appearance, or direction; Self-renewal. B Grade

An example of DESTROYING THE OLD can be seen in Jesus' message to his disciples when he says, *"Do not think that I have come to bring peace on earth; I have not come to bring peace but a sword. For I have come to set a man against his father, and a daughter against her mother, and a daughter-in-law against her mother-in-law and a man's foes will be those of his own household [49]."*

Jesus sees that acceptance of his message with its promise also brings destruction. Only those who believe in his teachings and accept the threat of destruction will find life. His words are direct and essentially tell his followers not to expect a warm. Teaching the gospel reveals the truth, and people become your enemies. The kind of spiritual sword that Jesus is talking about invisibly severs a man from his father, and daughter from her mother and so on. He says that no matter what the cost, one must follow him to the end, even if it means giving up one's family. However, this applies only if the family rejects the new covenant, not if the family accepts him. Examples of the sobering warning in Jesus' message appear in the ongoing acts of releasing your thoughts to catch God's ideas. In this teaching, your position resembles the faithful disciple who leads others to Divine truth.

DESTROYING THE OLD is a sign that says, "the world is changing" or is going to change so much that your experience of the circumstances at hand will no longer have the meaning they once had. It is a message to learn about the coming new environment instead of resisting the opportunities this wisdom will bring. By letting go of old approaches to leading others you open the door to learning what is new and right. Here, your success will depend on moving at the right time, while failure will come from premature changes or changes that come too late. Since it is difficult to see what will happen in the immediate future, it is best to err on the side of caution and then make changes as soon as possible after things begin to change. In this way, your change is well timed but not the first evidence of change.

DESTROYING THE OLD is a message that your attempt to take charge has come face-to-face with those who represent a philosophy of that may not agree with you. Although you want to direct people, the knowledge of those wiser than you must be recognized and supported if you are to be effective. In general, you can only lead other people when they respect your status as a person of knowledge. If you know less than they know, it is better to define yourself as a student. When and if your awareness is on the same level or greater, leadership may be possible. In Jungian terms, the presence of extroverted thinking below and introverted intuition above depicts situations where your interest in facts and practical problem solving is expressed in an environment where people make changes based on their intuitive understanding. The combination of Fire below Lake produces an interest in "big picture" ideas rather than detailed procedures or facts. When this hexagram comes up it is likely that your will attract others whose goals compliment your goals.

50
BUILDING THE NEW

Above: Fire *(Jacob, Extroverted Thinking)*

Below: Wind *(Aaron, Introverted Thinking)*

Summary: Improvement; Cauldron; Cosmic Order; Transformational work; A gathering between leaders; Significant effort to bring peace and order. B Grade

The third Beatitude near the beginning of the Sermon on the Mount gives us an illustration of BUILDING OF THE NEW. In it Jesus says, *"Blessed are the meek for they shall inherit the earth [50]."*

While those who are strongly competitive and assertive are the ones who receive outer recognition, admiration, and rewards, while meekness is the virtue blessed by the Divine.

A meek person is gentle, tenderhearted, patient and submissive on the one hand, but cool, calm and collected on the other hand. True meekness is power under control: for instance, a domesticated horse is useful but an undomesticated one is destructive; a gentle breeze cools and soothes but a hurricane kills. As strength under control, meekness goes beyond simply being nice. The truly meek admit that they are insufficient to cope with the complexities, pressures and obstacles of life, and they trust that God will guide their actions. Your position in the saying by Jesus resembles the meek individual who understands and serves the will of God. Because your approach is one of meekness in the current situation, significant work in your community can be advanced with a spirit of cooperation.

In general, BUILDING THE NEW refers to meetings between leaders and influential people. When it comes up your position is like the leader who works with other leaders in positions of power and authority. The state of affairs it represents resembles a gathering of rulers such as department heads, spiritual leaders, CEO and individuals who hold sway over others. The combination of Wind below Fire brings together your friendly communicative style of Wind with the recognized authority figures represented by Fire. Your effort to extend the hand of fellowship may lead to the result of a summit or gathering of important people with the shared vision of exploring new ideas. This paring suggests warm atmospheres in nature and human interactions, and the potential for clarity. In Jungian terms, your perspective of introverted thinking seeks to express itself in an environment that demands a focus on concrete facts and practical solutions to problems.

BUILDING THE NEW suggests that you are able to understand your duties and responsibilities for helping those who lead other people. In addition to cooperation and unity, it also associated with the establishment of new orders. In the situation at hand, unity extends from your private world to your immediate circle, and to the universe at large. This hexagram points to flashes of inspiration that help you solve problems in the larger social order. If you continue to have faith and understanding about the subject at hand, your purpose will remain clear. Getting this hexagram is a message to heal the social order instead of limiting your focus to personal concerns. It also suggests that you would do well in work that engages people in leadership positions.

51
SHOCKING

— —
— —
——— Above: Thunder *(Isaac, Extroverted Feeling)*
— —
— —
——— Below: Thunder *(Isaac, Extroverted Feeling)*

Summary: Arousing; Mobilizing; Shaking; A challenge to one's sense of order; Affected by external factors; Earthquake, alarm, or sudden awakening. <u>C+ Grade</u>

The life of Isaac as presented in the book of Genesis personifies the meaning of SHOCKING and serves as an example of how the events represented by this hexagram are expressed in the lives of those who receive it. Of the three patriarchs Abraham, Isaac and Jacob the least is recorder about Isaac, not because he was any less significant or righteous, but because he lived in a more settled time. The whole meaning of his life is bound up with his father Abraham and Isaac's son Jacob in that his importance consist less of his actions than in the unexpected, shadow-like, ways he is acted upon by others. First, his life begins when God makes and keeps a promise to Abraham that he and his wife Sarah will have a son even though they are stricken with old age [51]. God tells Abraham that this son will be father of a nation and that his seed will appear in all nations on earth. Second, God tests Abraham's faith and love by commanding him to kill his son Isaac. After Abraham agrees to God's demand and nearly kills his son as requested, he passes God's test, averts the moment of crises, and does not have sacrifice Isaac. Third, Isaac's blindness and senility allows his second son Jacob to trick him, steal his blessing, and inherit God's covenant. By speaking to the unexpected, dark events of Isaac's life, these stories offer insights into your experience with the circumstances represented by this hexagram. In this narrative, your position resembles the role played by Isaac in that you are a catalyst for sweeping change, but not in control of the forces working through you to create them.

When SHOCKING comes up an event in the flow of your life has crystallized into a rigid pattern that no longer allows for change. As a result, change is taking place whether you like it or not. Its presence is natural and calls you to re-examine your view as well as the views of others. You may experience what is taking place as a threat to your way of life or some structure that has become routine and comfortable. Relationships often change in unexpected ways, but this will depend upon how much each partner is open to new and challenging experiences. Although most people react with shock, fear, and panic when this hexagram comes up, it is possible to accept the present moment without drama. On one hand, the elements in your situation may create the life-giving energy to produce advancement; on the other, it signals letting go of something significant.

SHOCKING is the archetype that reveals the sudden result of God's manifestation into the conscious realm. The symbol of Thunder below and above serves the purpose of first identifying and then completely discarding patterns that have blocked the way for personal and social growth. While the events expressed through it are often feared, and unexpected, their existence clears the air and can be an asset once they are accepted. From the perspective of Jungian types, extroverted feeling is mainly dependent upon and usually accepts the ideals, conventions and customs of their environment. As such, your feelings and the feelings of the people related to you will tend to mirror those reflected by the community.

52
KEEPING STILL

———
— —
— — Above: Mountain *(Moses, Extroverted Sensing)*
———
— —
— — Below: Mountain *(Moses, Extroverted Sensing)*

Summary: Immobility; Bound; Submitting to tangible forms; The five senses; The absence of motion; Influenced mainly by appearances and outer events; Situations that prevent passage; Retreat, stop. C- Grade

The events in the life of Moses personify KEEPING STILL [52]. He represents the first true hero archetype in the bible. He is the shy and reluctant savior of Israel who reflects all of the traits of a traditional hero. Moses mediates between God and the people of Israel as he leads them from Egyptian bondage to the Promised Land and transforms them from an oppressed ethnic group into a nation founded on religious laws. He is the only person in the bible ever to know God "face-to-face." Moses is God's representative and in time makes God's relationship with the people of Israel a personal one. The circumstances represented by this hexagram have straight-forward connections to following the law in that four of the first five books of the Old Testament are devoted to activities under the leadership of Moses, the primary law giver in the bible. A few months after Moses and the Israelites arrive at Mount Sinai, he climbs the mountain to commune with God for forty days, and God gives him two stone tablets with Ten Commandments inscribed on them. They deal with ethical behavior as well as an extended series of laws regarding worship, sacrifice, social justice, and personal property. Those who receive this hexagram are should be still and recognize the presence in God before taking action. At the highest level, your position resembles that of Moses: leader of an established group, someone who listens to and acts for God, to convey a new way of life.

KEEPING STILL stands as a symbol of being still, centered, and focused. It suggests that without understandable rules for behavior it is foolish to advance. By waiting for clear signs on when to act, you can increase the possibility for growth and progressive action. Since thoughts about the future will only cause agitation and worry, it is better to pay attention to the present and dispel illusions of what can or will be. Getting this hexagram implies that the call to be still, centered, and rise above appearances is best dealt with by taking no action until the signs for doing so have been made clear. More than at other times, the present state of affairs demands greater control over your desire to act and take matters into your own hands.

KEEPING STILL refers to following established traditions, authority and ways of life from both private and public perspectives. It represents the development of regulations and the way of life regarding these regulations. It is not merely following a set of rules and restrictions given as guidelines, but rather a notion of rules as a way of life for all concerned parties. Social traditions and time-honored laws about how you should behave and treat others are signs of the Mountain trigram that you can recognize and share. In this sense respecting culturally defined laws are less a means of achieving actions of goodness than it is a way for people to show their commitment to practical agreements.

53
DEVELOPMENT

———
———
— —   Above: Wind *(Aaron, Introverted Thinking)*
———
— —
— —   Below: Mountain *(Moses, Extroverted Sensing)*

Summary: Gradual progress; Growth that proceeds unhurried in degrees; Steady step-by-step improvement; Evolution; Progression from a simple form to a more complex form. B Grade

An example of DEVELOPMENT is seen in one of the of the most popular New Testament verses in the Gospel of John that says, *"For God so loved the world that he gave his only Son that whoever believes in him should not perish but have eternal life [53]."*

The subject of God's love includes the sum total of the material universe and all the people living in the world. The word Son refers of all people who show maturity in expressing their relationship and likeness to God's character. The phrase only Son refers to one's Divine Self. Taken as a whole, the verse tells us that God loved the world and the people in it enough to join in their lives. Repeatedly in the New Testament God says that whoever believes shall obtain salvation and have eternal life. The call to come to Christ or reunite with God is an invitation to all. It is also evident that the believers who consistently seek God's ideas are fulfilling God's purpose for his or her life, and becoming one of God's elect. The message of this verse is one of following the ways of life spelled out in the teaching of Christ and the direct discernment of God's ideas. You can sustain your connection with God by fellowship with others and through growth in your in spiritual awareness. While God alone knows the point at which a person receives the message of salvation, your job is to lay the foundation for salvation to take place. The gift of salvation is free and available to all, but you must take the invitation and exhibit great patience to receive it.

DEVELOPMENT refers to steady improvement and growth that proceeds bit by bit toward the same goal. The gradual and unexciting course ahead demands caution and endurance from those who work toward their objectives. While this process is not glamorous and the ability to influence others is small, divinely guided actions along this course lead to lasting accomplishments. As a whole, the situation at hand contains an opportunity for growth in consciousness toward what is good for you and all concerned parties. In time, this kind of development reaches the highest levels attained by the intellectual and spiritual leaders of all time.

DEVELOPMENT emerges as a message to persuade and control the people in your circle in a friendly manner. It implies that you can achieve the results you are seeking by using the sensible, realistic approach to direct individuals in accord with you. The presence of Mountain below Wind is symbolic of the working relationship between the strong but humble Moses and his friendly brother Aaron. As a team they lead the Israelites out of Egypt and toward the Promised Land, and laid the foundations for new laws and customs as a way of life for their people. In the circumstances represented by this hexagram, you are called upon to use your inner sense of authority to direct the people in your group in an agreeable manner. To achieve the progress you seek requires deliberate and consistent efforts to communicate with the people who share your vision.

54
THE OUTSIDE PARTNER

___ ___
___ ___
_______ Above: Thunder *(Isaac, Extroverted Feeling)*
___ ___
____
_______ Below: Lake *(Abraham, Introverted Intuition)*

Summary: The Marrying Maiden; An improper match; Subordinate; A mistress or second spouse; Inferior partner; A secondary relationship outside the primary one. C- Grade

An example of THE OUTSIDE PARTNER can be seen in the verse where Jesus says, *"But who ever causes one of these little ones who believe in me to sin, it would be better for him to have a great millstone fastened around his neck and to be drowned in the depth of the sea [54]."*

In this verse and three just before it Jesus teaches that every believer is important and every effort is put forth to preserve their spiritual well-being. He encourages his followers by telling them that while their role as believers will draw insults from the world upon them God will not abandon them. Believers in both the teachings of Jesus and God's truth revealed through their intuitive and spiritual nature often find themselves in environments surrounded by people with different beliefs. The offending party in the verse is any one causing another to sin, and the lesser party is the "little one" or believer. People disrespect the godly and modest when they treat them with distain. We offend believers when we cause them to stumble or fall off the right course. Your position resembles one of the little ones who are preyed upon by an offending party in spite of having faith in Christ. You should make every effort to keep your faith alive, even though those outside of your relationship may not respect your faith in God. Even though you may have stumbled in the situation represented by this hexagram or made a poor choice you should know that God's help is available to you at all times.

THE OUTSIDE PARTNER refers to relationships where you are in an inferior role that is fraught with difficulties. This position is not the result of conscious effort, promotion or demotion, but rather by unwittingly making a poor choice. Apart from meeting certain of their needs, those in control have little concern for what you can offer. To avoid the conflict implied by this hexagram it is best to look toward the big picture and choose what is right within this framework. Since your previous knowledge is of limited use in the current situation, it is better to stay in the background and remain quiet. Troubles are inevitable when you are in the restricted role of being a lesser partner and all that this entails.

Getting THE OUTSIDE PARTNER implies that your position as a subordinate is similar to that of a knowledgeable person who has come face-to-face with unwanted and unexpected behavior. The combination of Lake under Thunder suggests that your awareness of right and wrong is a challenge to your sensibilities. Even though you have good judgment about most things this situation has usurped this power. It's as if you suddenly find yourself in the role of the prey cornered by a feared predator. When this hexagram comes up you should attempt to grasp the nature of events as they come into view. In personal relationships, for instance, your faith in the powers of Spirit may be tested by external "pressure-cooker" conditions that cause you to lose your commonsense.

55
ABUNDANCE

```
___ ___
___ ___
_______      Above: Thunder (Isaac, Extroverted Feeling)
_______
___ ___
_______      Below: Fire (Jacob, Extroverted Thinking)
```

Summary: Ambition achieved; Goal reached; The attainment of fullness; Peak; Summit; The highest possible point; Fulfillment beyond expectations; Relative wealth; Maximum. <u>B Grade</u>

The story of healing a Centurion's servant comes into view as an illustration of ABUNDANCE. In it, Jesus commends the great faith of the Roman Centurion, a Gentile, who came to him seeking healing for his paralyzed servant. When Jesus offers to come and heal the servant, the Centurion tells him that just speaking his word will heal the servant. The servants healing takes place within the hour and Jesus says to his followers, *"Truly I say to you, not even in Israel have I found such faith [55]."*

In curing the servant based on his master's faith, Jesus implies that his followers had too little faith in the Divine to receive their healing. The curing of the Centurion's servant through the faith of another, points to the possibility of a similar cure for believers. The miracle is not that the faithful Centurion approached Jesus on behalf of his servant, but that his faith is much greater than the faith of Jesus followers. By calling attention to the example of this one Gentile, Jesus promises all faithful Gentiles entry into the kingdom of God. In curing the servant, Jesus points beyond his ministry among Jews to all people of faith. This story teaches that faith is the key to participation in the kingdom and not status. It implies that anyone with great faith may become a revealer of the Divine and receive its blessings. In this story, your position is like that of the faithful Centurion who requested healing for his servant.

Getting ABUNDANCE refers to receiving an added blessing that extends the result of your effort beyond what was expected. It serves as a sign that events beyond your control bring greater recognition than anticipated for your effort. The present level of attainment has a lot to do with a natural unforeseen occurrence that coincides with your effort to lead, but is not dependent upon it. Although you do only what is needed, the events represented by this hexagram produce unexpected credit. In spite of this result, you should continue to communicate your interests and encourage others to support them.

ABUNDANCE implies that your effort to take the lead will bring changes that go beyond your intended goals. It's as if you are getting credit for creating positive outcomes that were waiting to happen. The combination of Fire below Thunder suggests that people perceived you to be the cause of a sudden and often far-reaching event. When this hexagram comes up you have the potential to direct people in making broad changes. Because people respect your intention to inspire others, your acceptance of this new role is should be well received. This hexagram has some connection to BITTING THROUGH (21) in which Fire and Thunder come together in reverse order. In Hexagram 21 some wrongdoing that needs correcting takes place, but here things are in their proper order and surprising growth takes place.

56
THE WANDER

Above: Fire *(Jacob, Extroverted Thinking)*

Below: Mountain *(Moses, Extroverted Sensing)*

Summary: Shifting in and out of focus; Changing; Rambling; Traveling; Indecision; Something present for a limited time; Having different feelings and views without resolving anything; Temporary. C- Grade

The story of a woman caught in adultery is an example of THE WANDER. Here the religious authorities bring an adulterous woman before Jesus to get his agreement to stone her to death according to the Law of Moses. As they corner Jesus and ask him to agree with the Law permitting stoning for punishment he replies, *"He that is without sin among you, let him cast the first stone at her [56]."*

Everyone became silent when Jesus spoke this one sentence, and everyone departs beginning with the eldest because he had the most sin to hide. These religious authorities brought the adulterous woman to Jesus not because they were shocked at her conduct or grieved that she broke God's holy law, but rather to use her to accomplish their intentions against him. They were anxious to discredit him before the people, but Jesus showed mercy. This narrative tells us that judging between right and wrong based on appearances is both necessary and forgivable. However, because we cannot see a person's entire life, judging to put someone to death is eternal damnation and reserved only for

God. This story is symbolic of your situation, and the religious authorities represent your position. By acknowledging the two extremes, and introducing a spiritual rather than literal judgment the conflict between the Laws on the one hand and Jesus' mission to fulfill the Law on the other hand the conflict gets resolved.

Getting THE WANDER is a sign that you feel the pull of different possibilities. On the one hand, there is an urge toward facts and the letter of the law and on the other hand, the urge toward principle and the spirit of the law. These attitudes are temporary and dissolve into unity in the end, but the dilemmas they present bring opportunities to scrutinize existing aspirations and circumstances. In the situation you face now, this is a poor time to make big decisions because of conflicting feelings, and you should not lose site of larger objectives. As you focus on one conclusion or course of action, other considerations come up that cause you to change your outlook. Since the desires to go forward, do nothing, and retreat are all present, it is best to look beyond appearances and seek the comfort of Divine guidance.

THE WANDER points to a clash between your intention to pursue a conventional path and conditions that call for thinking beyond the traditional order. Your desire to manage things according to traditional guidelines has come face to face with someone else or other information that pulls you in another direction. The combination of Mountain below Fire refers to a state of affairs where your conservative bit-by-bit approach does not support the expansive liberal perspectives help by other people. It brings to light the alternating pull between the inspired unrestrained style and the restricted matter-of-fact style of guiding people. This combination is stressful because the back and forth yearning to taking care of details must make room for an equal need to deal with larger goals.

57
THE GENTLE

Above: Wind *(Aaron, Introverted Thinking)*

Below: Wind *(Aaron, Introverted Thinking)*

Summary: Subtle influence; Progress through submission and mildness; Movement free from aggression; Effects produces by gradual and inconspicuous progress; Values ideas, theories, archetypes; Seeks similarities. C+ Grade

An illustration of THE GENTLE comes into view through the story of Aaron [57]. From beginning to end he used his excellent ability to communicate with the people, carried out the commands entrusted to him, and faithfully assisted his brother Moses in leading the Israelites out of Egypt.. Aaron is the bearer of intellectual light to the Israelites and personifies the power of communications and rational awareness of the Divine. Even though he is only the mouthpiece for his brother, he is able to express his thoughts in fitting language, and to bring out what his great brother had planned. Although he didn't have the patient endurance and calm self-command of Moses, he was earnest in his devotion to God and his people. God designated Aaron to be the first High Priest in Israel and father of the Levites who descended through him to become the priests of Israel for years to come. These priests and ministers acted as Gods ordained mediators to receive the gifts of the people and officiate over ceremonies. They represent religious thought and the love faculty in individual consciousness, more than spiritual wisdom. The service they provide becomes the directive power of a new state of consciousness. Your experience with the circumstances represented by this hexagram is like Aaron's in that your ability to communicate will have significant value to all. Like Aaron, your role calls for skilled communications to carry out the difficult work of moving toward freedom and a new way of thinking.

THE GENTLE refers to gradual and inconspicuous influence like spirit animating living matter and causing objects to move while it itself is invisible. It represents the kind of expansion that accumulates, builds up, and reinforces itself in the process of thinking and doing. This hexagram deals with person-to-person contacts, and has a certain connection to THE JOYOUS (58) which teaches us to communicate with the Divine. Hexagram 57 has a lot to do with personal development, while Hexagram 58 has more to do with spiritual development. Even though progress is nearly certain, it calls for sustained effort over the long run to eliminate those elements that have become unnecessary and limiting, replacing them with superior constructs.

THE GENTLE is the archetype of friendships, meetings, and social interactions. Your welcomed desire to connect with others suggests a pleasant and easygoing outcome. This hexagram represents gatherings between like-minded people, friends, and those with common interests. Additional examples of this pattern can be seen in gatherings such as partnership meetings, church fellowships and family gatherings. Like the seven other patriarch hexagrams made up of two identical trigrams (1, 2, 29, 30, 51, 52, and 58) this one shows accord between personal intentions and social circumstances.

58
THE JOYOUS

— —
———
——— Above: Lake *(Abraham, Introverted Intuition)*
— —
———
——— Below: Lake *(Abraham, Introverted Intuition)*

Summary: Understanding; Openness; Faith; Inspiration; Philosophical perspective; Intuitiveness; Teaching; Well-being; Encouragement; Centered; Happiness. B Grade

The story of Abraham personifies THE JOYOUS. Abraham represents the qualities through which humankind has faith in invisible forces, without seeing any objective evidence. Chosen by God, Abraham is the first patriarch and spiritual grandfather of Christians, Jews and Muslims. God established his covenant with Abraham, and developed an ongoing personal relationship with the Israelites through Abraham's descendants [58]. He represents faith and the intuitive powers of the mind to manifest God's ideas in unlimited expressions of matter. Getting this hexagram suggests that by faithfully paying attention to Spirit through your intuitive nature and following its wisdom, you can develop a partnership with the deeper mind and open your self to its nature. Nowadays, spiritually developed people of insight and vision are people of faith in God's promise. Like Abraham, your spiritual development must rely upon belief in the Divine in order to accept its wisdom and make things of substance.

THE JOYOUS is a sign of understanding the Divine either through rational methods, such as taking classes and reading books, or through experiential means such as intuition or meditation. It represents the making of bold plans, innovation, greater than usual perception, and the faith to believe in the unseen. Under its influence, people feel confident about their views and listen to others without feeling threatened by their views. Getting this hexagram is a reminder to share your intuitive insights about the Divine and reveal your deepest and most persistent private knowledge about the inner Self. The situation at hand serves as a message to think about whether your goals are internally generated, or adopted from other people.

THE JOYOUS is a symbol of perception and knowledge of the correct relationship between individuals and God. It stands for your intuitive and spiritual nature and entails the potential for direct contact with the Universal Mind. It deals with understanding Spirit and its ideas for humankind. The combination of Lake above and below points to faith, and to people who trust their insights about the relationships and meanings of things regardless of established beliefs. These trigrams often represent initiators, inventors, promoters and people having no taste for life as it is. In general, this hexagram describes a state of affairs where all parties have some knowledge of the same philosophical concepts. It deals with intuition and expressing oneself through subjective perceptions: the metaphor, imagination, symbols, and visions from the Divine. They are also a sign of excitement and self-expression, and imply little patience for the demands of daily routines and regulations.

59
RELEASING

———
———
— — Above: Wind *(Aaron, Introverted Thinking)*
— —
———
— — Below: Water *(Joseph, Introverted Feeling)*

Summary: Disintegration; Separation; Not seen by others; Scattering; Breaking up rigid thinking and opinions; Prejudged; Misperception; Gaining knowledge to overcome ignorance. C- Grade

An example of RELEASING appears in the verse of Scripture from John's Gospel that explains the existence of Jesus in the following way: *"He was in the world, and the world was made by him, and the world knew him not [59]."*

While there was some knowledge of Christ throughout the world in the beginning among Adam and his offspring it was forgot and lost. For many thousands of years nearly all of humankind didn't know the one true God and were without Christ until the time of Jesus. Throughout Jesus' life time just about all of the inhabitants of the world did not see him as their Creator: nor did they acknowledge the mercies they received from him; nor did they worship, serve, love or know Christ. After his death, a great number of people have come to know him as the Messiah, Mediator between God and humankind, Redeemer, and Saviour. This Scripture implies that Jesus lives in the body of ideas where the physical limitations of form do not exist. When we have grasped the power of his spiritual ideas, his appearance is understood. Your position in this verse resembles those who know, believe and have faith in Jesus. This knowledge, faith and belief is often expressed by catching God's ideas as revealed through your intuitive and spiritual nature. Even though you mingle with others and converse with them, they do not see or acknowledge what you have to offer. When this hexagram comes up your situation is one of being both invisible to and apart from the people in your environment.

RELEASING refers to situations where other people judge you by outer appearances rather than the content of your character. Under its influence your personal feelings, talents and goals are of little interest to other people as they have completely different interests. Even though most people have great value in the right milieu, they have no value or respect in the wrong environment. Getting this hexagram often gives an opportunity for personal growth because it brings to light many beliefs, attitudes, and perceptions that are simply not true. The situation here is often unsettling to all parties because each is unseen by the other and ignored by them as well. This outcome is not necessarily intentional, but rather the result of seeing only your own interests and views.

RELEASING comes about when the people you are trying to reach do not understand your views. This is frustrating because you are essentially invisible to them. In spite of revealing your true character and content, you are judged by other criteria and beliefs. The combination of Water below Wind refers to situations where your personal feelings and true character are of no consequence to people who can only accept your public and social value. Even though your private life is important to you and those close to you, it has little if any interest to people in the outside world. Additional illustrations of this hexagram comes into view in policies such as "don't ask, don't tell," in place for the military and the adage, "what takes place in your bedroom is none of my business."

60
LIMITATIONS

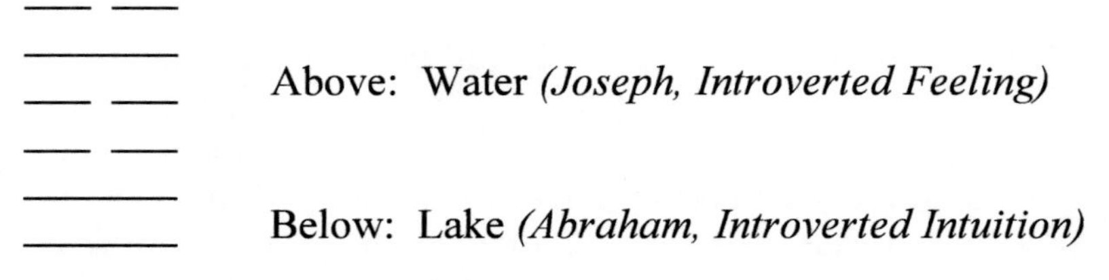

Summary: Making clear; Drawing conclusions; Educated guesses, predictions; Estimation, divining, sampling; Setting reasonable guidelines; Foretelling or prophesy. C- Grade

An illustration of LIMITATIONS comes to mind in one of the best-known biblical Scriptures where Jesus makes the statement in John's Gospel: *"You shall know the truth and the truth shall set you free [60]."*

Many aspiring believers in Jesus use this scripture to justify their separation from others over what they conceive to be the "truth." The meaning of all Scriptures, including this one, is the meaning represented by its text. If we throw out the context, we are without a guidepost to steer us in an accurate awareness of the author's intent. At heart, the writer is saying that when we know the truth, the nature, teachings, and historical context of Jesus, we are free, and not until then. We can never know "the truth" completely, and specifically the whole truth, implied by the life of Jesus and this penetrating passage. However, in spite of this limitation we can use our intuition and intellect to collect enough insights about Jesus and the truth he reveals. From this verse, your position is that of the truth seeker whose aim is to be free by knowing the nature and teachings Jesus. By directly seeking to answer the question, "What is God's idea about that which I want to know?" we can come to the truth as well.

LIMITATIONS refers to the need to study and gain insights about the nature of a groups of individual opinions or realities. It suggests doing research and drawing inferences in order to make estimates about an unknown body of thoughts or things. Because your knowledge of the whole is limited nature, you must make educated guesses about its character through intuitive and data sampling methods. When applied to receiving insights from the Divine these methods may include working visioning, dreams, the Book of Changes, tarot, etc. Even though this hexagram refers to efforts to understand the whole based on some of its parts, some distortions are inevitable. Even with the best of intentions, it is possible that too much emphasis will be placed on matters that don't deserve the focus or too little on important topics.

LIMITATIONS points to situations where your search for understanding will depend on gathering insights from and about the whole. You can do this by intuitively sensing another person's behavior or perhaps learning the nature of an entire group by getting to know some of its members. The combination of Lake below Water refers to having faith in intuitive methods such as visioning or some form of divining in order to help you catch God's ideas about your life. While it is valid to gain insights in this way and this approach can be helpful, your understanding may be limited to having faith in your inferences, educated guesses and hunches. Long story short, this hexagram calls for inductive reasoning: the process of learning about the whole by understanding some of its parts. While you cannot know everything, partial knowledge is always better than no knowledge.

61
INNER TRUTH

Above: Wind *(Aaron, Introverted Thinking)*

Below: Lake *(Abraham, Introverted Intuition)*

Summary: Faithful acceptance of inner knowledge; Confirming; Trust; Sincerity; Inner confidence; Staying focused; A Void; Misrepresentation; Following the Self; Understanding Spirit. C+ Grade

An illustration of INNER TRUTH comes to mind in the verse in John's Gospel where Jesus says, *"I am the vine and you are the branches. He who abides in me, and I in him, he it is that bears much fruit, for apart from me you can do nothing [61]."*

In this verse, Jesus implies that we are not required to do nor should we do anything without Christ. It points to a corresponding promise that we'll get the help we need to perform what God commands us to do. The statement "without me you can do nothing" means that without spiritual insight the attainment of holiness is impossible. The text suggests that the divine light you are given is proportional to your dependence upon and belief in Christ. To believe the truth, and that we are dependent upon Christ implies the continual remembrance of it. It requires that you make use of your spiritual and intuitive nature to gain access to God's wisdom on a daily basis. We must be in a constant attitude of depending, trusting, and seeking divine guidance in all that we do. In this verse, your position is like the vine with many branches or people dependent upon you for guidance. Like Jesus, you have an established connection with the Divine, and depend upon its wisdom and comfort, while the people in your community are dependent upon your interactions with them.

INNER TRUTH refers to joining with other people to gain inner knowledge or vision that goes beyond cultural developments, beliefs, customs, and doctrines. It denotes the opportunity to increase your knowledge of the Divine and sense of inner confidence. Its presence points to people learning significant truths about their lives and life in general that they are normally reluctant to face. This knowledge serves to prevent small problems from growing into big problems. In the situation at hand, individual participants get the benefits of seeking knowledge together. Even though the learning that takes place here is subjective, it is important to know that this study always expands your knowledge about the concrete and tangible aspects of the world. When you lack knowledge of the deeper dimensions of life, the outer world becomes meaningless.

INNER TRUTH is a sign that your effort to understand and explain spiritual insights is taking place in a gathering of likeminded people or within the context of a friendly interaction. The approach to life represented by this hexagram life relies on faith-based partnerships or social groups that depend upon intuition to explore the broad picture. Here the desire to share knowledge about the Divine happens in a fellowship and in relationships between two or more people. With a friendly and open manner, you can learn and teach spiritual matters to others. The combination of Lake below Wind suggests that the enthusiastic desire for wisdom will heighten the intellectual interests and curiosity about new ideas. In the situation at hand, you can interact with unseen forces through lighthearted contacts with the people in your environment.

62
SMALL CHANGES

Above: Thunder *(Isaac, Extroverted Feeling)*

Below: Mountain *(Moses, Extroverted Sensing)*

Summary: Small occurrences, improvements or progress at the end; Focusing upon small elements of a whole; An Emphasis on neatness and exacting details; Attention to final project elements. C+ Grade

An example of SMALL CHANGES can be seen in the Gospel of John's Scriptural verse where Jesus says, *"I am the resurrection and life; he who believes in me, though he die, yet shall he live, and whoever lives and believes in me shall never die [62]."*

This verse is the high point of the whole story about Lazarus and the place we need to locate ourselves. The raising of Lazarus is symbolic of youth restored to the conscious realm that has been asleep in the unconscious tomb of the body. The idea of youth is not dead, but sleeping until the "I am" understanding of Jesus comes along to awaken it. Those who want the youthful inner life to awaken in outer consciousness must believe in the reality of spiritual powers, have faith in this power, and rely upon its wisdom. Jesus clarifies that his reality as the resurrection and the life will persist even if the people who believe in him die. In the end we don't need to get temporarily raised the way Lazarus did, but rather to accept the gift of eternal life by believing in the Christ and seeking to do God's will. While everyone in our world expects death, Jesus tells us that death is a temporary state from which God brings life. Those who listen carefully to the Divine perform the rising of Lazarus every day. Whenever we release our will and we undergo a small death, and when we embrace God's will we experience birth. In this story, your position resembles the role played by the dead Lazarus resurrected by Jesus authority. Because Lazarus believed Jesus before his physical death, his unprecedented resurrection takes place.

Getting SMALL CHANGES refers to turning away from overall expansion and upward movement in order to complete specific details. In this way, significant and often long-term projects end. It's as if an overall venture such as the writing of a book, constructing a bridge, or concluding a long training program are ready for formal acceptance after finishing touches are added. This hexagram suggests that big changes in the project at hand will come through patient attention to closing details. Although this is not a glamorous time, modest and sensible actions can lead to lasting success. This is not a time for big ideas, but rather for thorough and persistent efforts aimed at perfecting incomplete tasks

With SMALL CHANGES, a matter-of-fact and controlled approach will produce sweeping changes. It often represents unexpected and perhaps feared changes taking place in the process of ending a significant undertaking. As you take charge and work within the guidelines, the effect of your effort on others will be astonishing. Far-reaching results are likely when your approach to the events before you is cautions and bit by bit. The combination of Mountain below Thunder points to a talent for adapting to routines and taking command of unexpected events such as epidemics, natural disasters or accidents.

63
PARTIAL COMPLETION

___ ___
____
___ ___ Above: Water *(Joseph, Introverted Feeling)*
____
___ ___
_______ Below: Fire *(Jacob, Extroverted Thinking)*

Summary: After completion; Attainment of an important milestone; Success in completing a significant part of an endeavor; Successful in part of an endeavor; Need for divine guidance. C+ Grade

An example of PARTIAL COMPLETION can be understood in Jesus' parable about the duties of Christ's Ministers when he asked the question, *"Who then is the faithful and wise servant, whom his master has set over his household, to give them their food at the proper time? Blessed is that servant whom his master when he comes will find so doing. Truly, I say to you, he will set him over all his possessions [63]."*

Here the faithful represent believers in God who are taking the lead in helping others come to a correct understanding of His written words, ideas revealed through intuition, and purposes. They take the lead in providing for the spiritual needs of other believers. Jesus makes the point that those who are in charge of his household should always be alert, and never let themselves to fall asleep to this responsibility. By implication, anyone who serves God has a permanent relationship of servitude to other people. The blessed person is one who is fully satisfied, not because of favorable circumstances but because God indwells them.

These people are in the world yet independent of it; their satisfaction comes from God and not from favorable circumstances in the world. While the job of assisting the divine in providing spiritual sustenance is never completed, greater responsibilities come as you carry out the ones given to you.

PARTIAL COMPLETION refers to reaching an important stage in an endeavor such as writing the first draft of a new book or framing a new structure. Because the conclusion is unknown until the end is reached it is best to remain humble, cautions, and realistic. If those involved don't make the best of the present circumstances they won't make the most of what lays ahead. While you have reached a state of new understanding and things seem to be in order, this is not the time to relax. Rather, the time calls for continued awareness, inner guidance and commitment. When you are open to other viewpoints or guidance, and willing to make adjustments as needed, the chaos that often follow this hexagram can be avoided.

PARTIAL COMPLETION suggests that you are taking the initiative to understand the Divine and carry out its directives. The best results come into view when you get your inspiration and power from the Divine. Examples of this inspiration are present in the character of every spiritual leader from Abraham to Jesus. In the secular world, inspiration is present when the person in charge makes it his or her mission to serve a particular group, e.g. head of household, judges, ship captains, and teachers. The combination of Fire below Water points to the widest expansion of awareness, the capacity to understand people, and the ability to communicate this understanding. Here the conscious and unconscious aspects of the mind work together to put you in touch with both realms. This takes place by giving emotional depth to your ideas and at the same time a degree of emotional detachment and clarity.

64
BEFORE COMPLETION

———
— —
——— Above: Fire *(Jacob, Extroverted Thinking)*
— —
———
— — Below: Water *(Joseph, Introverted Feeling)*

Summary: Incomplete but approaching a conclusion; Almost there; Anxiety, anticipation, deliberation and caution about the end; Close but not ready; Prior to the final stage. C- Grade

An illustration of BEFORE COMPLETION comes to mind in Luke's Gospel where Jesus' gives a teaching parable on humility. In it he says, *"He who exalts himself will be humbled, and he who humbles himself will be exalted [64]."*

The first prerequisite for humility is admitting our inadequacy to function without God's help. If you exalt yourself its like saying you have no sin, make no mistakes, and have no need of God. If you trust in your own righteousness to save you, then one day you will find your righteousness to be your prison. In this verse, the message is that if you pursue earthly things, you may have earthly rewards, and if you pursue eternal things, you will have eternal rewards. Although most times the humble things we do go unnoticed, the Universe takes note. Here Jesus is saying that the greatest people among us are those who serve us. The idea of humbling oneself is to recognize ones ignorance of the truth. True humility is coming to the end of yourself, and telling God and others that you need a savior. When you humble yourself, you admit that you can't save yourself or find your way alone. In short, you're saying you need God to help you. Your position in this verse resembles the person who humbles him or her self by serving others. Your humility in accepting Divine approval is the rite of passage for the successful completion of your endeavors.

BEFORE COMPLETION points to the complete manifestation of something new and holds great promise for the future. It suggests that the receipt of new insights or knowledge will require change or adjustment in your intended course. While the preceding hexagram offers the analogy of writing the first draft for a book, this one offers the analogy of marketing the completed book. The time before any significant endeavor has conscious form and solidity brings natural anticipation and worry. Although some success is certain, the situation at hand calls for caution until you reach the end goal. This hexagram brings a sobering message, "don't count you chickens before the eggs hatch."

BEFORE COMPLETION has a certain connection to PARTIAL COMPLETION (63). Here some missing information or step is required to complete the final form but in Hexagram 63, you are seeking wisdom on how to deal with the intermediate stages in a longer journey. Here we have Water below instead of above Fire and this reversal points to a similar but reverse interpretation. Whereas Hexagram 63 refers to people who bring their inspiration to the table here, the people who inspire you tend to exist in your environment. As someone in touch with the Divine or specialized knowledge you may find it helpful to offer guidance to others and those in charge as well.

Notes

Introduction

1. Rhonda Byrne, et al., *The Secret* (New York, NY: Atria Books, 2006)
2. Michael Bernard Beckwith, *The Life Visioning Process*, Session One on CD (Boulder, CO: Sounds True, 2008)
3. Byrne, et al., ibid.
4. Howard Thurman, *Mysticism and the Experience of Love* (Wallingford, PA: Pendle Hill Pub., 1973)

1. Seeking God

1. Joseph S. Benner, *The Impersonal Life* (Marina del Rey, CA: DeVorss & Co., 1941)
2. Ernest Holmes, *The Science of Mind* (New York, NY: Dodd, Mead & Co., 1938)

2. Accepting the Mystery

1. Isaiah 45:7.
2. Luke 15:11-32.
3. Mark 12:29-31.
4. Stephen Hodge, *Tao Te Ching: A New Translation and Commentary*
(Hauppage, NY: Barron's Educational Series, Inc., 2002).
5. Mark 11:15-17.
6. Mark 3:4
7. Dr. Wayne W. Dyer, *Excuses Begone!* (Carlsbad, CA: Hay House, Inc., 2009).
8. Forward by C. G. Jung, in Richard Wilhelm and Cary F. Baynes, *The I Ching or Book of Changes,* (Princeton, NJ: Princeton University Press, 1985)

3. Catch the Visioning

1. Genesis 2:7-3:24.
2. Larry Dossey, M.D., *Healing Words: The Power of Prayer and the Practice of Medicine* (San Francisco, CA: Harper Collins Pub., 1994)
3. Ibid.
4. Ibid.
5. Michael Bernard Beckwith, *The Life Visioning Process,* Session Two on CD (Boulder, CO: Sounds True, 2008).
6. Howard Thurman, *The Creative Encounter* (Richmond, IN: Friends United Press, 1972)

4. Manifest the Vision

1. Ernest Holmes, *Creative Mind and Success* (Los Angeles, CA: DeVorss Publications, 2004)
2. David Spangler, *The Laws of Manifestation* (San Francisco, CA: Red Wheel/Weiser, LLC, 2009)
3. Ken Wilber, *Up from Eden* (New York, NY: Anchor Press/Doubleday, 1981)
4. Michael Bernard Beckwith, The Live Visioning Process, Session One on CD (Boulder, CO: Sounds True, 2008)

5. The Change and Visioning

1. Joseph Murphy, PhD and Ken Irvin, *Secrets of the I Ching* (Paramus, N.J.: Reward Books, 2000)
2. Isabel Briggs Myers with Peter B. Myers, *Gifts Differing* (Palo Alto, CA: Consulting Psychologists Press Inc., 1983)
3. John Blofeld, *I Ching: The Book of Change* (New York, N.Y.: Penguin Books,1991)
4. Richard Wilhelm and Cary F. Baynes, *The I Ching or Book of Changes* (Princeton, NJ: Princeton University Press, 1985)

5. Forward by C. G. Jung in Wilhelm/Baynes, *The Ching or Book of Changes.*
6. Stephan A. Holler, *Jung and the Lost Gospels* (Wheaton, Il: Quest Books, 2002).
7. C. G. Jung, *Psychological Types* (Princeton, N.J.: Princeton University Press, 1976).

6. Elements of the Change

1. Genesis 17:1 ff.
2. Genesis 21:1 ff.
3. Genesis 25:19 ff.
5. Genesis 37:1 ff.
6. Exodus 2:1 ff.
7. Exodus 4:10 ff.
8. I Samuel 16:1 ff.
9. John 1:1-16; also see Matthew 4:17 ff.

7. Vision Centered Counseling and Healing

1. Howard Thurman, *With Head and Heart* (New York, NY: Harcourt, Brace Jovanovich, Inc., 1979)
2. Matthew 7:7-12.

8. Well-known Personalities

9. Spiritual Solutions for Social Problems

10. Consulting the I Ching

1. *The Creative,* The Pre-existence of Jesus and the Word becoming Flesh, John 1:1 ff; also see The Beginnings of Jesus activity in Galilee, Matthew 4:17 ff.
2. *The Receptive,* The life of King David, I Samuel 16:1 ff.
3. *Beginning in Difficulty,* Hypocrisy Will Be Revealed, Luke 12:1-3, Matthew 10:26-17.
4. *Youthful Folly,* Treasures in Heaven,

Matthew 6:19-21; Luke 12:23-24.

5. *Waiting,* Thomas Unbelief, John 20:24-29.
6. *Conflict,* Putting God's Kingdom First, Matthew 6:24.
7. *Teamwork*, Love Jesus More than Yourself, Luke 14:31-33.
8. *Holding Together,* Watchful Servants, Luke 12:35-36.
9. *Minor Restraints,* Parable of the Unrighteous Steward, Luke 16:10, Matthew 25:21; Luke 19:17.
10. *Conduct,* Paying Taxes, Luke 20:25; Matthew 22:21; Mark 12:17.
11. *Prospering,* Parable of the Sower, Matthew 13:1-9; Mark 4:1-9; Luke 8:4-8.
12. *Standstill,* Jesus Is the True Light, John 8:12.
13. *Fellowship,* True Family of Jesus, Matthew 12:47-50; Mark 3:32-35; Luke 8:20-21.
14. *Great Possession,* The Great Commission, Matthew 28:16-20; Mark 14-18; Luke 24:36-59.
15. *Modesty,* The Golden Rule, Matthew 7:12; Luke 6:31.
16. *Enthusiasm,* Jesus Cleanses the Temple, Matthew 21:12-13, Mark 11:15-17; Luke 19:45-46; John 2:15-16.
17. *Following,* Father and Son, John 5:19-20.
18. *Repair,* Jesus Heals a Man on the Sabbath Day, Mark 2:27; Matthew 12:10; Luke 6:9.
19. *Approach,* The Greatness of Humility, Mark 9:35-37; Matthew 18:2-5; Luke 9:46-48.
20. *Contemplation,* Man with the Jar of Water, Luke 22:10-12; Mark 14:13-15.
21. *Biting Through,* False Prophets, Matthe7:15-16; Luke 6:43-44.
22. *Grace,* Jesus Is Baptized by John, Matthew 3:13-17; Mark 1:6-11; Luke 3:21-22.
23. *Splitting Apart,* Jesus Walks On Water, Matthew 14:22-31; Mark 6:45-52; Jn 6:15-21.
24. *Return of the Light,* Weed in the Wheat,

Matthew 14:24-30.

25. *Innocence,* Dream Announcing Jesus Birth, Matthew 1:18-25; Luke 2:1-7
26. *Accumulating Wisdom,* The Great Commandment, Mark 12:29-31; Matthew 22:37-40; Luke 10:27.
27. *Nourishment,* Parable of the Barren Fig Tree, Luke 13:6-9.
28. *Yang in Excess,* Magi Warned by God in Dream, Matthew 2:7-12.
29. *The Abyss,* The Life of Joseph, Genesis 37:1 ff.
30. *Attachments,* The Life of Jacob, Genesis 25:19 ff.
31. *Influence,* Teaching About the Law, Matthew 5:17
32. *Duration,* Return of the Unclean Spirits, Luke 11:24-26; Matthew 12:43-45.
33. *Retreat,* The Buried Treasure, Matthew 13:44.
34. *Great Power,* The Lost Coin, Luke 15:9-10.
35. *Progress,* Parable of the Talents, Matthew 25:14-30
36. *Darkening of the Light,* Put God's Kingdom First, Matthew 6:33; Mark 10:30; Luke 12:31.
37. *The Family,* Jesus Ministers to the Multitude, Matthew 4:23-25.
38. *Opposition,* The Narrow Way, Matthew 7:13-14; Luke 13:24.
39. *Obstacles,* Jesus Sentenced to Death, Matthew 27:15-26; Mark 15:6-15; Luke 23:13-25; John 18:39-19:16.
40. *Deliverance,* Wise and Foolish Builders, Matthew 7:24-27; Luke 6:47-49.
41. *Decrease,* Jesus Is Tempted, Mark 1:12-13.
42. *Increase,* Reason for Parables, Matthew 13:10-17; Luke 8:9-10; Mark 4:10-12.
43. *Breakthrough,* Jesus Appears in Galilee after Resurrection, John 21:3-6.
44. *Coming to Meet,* Parable of the Prodigal Son, Luke 15:11-32.
45. *Gathering Together,* Saving Zacchaeus, Luke 19:1-10.

46. *Ascending,* Widows Offering, Luke 21:1-4; Mark 12:41-44.
47. *Adversity,* Beatitude on Righteousness, Matthew 5:6.
48. *The Well,* The Lords Prayer, Luke 11:2-4; Matthew 6:9-15.
49. *Destroying the Old,* Change Bring Conflict, Matthew 10:34-35; Luke 12:51-53.
50. 50. *Building the New,* Beatitude on Meekness, Matthew 5:5.
51. *Shocking,* The Life of Isaac, Genesis 21:1 ff.
52. *Keeping Still,* The Life of Moses, Exodus 2:1 ff.
53. *Development,* Gods Love for the World, John 3:16.
54. *The Outside Partner,* Stumbling Blocks, Matthew 18:6.
55. *Abundance,* Faith Greater Than All Israel, Matthew 8:5-13; Luke 7:1-10; John 4:43-54.
56. *The Wander,* Woman Taken in Adultery, John 8:2-9.
57. *The Gentle,* The Life of Aaron, Exodus 4:10 ff.
58. *The Joyous,* The Life of Abraham, Genesis 16:1ff.
59. *Releasing,* Explanation of Jesus Existence, John 1:10.
60. *Limitations,* The Truth Frees You, John 8:32.
61. *Inner Truth,* Jesus Is the True Vine, John 15:5.
62. *Small Changes,* Lazarus Resurrection, John 11:25
63. *Partial Completion,* Faithful and Unfaithful Servants, Matthew 24:45-47; Luke 12:42-44.
64. *Before Completion,* Jesus Teaches Humility, Luke 14:11; Matthew 23:12.